Reimagining Business History

Reimagining
BUSINESS HISTORY

Philip Scranton
and Patrick Fridenson

The Johns Hopkins University Press
Baltimore

© 2013 The Johns Hopkins University Press
All rights reserved. Published 2013
Printed in the United States of America on acid-free paper

2   4   6   8   9   7   5   3   1

The Johns Hopkins University Press
2715 North Charles Street
Baltimore, Maryland 21218-4363
www.press.jhu.edu

Library of Congress Cataloging-in-Publication Data

Scranton, Philip.
Reimagining business history / Philip Scranton and Patrick Fridenson.
p. cm.
Includes bibliographical references and index.
ISBN 978-1-4214-0861-3 (hdbk. : alk. paper) — ISBN 978-1-4214-0862-0
(pbk. : alk. paper) — ISBN 978-1-4214-0863-7 (electronic) — ISBN
1-4214-0861-9 (hdbk. : alk. paper) — ISBN 1-4214-0862-7 (pbk. : alk.
paper) — ISBN 1-4214-0863-5 (electronic)
1. Small business—United States—History.   2. Business—Research.
I. Fridenson, Patrick, 1944–   II. Title.
HD2346.U5S37 2013
338.6′420973—dc23   2012027069

A catalog record for this book is available from the British Library.

*Special discounts are available for bulk purchases of this book. For more
information, please contact Special Sales at 410-516-6936 or
specialsales@press.jhu.edu.*

The Johns Hopkins University Press uses environmentally friendly book
materials, including recycled text paper that is composed of at least 30
percent post-consumer waste, whenever possible.

Contents

Preface

In the late summer of 2007, we shared the privilege of being faculty members for the European Business History Association's Dissertation School, joining colleagues and about fifteen PhD candidates for a week's work together in the Umbrian hills. One day the graduate students were scheduled for a break: a bus tour of the region's stunning landscapes and towns. The two of us fell to talking about the state of the discipline, as veteran academics will do. Inside an hour, we began speculating about quickly pulling together a chapbook presenting our opinions about, judgments of, and hopes for business history. This is that book, six years later. We spent shared design and writing sessions in many cities, worked independently on drafts, and exchanged texts for comments and revisions. It has been an intellectually exciting process, as the work stretched our minds repeatedly, though it also stretched out far longer than we had planned. The result is an experimental text, ultimately the product of a high-uncertainty project by two senior scholars looking carefully around while leaning forward.

We hope this effort will stimulate discussion and reflection about business history's past and present, plus imagining and planning for its future. But first, one warning: we don't think this is a book to be read straight through, cover to cover. Nonlinear sampling would be a better strategy, or picking topics that appeal to you from its four sections, ignoring others. This is a book of perspectives and suggestions; it has purposes but not an argument, no arc of development or critique. Forty years ago, yippie anti-leader Abbie Hoffman published a classic activists' guide for American radicals, the title inviting potential readers to *Steal This Book*. Our title, *Reimagining Business History*, is formal and academic, but the subtitle could be *Browse This Book*. The "entries" (as we have come to call them) are all short, 1,200 to 2,500 words, just the right length to read on a commuter train, in a waiting room, or during TV commercials. There is no sequencing of segments, no building from small items to grander issues. Each entry stands on its own, even as some topics can intersect (though you get to draw the links); hence you'll find some repetition of concepts or references and some cross references. Given that readers will have variable familiarity with the themes addressed, many will find some sections obvious or banal, with others being, we hope, invigorating or challenging. This unevenness is what we anticipated in drafting the sections, for we expected our audience would principally be academic colleagues and graduate students in history and in other disciplines. We'd be glad to have readers' responses: just e-mail us at scranton@camden.rutgers.edu or pfridenson@gmail.com. Step right ahead now, and enjoy.

⎯◌ ◌⎯

The authors would like to express their appreciation to the organizers of the European Business History Association's Dissertation Summer Schools (Franco Amatori, Francesca Polese, and Andrea Colli, Bocconi University, Milan) for bi-annual invitations to discuss perspectives on business history with advanced doctoral candidates from Europe, Asia, and North America. We are equally in the debt of the fifty or more summer school fellows whose thoughtful questions and critiques helped shape our thinking. Our Bocconi colleagues also sponsored a spring 2012 seminar in Milan, at which sections of the draft were critically appraised. The EBHA scheduled a comparable panel at its late summer 2012 annual meeting, which we valued highly. Our thanks to those who joined in these efforts: Vera Negri Zamagni, Youssef Cassis, Claire Lemercier, Steve Tolliday, Francesca Polese, and Ray Stokes. We also thank the Johns Hopkins University Press editorial staff, particularly senior history editor Robert J. Brugger. Gratitude goes to our exceptionally acute copyeditor, Barbara Lamb, who saved us from innumerable gaffes.

Patrick Fridenson is grateful to colleagues and staff at the Ecole des Hautes Etudes en Sciences Sociales for their support and advice. Philip Scranton wishes to thank both the Board of Governors travel fund at Rutgers University, for underwriting multiple working visits to Paris, and the University Libraries, for their rapid responses to requests for research materials. Last and far from least, both authors benefited from their families' interest in (and tolerance of) the extended process that, after six years, yielded *Reimagining Business History*.

Reimagining Business History

Introduction

Devolved, business history becomes an instrument with surprising powers. Freely drawing on other social sciences, the historian of business may choose the portions of each he [or she] wishes to employ in his work. There is not a universally correct mixture of economics, sociology, political science or administration in the study of business history simply because the role of business in history has not been universal.

—Mostafa Hefny, "On Business History"

Business history offers an inside look at economic institutions, one that is "peopled" in the social history sense. . . . Business history offers a pragmatic institutionalism. Since the 1970s, the interdisciplinary "new" business history has emerged as a growth pole in the United States and Britain. . . . As the field flexes its interdisciplinary muscle, almost everything becomes a part of business history. . . . Yet that is its virtue as well: new business historians are true to the ecumenical sweep of prior economic historians.

—Paul Gootenberg, "Between a Rock and a Softer Place"

Business history entered the twenty-first century with a flourish, adding a new and energetic professional organization (the European Business History Association) and, in recent years, a new journal (*Enterprise and Society*), even as scores of colleagues from collateral disciplines contributed in greater numbers to annual meetings, symposia, and publications, broadening the field's scope and extending its reach. Both of us can recollect gatherings fifteen or more years ago that "rounded up the usual suspects"—conferences featuring scholars who knew one another well, agreed on the discipline's boundaries, and had a core mission: analyzing the modern corporation, its genesis, development, and significance. Much has changed since the 1990s, and we judge it timely to step back in order to look ahead, to ask questions about what's fresh, about where intriguing silences remain, about classic concepts that might profitably be unpacked, and about new perspectives that might offer avenues to unanticipated insights. We begin by inquiring briefly about the utility of history, particularly business history, before sketching this short book's character and purpose. We then outline several problems a reimagined business history can and should address, previewing this volume's four sections.

What are historians good for? What are business historians good for? These questions represent our first reframing, as it is customary to ask about the value of history, not historians. We narrow the focus here because citizens, advertising agencies, antique dealers, and politicians all construct historical narratives, find value in employing them, and modify them as the years pass. Historians are academically trained to do something different from these casual or occasional appropriations. We ask focused questions of the past, questions often rooted in present concerns. We determine the relevant evidentiary bases, rigorously explore documents, images, and artifacts contemporary to the problem, as well as later reflections on it ("the literature"), devise an analysis, share it with knowledgeable critics, reconsider and revise, then disseminate our findings and interpretations, in print, through exhibitions, or online. Historians matter because what they produce is "good to think" and because their findings also offer contestable, but intersubjectively tested grounds for action.[1] Arguably, business historians have long been good for business thinking, in that traditional research has focused on enterprises as the core subjects and has often originated in and been used at business schools, aimed at informing business planning and action. Even so, we welcome rising trends toward broadening that focus, employing varied units of analysis, and enriching two-way connections with general history and with specialist fields like political, social, cultural, environmental, and global history. Professional historians interrogating the past initiate a disciplined, collective, corrigible, and open-ended process that draws upon scholarly competences and provides empirically refined bases for reflection and action by citizens, policymakers, colleagues, and multiple publics.

As well, historians craft models for their own and others' use, including narrative frameworks like "rise and fall," the *"longue durée"* versus *"l'histoire événementelle,"* concepts of multiple and complex causality, diverse schemes for periodization or for grasping the ironies and unintended consequences of action, along with notions of coexisting, parallel processes operating across time and space, with different cycles or speeds and in which "events" are embedded. Historians have also recognized that human and natural processes must be analyzed at different scales (micro, meso, macro), each of which calls for particular modes of questioning and identifying distinct classes of relevant evidence. Dynamics at various sociopolitical or market scales also interact in ways that need to be specified. Actors not infrequently misunderstand or misrepresent these dynamics as they create documents we later consult, which compels historians to contextualize and critique these sources, another professional skill. In this environment, reimagining business history will be an ongoing process seeking to integrate with the historical profession's larger projects the particular concerns of those who explore enterprise historically as practice, institution, metaphor, ideology, or constraint.

In our view, as historians of business engage the challenges of accounting for business *in* history, they will provide insights and models complementary to those that general historians fashion. As *History and Technology* editor Martin Collins argues, technology, like business, "is a crucial site through which to query and investigate problems of elemental cross-disciplinary importance, [starting] from this proposition: that technology [or business], in its materiality, practices, modes of knowledge production, and use, has been deeply implicated in creating and sustaining particular orders of perception, power, and social relations, at ever-larger scales."[2] Acknowledging this offers business historians a conceptually robust point of departure that incorporates traditional projects while opening new vectors for research.

In this spirit, this short book sets out an array of cautions and suggestions, based on what its authors consider to be the character and problems of our time. What is that character and what are these problems? We live in an era defined by the triumph and crisis of neoliberal politics and economics in leading English-speaking nations and by the intersecting globalizations of finance, technology, and information flows. This historical period may plausibly date from the early 1970s, with the waning of the Cold War, the gold reserves crisis in developed nations, the arrival of floating exchange rates, and the ensuing stagflation. These, along with US political reversals (defeat in Vietnam, a dishonored presidency, Iran's Islamic Revolution and hostage taking), brought Ronald Reagan to power in 1980–81, shortly after Margaret Thatcher became Britain's prime minister. Both leaders presented political programs emphasizing diminished state capacities, reduced expectations of protection for both workers and firms, and heightened reliance on private market solutions for collective problems. Though Anglo-American neoliberal goals were contested and adjusted (not least the notion of shrinking government's roles), discursive spaces and policy agendas did shift markedly and durably, as the behavior of "New Democrat" and "New Labour" governments illustrated.[3] Globalization proceeded in tandem with these organizational reconfigurations, transforming the options businesses faced for sourcing, finance, or investment as well as forms of competition and routes to success/failure, while increasing both the speed of information and money transfers and the scale of human displacements, relocations, and resettlements.[4] The rapid collapse of financial relations and share values worldwide and the breathtaking volatility of commodity and stock markets since 2008–9 confirm the ubiquity of these dynamics, as do widespread and equally challenging bankruptcies, foreclosures, and layoffs. In these contexts, business historians may contribute perspective and value through inquiries documenting and analyzing, for example, failure, rapid change, regulation, fraud, and crisis management, issues beyond the boundaries of traditional research into strategy and structure, governance, mergers, or business-state relations.

At the same time, individuals currently confront a future whose uncertainties are mapped differently than was the case in the Depression and Second World War decades or the ensuing Cold War–Bretton Woods era. In North America, workers' tracks to durable business careers have morphed into segmented, serial employments, as doubts rise about the efficacy of business degrees and general education in increasingly unsteady institutional contexts. Europeans face multiple challenges to the social democratic pacts that have assured basic health care and pensions since the mid-twentieth century, along with structural unemployment patterns arguably more serious than American job churning. All are enmeshed in extensive environmental challenges whose complexity suggests, on one hand, the urgency of transnational action by citizens, consumers, businesses, nongovernmental organizations (NGOs) and governments, and on the other, limits to our capabilities to model, quantify, calculate, and understand rationally, much less influence or control, key trends. Phenomena like these, emergent over the last generation (at least), have recently gone critical, becoming more intense, with consequences for business and for business history.

With others, we believe that such transitions, events, and disruptions represent a fresh phase in the history of capitalism, as global markets and financial flows steadily displace and evade regulation and management at national levels, by states and enterprises alike. That this system's maintenance and growth has depended increasingly on returns from financial transactions, which have

generated innovation and momentum, is notable. Hence, in the wake of globalized business's first seismic crisis (launched in the United States, unlike earlier
tremors, testing the American economy's and state's response capabilities,
along with those of other developed nations), the questions, categories, and debates that animate traditional business history strike us as tangential to the
new century's emergent problematics.

Traditional business history matured during the Cold War, in the United
States at least, as a reaction to New Deal– (and earlier Progressive-) era critiques
of American capitalism. Drawing selectively on Max Weber's and Talcott Par-
sons's studies of institutions, bureaucracy, and social order, it reasserted the
legitimacy of capitalist managerial practices, organizational forms, investment
priorities, and political initiatives. Traditional business history normalized
and naturalized what had been in contention for the first half of the twentieth
century: the plausibility and viability of capitalist enterprise, the value of state
regulation and initiatives in crises (especially world wars), and the generation
of widening inequality as the price of prosperity and as a threat to democracy.
In this view, businesses optimized resource allocation and use (there is no alternative to free market capitalism that can perform better), state interventions are disruptive (even if at times necessary), and the distribution of wealth
reflects rewards for risk-taking and innovation. Such claims reinforced American corporations' and peak associations' counterattack on labor's New Deal
gains (crisply profiled in Howell Harris's *The Right to Manage*),[5] in part through
redescribing two generations of "robber barons" as organizational innovators
who collectively established managerial hierarchies that, governed by career-
minded executives, enhanced efficiency and enabled the triumph of "big business," mass production, and democratized consumption.

In the Cold War decades, this narrative rang true for many, even as its cele-
bratory tone generated broad indifference among political, social, and even
economic historians who regarded business history as descriptive and uncritical. Now, with the story's star players, U.S. Steel, General Motors, DuPont, Sears,
no longer dominant—indeed eclipsed, reconfigured, or in disarray—scholars
can draft a new narrative detailing the seeds of stagnation and decay amid the
capabilities that once brought profit and prosperity. This would be one plausible path, moving toward a reworked synthesis that restores contingency to traditional business history. That is not our object, however. Instead, we seek to
encourage (and undertake) research that will locate businesses in wider histories and view business people as creating histories, both drawing on cultural
practices and generating them. We regard businesses and related organizations,

individuals, and practices as integral elements in the moving landscape of capitalist development, crisis, and reorientation, alongside schools, churches, governments, and households, rather than as institutions separable into a field of inquiry or a subdiscipline. We reject any notion that business (or with Collins, technology) has or had a "civilizing mission"—to bring efficiency, order, growth, or rationality to society.

Three additional issues should be noted at the outset: the (now-ebbing) problem of American intellectual hegemony in business history, the question of a European perspective in the field, and the challenge of engaging globalization. In conducting the extended conversations that created this book's structure and focal points, we quickly recognized that a core problem with traditional business history was that "It's so American!" English-language business historians (and many colleagues in continental Europe and Japan) appropriated the big-business-centered "strategy and structure" approach, which dominated the field for three decades, and applied it to dozens of nations, compiling lists of the largest 100 corporations and redrawing them one or more generations later. Multinational firms came under special scrutiny, both for their organizational forms and for their foreign direct investment strategies. The layered assumptions about American primacy that this work entailed came to light in the early 1990s, when a major comparative work on US, German, and British corporate development triggered withering criticism.[6]

Presenting US practice as the standard against which business operations elsewhere were to be assessed was both arrogant and methodologically unhelpful. (Falling into this conceit represents one of the traps we highlight in Part I.) Recognizing and avoiding this silent gauging is important, but understanding its roots by historicizing traditional business history (TBH) is also crucial. As sketched above, we believe that TBH congealed amid Cold War interactions through which the United States asserted hegemony among capitalist political economies, while striving in its rivalry with the Soviet bloc to make capitalism globally dominant. Unsurprisingly, TBH sought to reveal the corporate route to American economic leadership (by the mid-twentieth century) but did this in a peculiar fashion—unconcerned with technological innovation and deployment or with the aggrandizing American state and its military capabilities, concretized in victorious warfare across two oceans. Rather, TBH's architects charted a route to hegemony defined by efficiency, predicated on formal organization, hierarchical divisions of labor, means for measurement, and consequently managerial discipline over work, planning, investment, design, and marketing. In this framework, the modern American corporation laid the foundation for America's

global power and thus represented a model for the world. Such simplifying notions are no longer workable, but the question of how, then, to anchor, conceptualize, and initiate business history remains. We offer a variety of responses.

Second, as an initial conjecture, how would a business history operate if it
were conceived on the basis of European practices and problems during the
twentieth century? Is there any such discipline or framework at present, at national or Europe-wide levels? If so, what are its key issues and characteristic
objects of research? If not, can this be related to ongoing linkages between
economic history and business history, with the former's agendas expected to
prevail? Given the complex and challenging relationships among business, the
state, and society in modern France, for example (powerful socialist and communist politicians, major state-run enterprises, a persistent rurality generating
world-class food and wines, along with deep divisions in polity and economy),
what sorts of general narratives about business and history have emerged, created by historians with what sorts of training, interests, and affiliations? One
could imagine, in France, rival scenarios depicting business people or capitalists as the enemies of the people, subverters of democracy, or as the architects
of modernity and progress, or as necessary evils, to be tolerated but never invited to dinner—contending narratives proposed by working-class, bourgeois,
and aristocratic observers. Do such class-based discourses exist in European
business history? Perhaps so and perhaps elsewhere, but they are rare in North
America, or have been at least since the dominion of TBH was concretized.
Decentering business historians' points of departure we believe will be a "good
thing" moving forward.

This brings us to a related issue: how to deal with globalization and business,
insofar as we move away from neoclassical economics and from presuming the
centrality of great firms. One way of conceptualizing this may be to anchor approaches to globalization by acknowledging the variety of flows and of transnational institutions that have transformed relatively autonomous (or reliably
dependent) nation-state and regional economies into vulnerable elements of a
worldwide, volatile, nonlinear drama, lacking a script. Flows include movements
of *capital* for investment, trade, speculation, bribery, subsidy, or influence, at a
minimum, activated by individuals (think of immigrants' remittances or art
collectors, alongside the world's Warren Buffets), nationally situated profit-
seeking and nonprofit enterprises (for the latter, universities and museums),
nation-state agencies (especially military forces), and multinational institutions
(the World Bank, HSBC, UNICEF, drug cartels). Flows likewise involve movements of *people* seeking opportunity, refuge, reconnection, revenge, education,

or comfort, shifting their locations frequently (corporate travelers, migrant farm workers), serially (job seekers moving up or down status ladders), or rarely (classic immigrants from state X to city Y, building communities, even enclaves). Human flows may involve individuals, families, and affiliated groups (ethnic or class clusters, usually) or desperate masses driven by famine, war, racism, or disease. Some of the transnational institutions featured here are air and ship lines, hotel systems, monitoring and aid organizations (Médecins Sans Frontières, CARE), labor recruitment agencies, religious communities, and ethnic or place associations (often crucial for chain migration). Last for present purposes, though not exhausting the range of possibilities,[7] flows involve movements of *information and artifacts*, both globally and along complex commodity chains. For instant news, market prices, or fresh research, electronic media have supplanted telegraphs, teletypes, and daily papers and are increasingly displacing hard-copy journals and reports. From silks to sculptures, materials and material culture travel farther and faster than they did generations ago, as do foods and foodways, creating decorative and dining eclecticism for the well-off and, for farmers and sharecroppers, global dependence on homogenized demand for genetically modified soybeans. Here transnational communications and transportation institutions are crucial, as CNN, Google, FedEx, or DHL support flows of words, numbers, paper, images, and the material of international exchange (and dominion).

For business historians who recognize these channeled instabilities, the challenges are, as elsewhere, to historicize their uneven dynamics and unexpected implications; to perceive and document their manifold business dimensions (many lying well beyond TBH); and to conceptualize interactions and patterns within these phenomena that may help readers and researchers to understand transnational, long-term transitions from relative isolation (with, for some, accompanying illusions of security and control) to radical connectedness (with, for others, accompanying fears of loneliness and helplessness).

To engage such challenges, we believe business historians will need to avoid a number of the "traps" we discuss in Part I, to reconnect with multiple streams of research in collateral historical disciplines, and to enrich their stock of conceptual tools. Reorienting our thinking toward general history opens a variety of research vectors not congenial to TBH approaches. The more speculative and as yet underdeveloped of these we term "opportunities" (Part II), and those that colleagues have already moved into exploring we gather as "prospects" (Part III). Of course, neither cluster is exhaustive. Finally, we put on offer a range of concepts and frameworks for organizing research that may add new tools to the business historian's constitutive imagination. Following Anthony Giddens, we regard theoretical notions as "sensitizing devices" that can trigger novel and productive questions, rather than as roadmaps for research, much less as short-cuts to answers. These we group as "resources" (Part IV). Each entry includes a variety of references to assist readers who wish to explore a particular topic further.

This book represents, in sum, the inverse of a historiographical analysis. Instead of retrospectively surveying, classifying, and evaluating a rich roster of completed studies, with an eye toward continuity, toward extending and reinforcing prominent trends, *Reimagining Business History* seeks to sketch a *prospective* historiography, signaling the possibility of novel questions, voiced and positioned beyond familiar queries, flowing out from times and spaces of rupture. Hence, what we offer here is a collection of *ordered, grouped assertions*, not a logical argument with a central spine. Some entries will offer unremarkable, well-known points we bring forward in order to reinforce their salience. Others may be more provocative. All are contestable, as is this project as a whole. Some colleagues have remarked that historians do not take well to being led or lectured to, but we seek neither to lead nor lecture, though we do slip at times. (Apologies in advance.) Rather, we aim to initiate a conversation about futures for our discipline, hoping that scholars and students of business history will find value added in this effort. If there is any foundational claim, it is that we regard advancing a dialogue with fellow historians as essential to the further development of the discipline, in tandem with stepping away from our decades-long reliance on economics, economic history, and management science.[8] Making such claims may also produce a second conversation—about the wisdom of such a shift in emphasis and in partners, the value of added themes and initiatives, and the usefulness of bringing in concepts from the social sciences and the humanities. We would of course welcome that discussion as well.

NOTES

Epigraphs. Mostafa Hefny, "On Business History" (paper presented at the Middle East Studies Association annual meeting, Washington, DC, 2005), quoted in Shakila Yacob, "Hidden Disciplines in Malaysia," *Australian Economic History Review* 49 (2009): 313. Paul Gootenberg, "Between a Rock and a Softer Place: Reflections on Some Recent Economic History of Latin America," *Latin American Research Review* 29 (2004): 246–47.

    1. See Martha Howell and Walter Prevenier, *From Reliable Sources: An Introduction to Historical Method* (Ithaca: Cornell University Press, 2001), and Mary Douglas, *How Institutions Think* (London: Routledge, 1987), referencing Lévi-Strauss.

2. Martin Collins, "Editorial," *History and Technology* 25 (Mar. 2009): 1–2.

3. For an effective, critical overview, see David Harvey, *A Brief History of Neoliberalism* (Oxford: Oxford University Press, 2005). For neoliberalism's core tensions and contradictions, see 79–81.

4. On globalization, see Ulrich Beck, *What Is Globalization?* (Cambridge, UK: Polity, 2000); Zygmunt Bauman, *Liquid Times: Living in an Age of Uncertainty* (Cambridge, UK: Polity, 2007); and Manfred Steger, *Globalization: A Very Short Introduction* (Oxford: Oxford University Press, 2003).

5. Howell John Harris, *The Right to Manage: Industrial Relations Policies of American Business in the 1940s* (Madison: University of Wisconsin Press, 1982).

6. This work was Alfred Chandler, *Scale and Scope* (Cambridge, MA: Harvard University Press, 1990).

7. Consider animals and plants, for example, plus disease vectors, weather and climate patterns, pollution (acid rain), or nuclear fallout, most of which have significant relationships to business activities.

8. For a useful, perhaps analogous effort within economics, see Erwann Michel-Kerjean and Paul Slovic, eds., *The Irrational Economist: Making Decisions in a Dangerous World* (New York: PublicAffairs, 2010), which is a set of short provocative papers from a post-crisis Wharton School, University of Pennsylvania, conference.

PART ONE

TRAPS

Practices Business Historians Would Do Well to Avoid

1. Misplaced Concreteness

Accountancy is a booming field, making possible a rigorous understanding of complex economic relationships and trends. Yet, "the *cost* of a good does not exist." This surprising statement is entirely true, because abstractions are immaterial and because costs are determined by human actions allocating expenses and organizing data. This process can be handled in many ways, so all costs are located in the dynamics of finding them, not in the world of experience. "What exists is the costs of a decision or an event, compared to a scenario of reference. To assess it, one needs to measure a difference between two actions, one of which may be not to act. For the same good, the costs may be different according to the use one wishes to fulfill, i.e., controlling past actions, choosing between several projects, or calculating a selling price."[1] Moreover, costs depend on who is doing the observing and the figuring. Accountants and business leaders generally believe that costs are real and not constructed and that they compel adoption of particular strategies and policies. This exemplifies misplaced concreteness, taking an abstraction, a process, or a relation as being things that have real force in society and history. In consequence, as business historians, we have to be careful about how we engage accountancy, in order to unpack the assumptions behind the totals. Similarly, management scholars who defined productivity as a concept and a goal created a new tool, often associated with a new politics, but in reality they captured only a small portion of the web of connections between capital, science, machinery, and labor.[2] Here too a misleading concreteness developed, as though productivity were a real object rather than a relation between past and future.

Three issues related to reification, another term for misplaced concreteness, concern us here: the use of numbers, the constitution of markets, and the assumption of progress. Numbers provide no objective description of the world, because counting is always intentional and positioned, not least politically. Beyond the age of three, we do not count for fun but to establish an argument or document a condition of interest. The critical challenge for historians is to pull back the curtain and determine who made the numbers, how, and why. Counting is not simply a language; it has multiple, uncoordinated authors, not the fluidity or reflexivity of a language. Numbers are a social product, whereas language has a social foundation. Ted Porter's work shows, for example, that gathering numbers was critical for the relationships between industrialists and the state in various nations.[3] Giovanni Favero, in recent research, has shown how late-nineteenth-century Italian factory statistics depended on personal links between a prominent textile mill owner and a government statistician.[4] The former provided such data as he felt comfortable gathering from colleagues and revealing to outsiders, whereas the latter, in the absence of formal procedures and legislation authorizing collection and publication, repeatedly pressed for fuller data. Hence, the content of official tables was determined by a private ordering that influenced public policy, the context for which must be understood.

Equally, the categories selected for assembling data and for choosing what is excluded may well be significant. Joan Scott examined mid-nineteenth-century reports on the Parisian workforce and discovered that "statistical reports were weapons in the debates on the social question that preoccupied French domestic politics under the July monarchy." Though historians have used the extensive Chamber of Commerce documentation, they have usually overlooked its origins and purposes. Instead of simply counting employees and workplaces, the French researchers classified them in a fashion that "showed" a huge number of small enterprises, rather than a huge number of home workers, subcontractors, and laborers on piecework. This framing helped them argue that the 1848 revolution was misconceived, as entrepreneurs were everywhere thriving in Paris—a political and distorted judgment based on a classification maneuver. Historians using the tables without recognizing that their authors' intentions are embedded in them are, in Scott's view, "unwitting part[ies] to the politics of another age."[5]

Next, there is no such thing as a rational market. Markets, being relations, not things, cannot present attributes like rationality or freedom. However, for business history, economic theories of rationality have often taken the place of empirical inquiry. It would help to build up analyses of markets from behavior and then develop theoretical positions.[6] Abstractions do not provide explanations, but in the best situations, they do evoke the principal characteristics of a historical environment or practice, attention to which may yield historical explanations. All markets are regulated, by the state, by the actors involved, by conventions, by clients and consumers. An unregulated market would be total chaos. Hence a historical question is: How can we determine the rules and routines of market activity, how these change over time, and in what directions and with what consequences? The markets for kosher food, for example, are as fully regulated as medieval markets, even if some people cheat(ed), in both contexts.[7]

Progress is the unacknowledged assumption behind virtually all business history and indeed a great deal of modern history. However, it is just one kind of outcome of complex processes, which commentators naturalize so that progress becomes transhistorical. Progress thus comes to be regarded as a natural potential, a collective momentum often mobilized through planning. Other outcomes (stasis, regression, collapse) figure simply as anomalies—exceptions to the rule or diversions from and impediments to resuming progress. Progress talk is also a key locale for confirmation bias,[8] a classic fallacy in explanation, in which evidence *for* a proposition weighs more heavily than evidence against it, or worse, in which the positive information is absorbed into an explanation and the negative is set aside or even not noticed. Thus we judge complicated systems prone to unexpected failure as exemplifying progress, until they fail, at which point we seek to punish those responsible, while rarely reevaluating our own categories.[9] Moreover, contest and change viewed from actors' perspectives is both ambiguous and equivocal, often lacking coherence and direction and presenting a messiness that progress-based frameworks suppress. We should not be content with the tidy linearities and uncritical genealogies that such a mechanical vision supplies. After all, the fax machine was invented four times over a century, rejected three times, and at last became successful as network capabilities reached adequate levels, yet it is now being superseded by pdf file transfers.[10]

In conclusion, effective business history narratives demand critically examined, historicized concepts. Under such conditions, concreteness can be a powerful tool for business history, yielding enriched accounts in which people act and create ideas, institutions, and conflicts. It is a mistake for scholars to employ concepts without recognizing their origins and the assumptions they carry into analyses. (See Resources, 1: Assumptions.) The price of misplaced concreteness is very high—concepts serving as actors and explanations disconnected from historical practice and process, an error that shrinks understanding nearly to the vanishing point.

NOTES

1. Claude Riveline, *Evaluation des coûts: Eléments d'une théorie de la gestion* (Paris: Presses de Ecole des Mines, 2005), chap. 6, para. 2.

2. Charles Maier, "The Politics of Productivity: Foundations of American International Economic Policy after World War Two," *International Organization* 31 (1977): 607–33, and Régis Boulat, *Jean Forestier, un expert en productivité: La modernization de la France (années trente–années cinquante)* (Besançon: Presses Universitaires de Franche-Comté, 2008).

3. Theodore Porter, *Trust in Numbers: The Problem of Objectivity in Science and Public Life* (Princeton: Princeton University Press, 1995).

4. Giovanni Favero, "Business Attitudes toward Statistical Investigation in Late 19th-Century Italy: A Wool Industrialist from Reticence to Influence," *Enterprise and Society* 12 (June 2011): 265–316.

5. Joan W. Scott, "Statistical Representations of Work: The Politics of the Chamber of Commerce's *Statistique de l'industrie à Paris*, 1847–48," in *Work in France: Representations, Meaning, Organization, and Practice*, ed. Steven L. Kaplan and Cynthia J. Koepp (Ithaca: Cornell University Press, 1986), 335–63.

6. Mark Casson and John S. Lee, "The Origin and Development of Markets: A Business History Perspective," *Business History Review* 85 (2011): 9–37, and Justin Fox, *The Myth of the Rational Market* (New York: HarperBusiness, 2009).

7. Roger Horowitz, *Putting Meat on the American Table: Taste, Technology, Transformation* (Baltimore: Johns Hopkins University Press, 2006).

8. John Staudenmaier, "The Perils of Progress Talk," in *Science, Technology, and Social Progress*, ed. Stephen Goldman (Bethlehem, PA: Lehigh University Press, 1989), 268–93.

9. Charles Perrow, *Normal Accidents: Living with High-Risk Technologies* (New York: Basic Books, 1984).

10. Jonathan Coopersmith, "Old Technologies Never Die, They Just Never Get Updated," *International Journal for the History of Engineering and Technology* 80.2 (2010): 166–82, and Coopersmith, "Pretty Good Technologies and Visible Disasters," *Technology and Culture* 42 (2001): 204–7.

2. Not Recognizing That the State Is Always "In"

If the market system is a dance, the state supplies the dance
floor and the orchestra.

—*Charles Lindblom*, The Market System

Almost thirty years ago, a group of American theoretical and historical sociologists convened a conference, "Research Implications of Current Theories of the State," which led to publication of a landmark essay collection, *Bringing the State Back In*.[1] In that volume's widely cited Introduction, Theda Skocpol argued persuasively that for much of the twentieth century, analysts had viewed "government . . . primarily as an *arena* within which economic interest groups or social movements contended or allied with one another to shape the making of public policy." From the mid-1960s, however, a cohort of young scholars, chiefly Europeans, some of them neo-Marxists, initiated a wide-ranging series of studies concerned with "the roles of states in the transition from feudalism to capitalism, with the socioeconomic involvement of states in advanced industrial capitalist democracies, and with the nature and role of states in dependent countries."[2] This terminological transition, from *government* as an *arena* to *states* as *actors*, has been decisive in reframing historical narratives in which states have both operating agencies and "agency" within the socioeconomic order, culture, transnational relations, and the organization of everyday life.[3] Consistent with this scholarly genealogy, we believe that wherever a state exists, it is already "in"—in markets, business, law, and more—and that business historians cannot without loss overlook this foundational condition for economic action and institutional development. Yet what (and where) is the state?

Alfred Stepan, a comparative political historian, offers this helpful outline: "The state must be considered as more than the 'government.' It is the continuous administrative, legal, bureaucratic, and coercive systems that attempt not only to structure relationships *between* civil society and public authority in a polity but also to structure many crucial relationships *within* civil society as well."[4] These systems have histories, and their capabilities have waxed and waned across many centuries.[5] The ambition of state managers to control populations and extract wealth—put perhaps more positively, for the public good and the common defense—have long affected businesses and their prospects, but the wider argument here is that state practices and provisions are fundamental to the possibility of *doing business at all*. Though state capacities are divided, incomplete, multiple, and at times contradictory, states matter to business history because they play many roles in building the markets and institutions necessary for enterprise.[6] Moreover, states are *extensive*, present, and active across space, focused on defining and administering boundaries, territories, and regions, even as they are *intensive* in regulating flows (traffic, waterways, immigration, revenues) and initiatives (licensing, incorporation, patents, illegalities).

Consider the following (historically emergent) state activities, each of which deeply conditions and structures business operations:

1. State consumption. Although historians of consumerism and consumer culture have yet to take note, states are huge purchasers of goods and services and have been for ages. Predatory, early modern "fiscal states," for example, not only squeezed their aristocrats and merchants for warfaring funds but

also spent those revenues on ships, arsenals, and weapons, provisions and horses, plus forts, ports, and all sorts of materials (rope, shot, sail cloth).[7] The modern state has far wider tastes for goods and services, though its military needs remain deep and diverse. Chasing the question of who supplies the state with what, and with what consequences, is surely a sound project, as Mark Wilson's work on Union procurement in the American Civil War has shown.[8]

2. Regulation. Despite complaints from neoliberals, regulation is rarely unilateral—states entangling enterprises for obscure, illegitimate reasons.[9] Rather, state decisions on laws or tariffs or taxes, which some segments of the business community fiercely oppose, are often supported or promoted by other elements in the same "community." For more than a century, chain store expansion and waste-disposal regulation pitted some business clusters against others: local merchants against national or international retailers, or riverside papermakers and water authorities against dye houses or chemical manufacturers.[10] Splits among enterprises and sectors over right behavior and the assumption of responsibility for outcomes beyond the firm are routinely the sources of conflict over regulation and hence are worth business historians' attention.

We must also remember that where there's regulation, there's also lobbying (and corruption), not only in the modern era. Such activities trigger an extended dialogue between political and bureaucratic agents and businesses, a series of discourses often preserved in documents that merit critical analysis. For example, when French, Italian, and Japanese governments considered authorizing the expansion of department stores in the 1920s, small shopkeepers aggressively lobbied to oppose such policies, generating rich documentation about interests in conflict over differently conceived notions of the proper character of competition.[11]

3. Research and education. In seventeenth-century Europe, education was more often clerical than secular, and scientific research was chiefly the domain of learned amateurs. At least in the latter case, monarchs fostered institutions— the Royal Society in London and the Académie Royale des Sciences in Paris—to encourage rigorous explorations of nature. Even if the Royal Society proved to be "more of a club than a college," an institution in which "shared ideals . . . did not as a rule translate into shared projects and programs of research," state patronage had long-term effects in sustaining inquiries that proved immensely valuable to business. In its second century, the society announced a huge prize for a precision timepiece that would help military and commercial ships navigate by calculating their longitude accurately and matching it with their more easily determined latitude. This scheme pulled forward John Harrison's imaginative

chronometers, which profoundly altered the business risks of ocean commerce by 1800.[12] In subsequent generations, state agencies, at various levels, increasingly took responsibility for providing, supervising, and funding education, not least as a means to train workers, literate and numerate, for business employment and leadership. State support of research ranged from cartography and natural resource assessments to technologies of warfare, measurement, or building (classically, France's Ecole Nationale des Ponts et Chaussées),[13] and in tandem, related sciences. Both efforts simultaneously served nation and empire, along with economic communities in both.

4. Property. Unquestionably, states are the ultimate guardians of property, including intellectual property,[14] through their record-keeping of land titles and transactions, wills, patents, copyrights, and incorporations; their certification of contracts, licenses, and professional credentials; their inspections of imports, factories, and immigrants; and their provision of forums for, and rules governing, reliable means toward resolving conflicts, punishing frauds and crimes, and unraveling shares in contested assets or liabilities. Moreover, mechanisms and institutions for performing these services may themselves become businesses, as with France's durable professional administrators of civil law, les notaires, or Britain's chartered accountants, established by royal decree in 1880, in response to "the growth of the limited liability company and large scale manufacturing and logistics."[15] (See Prospects, 1: Deconstructing Property.)

5. Finance and currency. States stand as guarantors of their national units of exchange, but in sharply different ways, with profound implications for business practice. From Isaac Newton, as warden and master of the Royal Mint, to the US Secret Service during the nineteenth century, powerful individuals and institutions have battled counterfeiting.[16] Other agencies gradually took responsibility for chartering and overseeing banks and, in time, insuring depositors against calamity or fraud, while also regulating securities markets and brokers. The diversity and relative effectiveness of state capacities in recent financial crises certainly present multiple issues for historical analysis, now that the flood of journalistic accounts may be ebbing. (See Prospects, 2: Fraud and Fakery.)

6. Consumption by citizens. States can (and do) shape the character and extent of household consumption. From the medieval Assize of Bread, in which English magistrates set the price of a loaf of bread,[17] through eighteenth- and nineteenth-century public markets, where only licensed victuallers could offer to provision urban families,[18] to contemporary retailing, in which state oversight and statute law offer protections to buyers, the state's involvement in routine consumption is widespread, though unevenly effective. Here a key state role is

the definition and promotion of fairness, a concept often naturalized but one that needs to be historicized, as in Matthew Hilton's research on postwar consumer movements.[19] Tax policy can also direct consumers toward or away from purchasing a home, depending on whether or not interest payments may be deducted from income and whether low-interest loans are made available to certain classes of citizens (in the United States, military veterans). State subsidies for producers of politically significant commodities and goods, and taxes on their use (such as Britain's television license), affect household choices and routines, and all have relevance to business history.

Perhaps no set of events in the last century has underscored the centrality of states to the possibility of effective business operations more than the transition of Eastern European nations from state socialism to market capitalism after 1989. Hungarian political scientist Lazlo Bruszt has summarized these dynamics. After ten years of ideologically motivated "freedom from the state" policies, based on the neoliberal notion that markets were self-regulating and that states were "the sources of economic disorder," several postcommunist nations found that "economic actors cannot have the expectation that transacting partners will honor contracts," generating a return toward "the most elementary form of economic exchange . . . barter." What has been learned? That "market order and competition are constituted by states capable of maintaining the rule of law, upholding rights, and enforcing obligations that guarantee that economic actors can safely profit from their economic transactions. . . . Once having solved this problem [securing market order], states can focus on policing and regulating competition."[20] Exactly so.

NOTES

Epigraph. Charles Lindblom, *The Market System: What It Is, How It Works, and What to Make of It* (New Haven: Yale University Press, 2001), 42.

1. Peter Evans, Dietrich Rueschemeyer, and Theda Skocpol, eds., *Bringing the State Back In* (New York: Cambridge University Press, 1985).

2. Ibid., 4 (emphasis added) and 5. This introduction, according to Google Scholar, had been cited nearly fourteen hundred times by spring 2011. Traditional Marxists remained in general committed to the idea that states were extensions of capitalist class interests, but neo-Marxists had subtler understandings of the relationships between economics, ideology, and politics. See Bob Jessop, *The Capitalist State* (New York: NYU Press, 1982), which undertook to move beyond the more "instrumentalist" classic by Ralph Miliband, *The State in Capitalist Society* (New York: Basic Books, 1969).

3. An opposed philosophical tradition, methodological individualism, generally denies that agency can inhere in organizations. We do not subscribe to this position, which is tightly

linked to the microfoundations of neoclassical economics. For valuable commentaries, see Kenneth Arrow, "Methodological Individualism and Social Knowledge," *American Economic Review* 84.2 (May 1994): 1–9; Geoffrey Hodgson, "Meanings of Methodological Individualism," *Journal of Economic Methodology* 14 (2007): 211–26; and Christopher Cramer, "Homo Economicus Goes to War: Methodological Individualism, Rational Choice, and the Political Economy of War," *World Development* 30 (2002): 1845–64.

4. Alfred Stepan, *The State and Society: Peru in Comparative Perspective* (Princeton: Princeton University Press, 1978), xii (quoted in Evans, Rueschemeyer, and Skocpol, *Bringing the State Back In*, 7). Alex Preda similarly observes that "the theoretical underpinnings of this position are developed, among others, by Neil Fligstein (1996), who argues that states create markets by setting in place regulatory frames that comprise property rights, governance structures and rules of exchange." Alex Preda, "The Sociological Approach to Financial Markets," *Journal of Economic Surveys* 21 (2007): 515. The Fligstein reference is to Neil Fligstein, "Markets as Politics: A Political-Cultural Approach to Market Institutions," *American Sociological Review* 61 (Aug. 1996): 664–65.

5. For an incisive early modern European example, see Jacob Soll, *The Information Master: Jean-Baptiste Colbert's Secret State Intelligence System* (Ann Arbor: University of Michigan Press, 2009). Taking the long view is James Scott, *Seeing Like a State* (New Haven: Yale University Press, 1998).

6. For an effective and accessible overview, see Lindblom, *The Market System*.

7. Patrick O'Brien and Philip Hunt, "The Rise of a Fiscal State in England, 1485–1815," *Historical Research* 66 (June 1993): 129–76; Richard Bonney, ed., *The Rise of the Fiscal State in Europe, c. 1200–1815* (New York: Oxford University Press, 1999); and Jan Glete, *War and the State in Early Modern Europe: Spain, the Dutch Republic, and Sweden as Fiscal-Military States* (London: Routledge, 2001).

8. Mark Wilson, *The Business of Civil War: Military Mobilization and the State, 1861–1865* (Baltimore: Johns Hopkins University Press, 2006).

9. See David Harvey, *The Enigma of Capital and the Crises of Capitalism* (New York: Oxford University Press, 2010).

10. Paul Ingram and Hayagreeva Rao, "Store Wars: The Enactment and Repeal of Anti-Chain Store Legislation in America," *American Journal of Sociology* 110 (2004): 446–87, and Michal McMahon, "Makeshift Technology: Water and Politics in 19th-Century Philadelphia," *Environmental Review* 12.4 (1988): 20–37.

11. Nobuo Kawabe, "The Development of the Retailing Industry in Japan," *Entreprises et Histoire* 4 (Nov. 1993), 19 (law of 1937); Alain Chatriot and Marie Chessel, "L'histoire de la distribution: Un chantier inachevé," *Histoire, économie et société* 24 (Jan.–Mar. 2006): 67–82 (French law of 1936); and Emmanuella Scarpellini, *Material Nation. A Consumer's History of Modern Italy* (Oxford: Oxford University Press, 2011), 123 (law of 1938).

12. Peter Dear, "*Totius in Verba*: Rhetoric and Authority in the Early Royal Society," *Isis* 76 (1985): 147, and Dava Sobel, *Longitude: The True Story of a Lone Genius Who Solved the Greatest Scientific Problem of His Time* (New York: Walker, 2005). (Sobel's subtitle is misleading, however.)

13. Frederick Artz, *The Development of Technical Education in France, 1500–1850* (Cambridge, MA: Harvard University Press, 1965).

14. Adrian Johns, *Piracy: The Intellectual Property Wars from Gutenberg to Gates* (Chicago: University of Chicago Press, 2010).

15. Quote from entry: "Institute of Chartered Accountants in England and Wales," at http://en.wikipedia.org/wiki/Institute_of_Chartered_Accountants_in_England_and_Wales.

16. Thomas Levenson, *Newton and the Counterfeiter* (Boston: Houghton Mifflin, 2009), and Stephen Mihm, *A Nation of Counterfeiters: Capitalists, Con Men, and the Making of the United States* (Cambridge, MA: Harvard University Press, 2007).

17. Stanley Webb and Beatrice Webb, "The Assize of Bread," *Economic Journal* 14.54 (June 1904): 196–218.

18. Sean Adams, "How Choice Fueled Panic: Philadelphians, Consumption, and the Panic of 1837," *Enterprise and Society* 12 (2011): 761–89.

19. Matthew Hilton, *Prosperity for All: Consumer Activism in an Era of Globalization* (Ithaca: Cornell University Press, 2008).

20. Laszlo Bruszt, "Constituting Markets: The Case of Russia and the Czech Republic," in *Democratic and Capitalist Transitions in Eastern Europe*, ed. Michel Dobry (London: Springer, 2000), 197–98.

3. Periodization as a (Necessary) Constraint

Creating accounts of business history involves, at a minimum, locating patterns, crises, and events within a range of domains: organizational strategies, political environments, technological trajectories, place/space, and so forth. Yet crucially, one additional, especially salient arena is too rarely discussed critically: period. Periodization concisely evokes both context and situation yet simultaneously privileges the political (most times) and injects significance and sequence into the affairs being reviewed *before* we have investigated in depth. Briefly reviewing these claims, their implications, and possible remedies is the task at hand.

Ancient, medieval, and modern are the classic big-box periods, yet the first two are sharply European: Egypt and Sumer participate in ancient histories but neither was medieval, unlike Rome. The Americas exhibit neither ancient nor medieval ages but rather "precontact" eras and civilizations, then colonial, national, and perhaps globalizing periods. "Modern" may mean little, other than a problem or a threat, to Central Asian peoples, Zulus, or Inuits. Nor do any of these periods link to East Asian or South Asian histories. These classic labels establish sequences that enable the notion of progress to operate in our consciousness and in our research and writing. Moreover, such progress derives from rationality, not randomness or accident. We would argue that it is essential to remember the assumptions and baggage that come with even the most "basic" periodization.

Periodization is both compelling and controlling. It is *compelling* because historians seem obliged to chop time into segments, a point brilliantly illustrated by Marco, the Swiss history teacher in the film *Jonah Who Will Be 25 in the Year 2000*. Having brought a long piece of sausage and a cleaver into class, Marco whacked the sausage into chunks: Voila!—periodization.[1] It is *controlling* because shifting the chunks, stitching some back together, or reslicing others proves to be terribly difficult. Moreover, in most fields, the chunks that have been precut by others become expansionist: in US history, presidential terms have become templates for general histories and colonize specialties, highlighting elections as turning points. Yet of course they often are not: consider Calvin Coolidge succeeding Warren Harding or even Jimmy Carter replacing Gerald Ford.

In other domains, as Patricia Clavin notes, "The new transnational and international histories . . . have not been able to escape the big periodizations of European and world history. At best they have put a few dents in historical containers like the First and Second World Wars."[2] Gender historians, similarly, in general "accept, rather than modify, the traditional framework and periodization of European history," especially in syntheses and textbooks, even though "the periodization of such important events in European history as the industrial revolution changes when women's work and industries are included."[3]

What is to be done? When considering the past as business history, it seems to us worth trying to discern rhythms of innovation and consolidation, speed-ups and slowdowns in organization that may intersect with but do not derive from "big moments," which happen differently in widely separated places. How would we periodize the infilling of transnational European infrastructures for rail, telecom, power, water, air traffic, and information flows (rather than, or supplementary to, their internal national developments)? It's also plausible to see near simultaneity or ready emulation in aspects of class-divided European urban consumption (product development, marketing, shopping, fashion, transit, utilities), but how might we periodize consumption's outreach to

Europe's rural domains and enterprises' roles in this? Moreover, to what extent are phases of consumption connected with an independently derived periodization of women's European history, given that women of all classes anchored purchasing to provision households? On another front, how could we chop the more than 160-year time sausage of "Europe since 1850" into periods that resonate with practices and institutions essential for relations not just with Asia, the Western Hemisphere, and colonies but also with markets, import/export linkages, resources, ideas, and migrants in, to, and from noncolonial territories?

Another approach, perhaps better attuned to transnational thinking, would build out from considering a global history query: When did the Second World War start? Some European scholars might argue for Mussolini's assault on Ethiopia (1935) or Franco's coup triggering the Spanish Civil War (1936), but I expect most would settle on September 1939, the German invasion of Poland. By contrast, Asian historians would likely see Japan's 1931 invasion of Manchuria as a more sensible opening salvo, precipitating a fifteen-year war that became ever more "worldly" through 1941–42, when the Soviet Union and the United States joined the struggle (though the Soviets waited until 1945 to declare war on Japan). For the "great powers," world war only commenced once *their* involvement did. From a business history platform, the war's beginning lay in cascading contracts for rearmament, with Axis demand spiking in the early- to mid-1930s and the Allies trailing only a bit, except for the United States.[4] This example suggests the plausibility of stretching containers by looking more widely at diverse historical actors and their perspectives. Challenging derived periodizations is fundamental to reimagining histories.

More directly germane to most business histories are smaller-scale but no less positioned periods: in the United States, the Antebellum, the Gilded Age, the Progressive Era, the New Deal, and the Cold War (which has wider spatial reach, to be sure), and elsewhere, the Victorian Age, Austerity Britain, the Second Empire, Les Trente Glorieuses, postwar Europe, Stalin-era USSR, and Meiji Japan. With just occasional exceptions, these parentheses enclose ostensibly coherent time blocks defined by political or military actors or actions, presuming a useful extension of that frame to economic, institutional, cultural, demographic, or spatial dynamics. Sometimes and in some places this works quite well: in the Cold War United States, a demographic surge of "baby boomer" births reversed fifteen years of family limitation. But hardly reliably: Austerity

Britain cannot contain either the longer trajectories of decay in classic consumer goods production (textiles, clothing, shoes) or the business and technological initiatives the war unleashed, many carrying over into the 1970s.[5]

Prior commitments encoded in business and economy-oriented periods pose other problems. In the United States the Second Industrial Revolution is a common scholarly referent, generally the decades from the 1880s to the 1920s, during which big businesses rose to international significance through financial, technical, managerial, and marketing prowess and through mergers. The embedded assumptions here are dazzling: that this outcome was on balance a logical and natural development, that state actions were tangential to the process, that little else of comparable significance was occurring among US businesses, that there was a prior Industrial Revolution, and that this period was "revolutionary" in some nonrhetorical sense. Adopting the period and its quiet implications sets these issues aside as insignificant and leads scholars to look for later revolutions—in information, or in variously configured Third Industrial Revolutions.[6]

But why should we accept such a logical succession of disjunctures and advances, when disorder, scrambling about, and failure are so persistently central to business practices? More troubling, framing periods like the Information Revolution reifies one sector's practices, which in turn informs research initiatives. (In researching the Second Industrial Revolution, big manufacturing businesses long drove agendas.)[7] So if the American Information Revolution runs from the late 1940s through the mid-1970s (from vacuum tube prototypes to integrated-circuit personal computers), what else of significance was happening in the US business system over those decades? How do we describe this in periodization terms? Was information processing the axis around which investment and innovation rotated in the 1940s and 1950s? If not (or not yet), how do we frame treatments of finance, patenting, creativity, or entrepreneurship external to computer trajectories?[8] Do we easily move from one IR to another IR (the Internet Revolution), extending the metaphor and to some degree crowding out conceptualizing and researching the transformation of the professions, the emergence of biomedical enterprises and pharmacological innovations, or the transformation of basic materials and of the firms creating and marketing them? Most radically, if we generate juicy questions that trigger substantive research with fresh perspectives on and implications for business history, why can't we just tag this work with dates, rather than striving to link it to conventional or convenient periods?

Periods are boxes that can become traps; explore them carefully before putting your valuable research into them. This is an injunction your authors have learned the hard way.

NOTES

1. For this clip, see www.youtube.com/watch?v=N8fhqHyRj6M.

2. Patricia Clavin, "Time, Manner, Place: Writing Modern European History in Global, Transnational, and International Contexts," *European Historical Quarterly* 40 (2010): 628.

3. Jitka Maleckova, "Gender, History and 'Small Europe,'" *EHQ* 40 (2010): 688, 690.

4. David Edgerton, *Britain's War Machine: Weapons, Resources, and Experts in the Second World War* (London: Penguin, 2011), chap. 2.

5. See, for example, David Kynaston, *Austerity Britain, 1945–51* (London: Bloomsbury, 2007), or Jean Fourastié, *Les Trente Glorieuses, ou la révolution invisible* (1979; Paris: Hachette, 2004), along with Edgerton, *Britain's War Machine.*

6. Journalism favors this repeatedly. For a recent example, see "The Third Industrial Revolution," *New Scientist*, 13 Feb. 2010, 46 (an interview with economist and futurist Jeremy Rifkin).

7. But see Philip Scranton, *Endless Novelty: Specialty Production and American Industrialization, 1865–1925* (Princeton: Princeton University Press, 1997).

8. For an alternative view, which highlights automobile production technology, see David Hounshell, "Automation, Transfer Machinery, and Mass Production in the U.S. Automobile Industry in the Post–World War II Era," *Enterprise and Society* 1 (2000): 100–138.

4. Privileging the Firm

Business history has for some years been exiting a period when its inside-outside boundary could be detected by determining whether a study revolved around profit-oriented enterprises as the central object of analysis. Given that most archival collections are deposited or preserved by firms and that case studies remain a major format in business school readings, starting research with a company and its records can be a compelling prospect. However, we believe that effective business history now involves beginning with broader questions and more inclusive visions that reach beyond the firm to include a wide range of organizational agents and actors. Consider Matthew Connelly's synoptic assessment of transnational efforts at population control across the twentieth century, but especially in the wake of World War Two and decolonization.[1] What Connelly terms the "population establishment" developed as a loose coalition of university experts, businesses, NGOs (especially foundations), and organized activists seeking to avert a possible Third World Malthusian crisis that could overwhelm industrialized nations. Had he taken firms as the starting point, Connelly's central questions could not have been framed effectively or at all, yet businesses were crucial to developing adequate means of contraception as well as higher-yielding crops, each tackling overpopulation from different angles. Commencing with significant issues and problems involving business and addressing them through inclusiveness concerning actors and institutions can trigger a creative investigative strategy.

Moreover, as Akira Iriye argued at the turn of the millennium, both scholars and administrators might pay closer attention to the history of not-quite-business organizations, which have expertise and funds, make investments and policies, interact with both governments and enterprises to shape theory and practice alike, and which were crucial to Connelly's account.[2] Indeed, given this perspective, we might well wish to recode our conventional notions of "business-government relations" as a subfield, in order to consider, at a minimum, *triadic* enterprise-nonprofit-state interactions, which may surface as "adventurer-church-monarchy" complexes in one century and as "MNC–NGO–national government" dynamics in another—all dealing with projects, funds, power, technologies, conflicts, and the production of knowledge, goods, and control.[3] A further recoding would invite us also to seek out relations between firms and society's nonbusinesses (charities, foundations, and cultural, religious, and environmental associations) as well as to frame NGOs, for example, as enterprises, before proceeding to explore their relations with states and agencies, national and international. (See Opportunities, 7: Nonprofits and Quasi Enterprises.)

More possibilities for research open up once we consider what might be termed the broader ecology of organizational life forms appropriate for business historical analysis: cartels, clubs, chambers of commerce, trade and professional associations, networks of collaborators (lateral) and networks of contractors and subcontractors (vertical), industrial clusters, cross-jurisdictional agencies (e.g., regional port or transportation authorities and the IMF), private-public partnerships (not least in R&D), consultants and expert advisers, nonprofit enterprises and consortia, and so forth. (See Opportunities, 8: Public-Private Boundaries.) Currently, for example, Gail Radford is completing a study of "public authorities," which built much of the United States' urban and transport infrastructures (ports, toll roads, hospitals, state universities) through delicate legal maneuvering that opened capital markets through the creation of tax-free revenue bonds.[4] This strikes us as pathbreaking research at the boundary of business and political histories.

On a different front, in the early 1990s, a group of senior managers from major North American and European multinationals gathered in Montreal to try collectively to understand why their development and research projects so consistently failed to meet expectations. They quickly realized that this challenge would extend beyond one meeting, so they formed the Club de Montréal as an ongoing forum to address questions about rules, integration of functions and skills, performance metrics, and communications, to name but a few concerns. Here again we find a quasi institution of significance to business practice and history, a collaboration that is far from being a firm and indeed, doesn't "do business."[5] Another tempting collection of historical themes reaches beyond the firm, some of which have little to do with individual enterprises, for example, accounting and technical standards (especially internationally), cultures of entrepreneurship, transnational flows in management practice, training, and education, and varieties of project management, across sectors, spaces, and eras. (See Prospects, 6: Projects.) Work along a number of these lines is proceeding, suggesting at least two plausible trends extending classic business history formats.

First, consistent with the ecology of organizations notion and Iriye's appeal, one broadened vision would view many kinds of organizations through the lens of business history, noting that they face some, if not most, of the challenges firms encounter: identifying core projects and commitments, engaging competition, seeking funds, developing strategies and innovations, managing staff and resources, accounting for failures and successes, and dealing with the state, just for a start. Reciprocally, business historians can profit from greater familiarity with concepts and theories in organizational studies, a vital cross-disciplinary field. Second, another vision leads toward repositioning business history as the history of capitalism.[6] This draws on scholarly work recognizing that: (1) varieties of capitalism have emerged over the last four centuries; (2) economic history in its high-quantitative garb has rarely sustained interest in complex systems and contingent institutions; and (3) "capitalism" is a concept that business historians are well-positioned to critique, dissect, and refashion. Both paths have their drawbacks, of course. Working on organizations triggers boundary questions resonant with those a narrower business history once confronted (Aren't families organizations? Is business history therefore also family history, or should both be subfields in a broader "organizational history"?). Focusing on capitalism reinscribes a Western, indeed Western European, origins story into the heart of developing projects, while again inviting questions about what one means by capitalism (when and where?). Still, given the ambiguity of "business" as an English-language term,[7] we believe that exploring these openings will prove well worth the hard thinking and lively contestations the effort will bring. Moving beyond privileging the firm is already a work in progress, and rewarding work at that.

NOTES

1. Matthew Connelly, *Fatal Misconception: The Struggle to Control World Population* (Cambridge, MA: Harvard University Press, 2008). See also the *History and Technology* forum on this study, in its first 2010 issue: 26 (2010): 59–88.

2. Akira Iriye, *Global Community: The Role of International Organizations in the Making of the Contemporary World* (Berkeley: University of California Press, 2002).

3. This evokes the arena that Foucault delineated with his concept of "governmentality," which involves, as Michelle Murphy puts it in relation to Connelly's efforts, "techniques of management, demography, accounting and surveillance," all of which are familiar to management, marketing, and advertising historians. See Michelle Murphy, "Technology, Governmentality, and Population Control," *History and Technology* 26 (Mar. 2010): 69–76; for the basic texts, see Graham Burchell, Colin Gordon, and Peter Miller, *The Foucault Effect: Studies in Governmentality* (Chicago: University of Chicago Press, 1991).

4. Gail Radford, "Public Authorities When There's Nothing to Sell: The Evolution of Quasi-Public Agencies in the US after World War Two" (paper presented at the Business History Conference, St. Louis, 1 Apr. 2010). Professor Radford teaches at the University of Buffalo, New York.

5. Christian Navarre, "Planifier moins et communiquer plus," *Communication et organisation*, n.v., premier semestre, 1998, 25–40.

6. This in part derives from the series of conferences entitled "History of Capitalism in North America," begun in 2006 and sponsored by graduate students at Harvard University. For materials related to the initial conference, see www.fas.harvard.edu/~polecon/conference/index.shtml (accessed 13 Apr. 2011).

7. Business can refer to an organization (General Motors), a process and practice (doing business), activity in general (the nation's business), or an array of personal attitudes and relations ("my private life is nobody's business"). These ambiguities can be very fruitful as well as maddening.

5. Retrospective Rationalization

Lived forward, history for individuals is usually an emergent mess, thick with indecision, false starts, dumb mistakes, and at times, inspired insights and profound achievements. British intelligence officer Norman Lewis offers a vivid military example of this unpalatable mix, along with his expectation of retrospective rationalization, in his daybook on the 1943–44 Allied invasion and occupation of Southern Italy:

> With . . . our .38 Webley pistols we were ordered to assist in the defense of Army Headquarters against the Mark IV and Tiger tanks that were now rolling towards us. What this [American] officer did not tell us was that he and the rest of the officers were quietly pulling out and abandoning their men. Outright panic now started and spread among the American troops left behind. In the belief that our position had been infiltrated by German infantry they began to shoot [at] each other, and there were blood-chilling screams from men hit by the bullets. . . . Then at 4 a.m., we started up our motor bikes . . . and, by God's mercy avoiding the panic-stricken fire directed from cover at anything that moved, reached this field with its rabble of shocked and demoralized soldiery. . . . Official history will in due time set to work to dress up this part of the action at Salerno with what dignity it can. What We saw was ineptitude and cowardice spreading down the command, and this resulted in chaos. What I shall never understand is what stopped the Germans from finishing us off.[1]

For institutions and enterprises, nothing less than incoherence is frequently in view. As Cohen, March, and Olsen trenchantly noted forty years ago, many "organizations [are] characterized by problematic preferences, unclear technology, and fluid participation," rather than rational planning, reliable technology, and effective hierarchies—a description as apt for family firms as for universities and conglomerates.[2] The historical experience of nations and economies is surely nonlinear, peppered with unintended consequences, unacknowledged influences and expectations, accidents, failures, and surprises (like Pearl Harbor or the 1918 global influenza). So how does it happen that business histories, like most histories, commonly show rational decision-making yielding growth, innovation, and control? Conflict, speculation, intuition, and nonrational decision processes surely bring failure, except perhaps in creative industries such as advertising.[3] (See Opportunities, 2: Creation and Creativity.) At least that's how we've trained ourselves to see this landscape.

Part of the problem is our informants, living or preserved on paper or microfilm; part of it is ourselves. Actors presenting the course of business (current or long past, to shareholders, successors, or clients) seek to fashion accounts that make rational sense of diverse happenings,[4] whereas historians tend to avoid drafting narratives that seem more like collages of conflict and misunderstanding than like professionally rigorous summaries and analyses of orderly dynamics. Together they and we retrospectively rationalize human and business performances that were often experimental, chaotic, indeterminate, and conflictual. This disorder can be difficult to document, but searching for problem-solving memos, transcribed managerial policy debates, or e-mail exchanges in crises, merger and acquisitions (M&A) ventures, and product redesigns will be rewarded. The British Air Ministry, for example, unlike US or French bureaucracies, had a practice of "minuting," in which proposals passed among specialists accumulated serially attached comments, each analyst adding reservations or modifications and replying to his predecessors' notes. When ten or twenty minutes are attached to a document, the ebb and flow of decision-making dialogues can be experienced anew. Multiple drafts of speeches, reports, or legal arguments can be equally revelatory, especially if annotated by individuals urging revisions.

On the informants' side of the problem, a story about commemorative speeches at Volvo is worth relating. In 1926, Volvo completed its first automobile, essentially hand-built on an island near Gothenburg. Ten, then thirty years later, Volvo's long-term leader twice presented clear and logical accounts of the firm's origins and path to success. However, they were substantively different, with the later presentation showing no recollection of the earlier one, expressing a different vision, and twenty years on, a different rationality. In 1936, Assar Gabrielsson observed that the firm had been lucky, had made serious design mistakes (by the time it was introduced, Volvo's first model was obsolete), and was unprofitable. In 1956, the origins story lacked these elements, emphasizing the generally good climate for starting automobile production in mid-1920s Sweden and efforts at securing export markets and building trucks.[5] Plainly, business actors may construct a default discourse summarizing historical developments, emphasizing decisiveness, intelligence and initiative, at times in direct opposition to the understandings and actions of their predecessors moving forward into the unknown, who lacked knowledge about how the process was going to turn out. The Volvo case is extreme, perhaps, with its contradictory retrospective narratives, but care in taking seriously such discussions is obviously warranted. We might imagine, by the way, that stories assembled not long after seminal events would preserve something of their contingencies and actors' uncertainties. However, motivation is crucial here (and difficult to establish), as hundreds of rapidly composed corporate cover-up tales and rationalizations suggest, especially when they are later exposed as fabrications.[6]

The retrospective rationalization phenomenon among historians also surfaced comprehensively at a Paris aeronautical history conference that both of this book's authors recently attended.[7] Paper after paper treated corporate roles in aircraft design, strategic change in air forces, France's adoption of jet propulsion, and technology transfers from military to civilian applications. All were nonlinear and underdetermined processes, in which outcomes could not be predicted from start-up conditions; all involved conflicts, emergent and incompletely understood technologies, and failures in policy, funding, design, and performance. Yet each paper's narrative unfolded as a smooth sequence of logical steps leading to success; the chaos and noise had been filtered out, so the signal (rational progress) could appear unimpeded. As we had both spent considerable time in French archives exploring several of these themes, encountering struggles, disasters, redesigns, and controversies, including the abandonment of multiple efforts at innovation, such narratives struck us as expressing traditional scholarly needs for order and coherence at the expense of fidelity to historical dynamics.

Reading such texts—they are legion in business and technological studies—other historians would derive a substantively false picture of the relationship between planning, budgets, and outcomes, whereas current-day practitioners would be stunned at how capable their predecessors were, given how often contemporary projects are mired in delays, overruns, and uncertainties. Thus, in our view, the capability to recognize a "tidied-up" account of process, development, growth, or decline for a firm, sector, region, or project is one of the core elements of skepticism toward sources that business historians, indeed all historians, need to build into their skill sets. Such caution is also well appreciated by oral historians.[8] When the messiness of the past is excised, the utility of the source is limited indeed.

Finally, the long connection between business history and economics plays a role in expectations of rationality. Yet as Bruno Latour reminds us, writing of Gabriel Tarde's alternative economic vision:

> The new economics observed by Tarde [in the late nineteenth century], that of class struggles, of the first great globalization movement, of the massive migrations of men, of frenzied innovations punctuated by the great World Fairs, and the carving up of colonial empires, in no way demonstrated the advent of reason. Rather it presented a spectacle of "passions of unprecedented intensity, prodigious ambitions of conquest, a sort of new religion, socialism, and a proselytizing fever unknown since the primitive Church." . . . Tarde is not saying that, alas, calculating economic reason finds itself distorted, kidnapped and perturbed by passions. . . . No, *everything* in economics is irrational, *everything* in economics is, we might say, extra-economic (in the everyday sense of the word). And this is because it [economics] is made up of passions whose astonishing development in the 19th century only amplified their interconnections.[9]

Rationality in history, in business, in the actualities of events large and small is but one passion, one process among many. Driving out the intensities and struggles by reducing them to plans and logics is comforting perhaps, but still a falsification.

NOTES

1. Norman Lewis, *Naples '44* (New York: Pantheon, 1978), 18.

2. Michael D. Cohen, James G. March, and Johan P. Olsen, "A Garbage Can Model of Organizational Choice," *Administrative Science Quarterly* 17.1 (1972): 1–25. The authors specifically researched universities, but their analysis has been generalized across organizations of all varieties; Google Scholar notes their essay having been cited 3,428 times.

3. See Jerry Della Femina, www.amazon.com/Those-Wonderful-Folks-Pearl-Harbor/dp/0671205714/ref=sr_1_1?ie=UTF8&s=books&qid=1267028594&sr=1-1, *From Those Wonderful Folks Who Gave You Pearl Harbor: Front Line Dispatches from the Advertising Wars* (New York: Simon & Schuster, 1970).

4. Karl Weick, *Sensemaking in Organizations* (Thousand Oaks, CA: Sage, 1995).

5. Nils Kinch, "Managing Strategic Illusions: The Volvo Strategy in Retrospect" (University of Uppsala Working Paper [1991]), 8, available at http://uu.diva-portal.org/smash/record.jsf?pid=diva2:128556 (accessed 25 Feb. 2010).

6. Malcolm Salter, *Innovation Corrupted: The Origins and Legacy of Enron's Collapse* (Cambridge, MA: Harvard University Press, 2008).

7. This was the International Conference on Aeronautical Culture: Artifacts, Imagination and the Practice of Aeronautics, 14–16 Nov. 2008.

8. See R. Kenneth Kirby, "Phenomenology and the Problems of Oral History," *Oral History Review* 35 (2008): 22–38.

9. Bruno Latour and Vincent Lépinay, *The Science of Passionate Interests: An Introduction to Gabriel Tarde's Economic Anthropology* (Chicago: Prickly Paradigm Press, 2009), 24–25.

6. Searching for a New Dominant Paradigm

Business history has started to emerge from a generation's dominance by the Chandlerian interpretive framework—its visible hand metaphor, a presumption of efficiency as a consequence of scale, the notion that strategy governs structure, an emphasis on the three-pronged investment in manufacturing, management, and marketing, and so forth. This book (and much else)[1] offers evidence that a reorientation has begun. In our view, rather than seeking a new anchor point for the discipline, business historians might usefully embrace the diversity of perspectives and prospects now surfacing, as colleagues within and outside the field explore businesses as institutions, as loci for culture (and cultural contests), or as key actors in political and social change at multiple levels, from the local to the transnational.[2] "Embracing diversity" will lead us to encounters with collateral disciplines other than economics (sociology, anthropology, organization studies, law) and to themes other than firms, growth, or progress. Scholarly fields, we realize, are anchored by conventions and in challenging times may seek a return to what we might call professional default settings. Our hope, however, is that multiple voices will articulate new visions for business history, taking the field into unfamiliar and even uncomfortable neighborhoods. Business history will benefit more from such a dynamic than from identifying a substitute leading voice or a dominant methodology.

We are far from alone in stepping away from a discipline's once-settled boundaries. Social anthropologists, several decades ago, experienced a comparable transition. Revisiting their experiences could be instructive. From roughly the 1940s to the mid-1970s, anthropology experienced its structuralist era, in which universal elements of kinship were presumed to be foundations for social order and social relations. Led by Claude Lévi-Strauss, this central framework adapted from linguistics the notion that a "deep grammar" silently organizes our social lives, much as the grammar of a language organizes thinking and speaking without our being aware of it. This approach eroded as the world it had queried changed and as critiques mounted. Anthropology as a social science had developed through assembling the building blocks of "primitive societies," and thus it depended profoundly on colonial relationships, which provided the capacity to probe into indigenous people's lives. When decolonization and rising political consciousness among "natives" undercut the bases for such work, anthropologists had difficulty bringing their methods home and adapting their practices to modern, urban, industrialized societies. Moreover, their standard framework drew criticism for being deeply biased toward utilizing Western codes and assumptions as means of assessing "others," for exploiting its subjects, and for seeking invariants and universals, thus rejecting history as little more than surface froth. Most troublesome, scientific-minded structuralists had failed to ground their methods in well-tested theories. That kinship was fundamental proved to be an assumption, not a foundation. Most social anthropologists gave up their apprenticeships to science in exchange for wide-open reappraisals of the discipline's central questions and means to address them.[3]

Similarly, practicing business historians face a transforming economic world; unsurprisingly, critiques of the Chandlerian approach's effectiveness and adequacy have mounted. All history is written from a present and a place, providing elastic yet genuine contexts for questioning the past. Chandler's priorities and judgments were those of the American Century; they legitimized corporations as worthy actors, not corrosive forces, and confirmed corporate history as central to understanding how Americans led the constitution of capitalist modernity. Those heralded corporations are not the ones we encounter today; many have failed, been acquired, or been comprehensively transformed and are unrecognizable.[4] Finance arguably has seized manufacturing's once-pivotal place; US manufacturing, while still vast, lags behind that of China and the European Union, at least in some of its classically strong sectors. Analysts watch debt, consumption, and commodities data as or more closely than industrial production figures.

What is to be done in business history? One track could follow other disciplines into the search for invariants, foundational principles that transcend time and space, as Lévi-Strauss attempted for anthropology. Management practitioners, business school researchers, accounting software makers, and organizational studies scholars in some numbers have turned to the concept of "performance" as foundational for firms, believing it applicable to nonquantitative dimensions of operations, as well as to budgets, investments, and the like.[5] We see such moves as scientistic (see Traps, 7: Scientism), a turn toward a failed positivism in the search for certainties. Quantifying everything has hardly revitalized economic history,[6] whereas stretching rationality and the search for efficiency across the social landscape has made sections of contemporary economics seem both quaint and peculiar.[7]

Our alternative is to encourage work toward recognizing and researching diversities that lie in everyday business life and hence in its history. Business people do not (and have not) simply operated by applying recipes or formulas; they were and are creators in their own right, under a bewildering array of circumstances, in a huge variety of institutional settings, and with a vast range of goals and understandings of success. (See Opportunities, 5: Microbusiness.) This diversity tells us something basic about business in general—that our priorities are arbitrary and situated. We choose them by fiat, tradition, logic, and emotion; to exclude any of these dimensions is not worthwhile, as a broader scope for thinking and inquiring opens doors we might otherwise miss entirely. There is no one way to do business well, and "well" itself has many dimensions; this insight provides an open-ended engagement with both competition and cooperation. Opportunities are everywhere for new research initiatives, after all.

Consider organic foods from the perspective of discourse analysis, which can allow us to see aspects of unfolding situations not otherwise accessible. The political dimensions of "organic" intersect with marketing appropriations of "organic." Clear distinctions between safe and hazardous farming and processing practices become objects of controversy and obfuscation, the former in public debates, the latter in advertising suites.[8] Words may indeed matter more than business historians sometimes think and more than firms imagine, in this environment. Also, odd initiatives may yield unanticipated results that don't match conventional categories very well. When European aircraft builders recognized in the 1960s that dominant US manufacturers Boeing and McDonnell-Douglas were uninterested in designing wide-body, short-route planes, which could carry more than two hundred passengers eight hundred kilometers, they collaborated to fashion an alternative. The result was Airbus, a private initiative and international alliance largely funded by three states (France, Germany, and Britain), which delivered the A300 as its first, and almost immediately successful, product. Further models brought Airbus into global competition with Boeing, which led its managers to attempt to achieve efficiency through privatization, chiefly in a joint venture between Lagardère and Daimler Benz during the 1990s. More recently, the hybrid company's private sector stakeholders, facing extensive redesigns and cost overruns with the double-decked A380, have voiced their wish to withdraw from the effort and return Airbus to state management, thus conceivably moving the firm from mixed private-public to all-public ownership.[9] Shoehorning this mildly bizarre sequence into one theoretical framework or another will be less productive, we believe, than recognizing it as one of many possible outcomes that large-scale and innovative technological enterprises may yield. Such diversity can encourage imaginative and instructive research, which is unlikely to materialize if what counts as business history is again narrowed to any particular channel.

NOTES

1. For example, the May 2011 invitation for submissions to a special issue of *Business History* focused on a critical appraisal of "strategy" is explicitly post-Chandler in its statement of purpose. Accessed 6 May 2011 at www.egosnet.org/jart/prj3/egosnet/data/uploads/CfP/CfP_Business-History_Strategy-Special-Issue.pdf.

2. One sign of this welcome "invasion" is the increasing numbers of papers and panels by scholars working outside business history (i.e., not defining themselves as business historians) presented at the Business History Conference in the United States and at the annual meetings of the European Business History Association.

3. See John Sturrock, ed., *Structuralism and Since* (New York: Oxford University Press, 1981), and Johannes Fabian, *Time and the Other: How Anthropology Makes Its Object* (1983; New York: Columbia University Press, 2002). For successor perspectives, see James Clifford and George Marcus, eds., *Writing Culture: The Poetics and Politics of Ethnography* (Berkeley: University of California Press, 1986), and Clifford Geertz, *The Interpretation of Cultures* (New York: Basic Books, 1977).

4. Interestingly, the great, Morgan-merged U.S. Steel Corporation has come full circle, closing many of its plants in the 1970s, then buying two oil companies in the 1980s, venturing into chemicals and real estate, and renaming itself USX, all before undertaking a full (and tax-free) reorganization in 2001. In this move, the energy divisions spun off the steelmaking operations, which then purchased assets from other bankrupt steel companies (including one in Serbia), and reappropriated its original name, U.S. Steel. Thousands of Pittsburgh steelworkers came from Central Europe; U.S. Steel now has integrated plants in Slovakia and Serbia and presents itself as the world's fifth-largest steelmaker. "What a long strange trip it's been" (The Grateful Dead). See www.uss.com/corp/company/profile/history.asp (accessed 29 Apr. 11).

5. For a collection of leading articles in this area, see the *Harvard Business Review on Measuring Corporate Performance* (Boston: Harvard Business School Press, 1998).

6. See, for example, L. Costa Dora, "Height, Weight, Wartime Stress, and Older Age Mortality: Evidence from the Union Army Records," *Explorations in Economic History* 31 (1993): 414–49.

7. This is the particular delight of the Nobel Prize–winning economist Gary Becker. See his *The Economics of Life: From Baseball to Affirmative Action to Immigration* (New York: McGraw Hill, 1998) (a collection of his *Business Week* columns), and Gary Becker and Richard Posner, *Uncommon Sense: Economic Insights from Marriage to Terrorism* (Chicago: University of Chicago Press, 2009). For dissenting views, see Frank Ackerman, "Consumed in Theory: Alternative Perspectives on the Economics of Consumption," *Journal of Economic Issues* 31 (1997): 651–64; Ackerman, "Still Dead after All These Years: Interpreting the Failure of General Equilibrium Theory," *Journal of Economic Methodology* 9 (2002): 119–39; and the classic by Paul Hirsch, Stuart Michaels, and Ray Friedman, "Dirty Hands" vs. "Clean Models": Is Sociology in Danger of Being Seduced by Economics?," *Theory and Society* 16 (1987): 317–36.

8. Oscar Broberg, "Labeling the Good: Alternative Visions and Organic Branding in Sweden," *Enterprise and Society* 11 (2010): 811–38.

9. Bill Gunston, *Airbus: The Complete Story* (1988; Sparkford, UK: Haynes Publishing, 2010); John Newhouse, *Boeing vs. Airbus* (New York: Vintage, 2008); Jean-Paul Callède, "Voies et voies autour de l'Airbus A380: réseaux et territoires en conflits," *Flux*, nos. 63-94 (2006): 71–74; and Christophe Barmeyer and Ulrike Mayrhofer, "Culture et rélations du pouvoir: Une analyse longitudinale du groupe EADS," *Gérer et Comprendre*, no. 88 (June 2007): 4–20.

7. Scientism

> In summary, while we can accept that human knowledge is always limited by our perception and experience, it does not logically follow that the world itself is so limited—this is the epistemic fallacy.
>
> —*John Mingers, "A Critique of Statistical Modelling"*

What is scientism, and why is it a trap for business history? Scientism represents a rigorous, if narrow and formalistic, application of an "empirical analytical approach" to securing knowledge, a protocol that "defines a fairly rigorous set of canons by which the practice of science has to proceed. . . . These constitute the only route to valid knowledge. Any human activities not following these methods may still be worthwhile pursuing, because they are practical or [involve] art or religious contemplation or whatever else, but they do not lead to valid knowledge and hence are not part of science."[1] These rules lead to privileging methods and findings anchored in mathematical formulations and models, the master tools of "hard" science. Practitioners regard as scientifically promising only those objects of study that can be encountered through, reduced to, or transformed into numerical data. Moreover, they strive to establish truths and regularities that are valid, independent of place or time, universals beyond history and culture. Those incapable of implementing this program cannot generate knowledge that allows both formal explanation and reliable prediction, the hallmarks of scientific achievements. They may be diligent, inspired, and creative, but they do not draw truths from nature.

Although for most business history research, such imperatives and judgments are tangential, we should not forget that colleagues in nearby social sciences (especially economics), management science, and the engineering sciences often trend strongly toward scientism and assess our work from that elevated (or constricted) perspective. Indeed, among historians positioning themselves as social scientists, this framework is at times adopted, viewed as bringing scientific values and practices into the "softer" environments of human subjectivities and interactions. Such aspirations have triggered sustained critiques for half a century, arguments that we shall reference but not rehearse here.[2] Given current research contexts, particularly in business disciplines, understanding scientism is imperative for business historians.

As one point of departure, it may be helpful to note that a more inclusive definition of science, widely current outside Anglo-American domains, refers to all systematic attempts to increase human knowledge of the material and the social world. As two analysts noted, this "'continental' definition [focuses on] the research procedures and the systematization of knowledge which make it communicable, codifiable and progressively updatable."[3] Hence, multiple routes to valid knowledge can be charted. In this section, we hope to reinforce this insight with some cautions about misleading uses of science and some encouraging thoughts about how social science as practice can become a resource for us.

Business historians will surely have heard of "the one best way," a touchstone of Frederick Taylor's "scientific management," and many will have read Robert Kanigel's detailed exploration of Taylor's world.[4] Taylor's methods, claims, and visions of work were scientistic; Taylor imagined a tight analogy between physical phenomena and human capabilities, one that would generate managerial control by way of detailed planning and worker efficiency through inculcating obedience and passivity. Though Taylor's direct impact on US industrial labor was modest, widespread international adoptions and adaptations followed, initiating what Judith Merkle termed "a systematic and massive industrial engineering crusade" that promised to "use 'science' to increase profits, get rid of unions, . . . and raise productivity." In the long run, scientific management "not only tend[ed] to promote the idea that democracy and efficiency are mutually exclusive, but it has left an additional legacy in the form of a problem solving approach that says potential conflict can and must be handled by the intervention of managerial elites."[5] Some "management science" scholars routinely critique Taylorism as crude and ineffective, but its line of descent is unmistakable, from his quest for control through science to contemporary mainstream managerial policies.

Other misestimations of science persist. The "linear model" of the relationship between science and technology, which regards technological change as derived from applying scientific principles, has been repeatedly unhorsed by researchers. It remains, however, a routine default setting,[6] as does the regular use of the words *science* and *rationality* as honorifics: "actuarial science," "finance as science," "accounting science," "rational markets." All embody the prestige of high-level quantification and the assumption that reason governs, or ought to do so, were human failings corrigible.[7] By extension, such scientism leads to *inappropriate appropriation*—analysts using scientific theories out of context, as with chaos, complexity, or evolutionary theories. It is common, in this vein, for scholars to invoke "evolution" when they are referring to gradual and incremental changes, without engaging evolutionary theory's requirement of randomness and reliance on stochastic events or the more complex variations contemporary formulations entail, an issue Edmund Russell has explored.[8] Whether searching for the perfect metaphor, analogy, or instrument, such thinking overlooks the reality that social or organizational relationships and business practices are not purely rational but a mix of logics, emotions, and histories, not effectively reducible to numbers and rarely single valenced.[9]

In another arena, decades ago in *Relevance Lost*, H. Thomas Johnson and Robert Kaplan outlined the multiplicity of accounting models operating in Second Industrial Revolution American manufacturing, deploring their failure to persist after the Second World War and their displacement by universalizing financial accounting systems (managing by the numbers) in the 1960s and '70s.[10] What was the central problem? As Johnson later explained, managers began expecting that accounting data could control operations and predict trends. Aided by new information-processing technologies, this scientistic shift diverted attention from production processes, employee capabilities, and client satisfaction. Unfortunately for US enterprises, "formidable competitors" did not subscribe to this approach, outpacing American firms that did. The Japanese and Europeans "were not managing by the numbers with top-down financial control systems that treated customers as objects of persuasion and employees as cogs in the gears of a deterministic machine." Running firms by "remote control," US top managers "abdicate[d] their strategic responsibilities" by seeking short-term cost reductions rather than searching for technological, organizational, or market initiatives to invigorate global competitiveness.[11] Such tactics contributed to the early end of "the American Century."

Certainly, science and technology have become ever more important to business operations, from the eighteenth century onward; it would be foolish to ignore or undervalue this and write histories bypassing such trajectories. Instead, business historians might well work to become more familiar with scholarship in the history of technology and the history of science, not least to dispel any remaining illusions about either (technological determinism is a partner to scientism). On both fronts, such investments will help us appreciate that neither science nor technology is a simple tool to solve business (history) challenges. Instead, each domain of systematic practice offers useful ways to think about the world—about institutions, the dynamics (and irregularities) of change, the limits to human knowledge, and the challenges involved in extending those boundaries, along with the costs and implications (across multiple parameters) of doing so.

Investigators who don't understand how sciences work (different standards in different domains) readily use science to explain change, as if computers changed businesses. Not so: people using computers changed businesses, and collections of enterprises using computers changed the environment for business as well. Equally, it is fairly easy to overestimate the importance of science to business. In France, companies focused on science and its applications have not been among the most profitable. Often, at troubled science-linked firms, takeover managers refocus enterprises on using their assets to meet clients' needs (not their own research goals), a strategy that resonates with Johnson's concerns. In consequence, two possible business roles for science can be noted, both of which have importance for business historians. First, in planning and operations, enterprises can regard scientific knowledge as a core asset and scientific practices as real skills, making both emergent, rather than passive, resources. Second, firms very often have to choose between mobilizing their capabilities to enlarge science (acting in a scientific fashion) and adapting science and technology to users' needs (acting in a commercial fashion). Situations requiring such decisions deserve close study; they generate conflicts and documents and may last for years and years. Both choices necessitate business actions, not just intellectual positioning, and each may strike success or subside into failure—contingency remains.

Finally, we turn to one of the social sciences that has embraced the "continental" motif for scientific work, after generations of chasing universality, namely, social anthropology.[12] In France, initial efforts to transfer ethnographies of rural or "primitive" peoples to researching businesses and bureaucracies failed to yield broad generalizations and testable theories, producing instead special issues of journals focused, for example, on tensions in aerospace labor-management processes. Yet the idea of *corporate culture* spread everywhere, legitimized through references to anthropology, localized and appealing. In time, researchers abandoned their earlier scientistic projects and focused on local domains and particular practices, whose patterns, rituals, and reinforcements could enable scholars to see things that *are* there but remain invisible without anthropological tools. Such investigations have opened the way to appreciating the voices of tradition, the uses of space, and the significance of ritual objects and practices in organizations. (See Opportunities, 10: Ritual and Symbolic Practices.)

Questions creative ethnographers have asked of current-day organizations may well inform historical investigations as well, to the extent that business historians become familiar with contemporary ethnographic methods and literatures.[13] If such efforts mature, business history will avoid the trap of striving to emulate hard science and will broaden its vocabulary for analysis and repertoires for inquiry. As with other social science approaches, however, there is no guarantee that protocols applied to working organizations can be reconfigured to engage historical records. We expect that challenge to test the creativity of business historians.

NOTES

Epigraph. John Mingers, "A Critique of Statistical Modelling in Management Science from a Critical Realist Perspective," *Journal of the Operational Research Society* 57 (2006): 202–19, quote from 204.

1. Heinz Klein and Halle Lyytinen, "The Poverty of Scientism in Information Systems," in *Research Methods in Information Systems*, ed. Enid Mumford, Rudi Hirschheim, Guy Fitzgerald, and Trevor Wood-Harper (New York: Elsevier, 1985), 123–51, quote from 124. See also J.M. Legget, "Medical Scientism: Good Practice or Fatal Error?," *Journal of the Royal Society of Medicine* 90 (Feb. 1997): 97–101, quote from 97.

2. See Harry Redner, "Science and Politics: A Critique of Scientistic Conceptions of Knowledge and Society," *Social Science Information* 40 (2001): 515–44; Herbert Reid and Ernest Yanarella, "Political Science and the Postmodern Critique of Scientism and Domination," *Review of Politics* 37 (1975): 286–316; and Josef Bleicher, *The Hermeneutic Imagination: Outline of a Positive Critique of Scientism and Sociology* (London: Routledge, 1982).

3. Augusto Carli and Emilia Calarescu, "Language and Science," in *Handbook of Language and Communication: Diversity and Change*, ed. Marlis Hellinger and Ann Pauweis (New York: deGruyter, 2007), 523–52. This view is also spreading among scientific critics of scientism.

4. Robert Kanigel, *The One Best Way: Frederick Winslow Taylor and the Enigma of Efficiency* (New York: Viking, 1997), and the classic by Daniel Nelson, *Managers and Workers: Origins of the Twentieth-Century Factory System in the United States, 1880–1920* (Madison: University of Wisconsin Press, 1975).

5. Judith Merkle, *Management and Ideology: The Legacy of the International Scientific Management Movement* (Berkeley: University of California Press, 1980), 1, 2, 298.

6. David Edgerton, "'The Linear Model" Did Not Exist: Reflections on the History and Historiography of Science and Research in Industry in the Twentieth Century," in *The Science-Industry Nexus: History, Policy, Implications*, ed. Karl Grandin, Nina Wormbs, and Sven Widmalm (Sagamore Beach, MA: Science History Publications, 2004), 31–57.

7. Justin Fox, *The Myth of the Rational Market: A History of Risk, Reward and Delusion on Wall Street* (New York: HarperBusiness, 2009).

8. It is not encouraging that similar misunderstandings are evident in medical circles. See the comment by Nathaniel Robbin, "Why Physicians Must Understand Evolution," *Current Opinion in Pediatrics* 21 (2009): 699–702. For a sophisticated corrective, see Edmund Russell, *Evolutionary History* (Cambridge, UK: Cambridge University Press, 2011).

9. Gabriel Tarde, the renegade French sociologist and judge, argued that social scientists were insufficiently aggressive in attempting to quantify emotional states, relationships strengths, and attachments. Bruno Latour notes that contemporary data gathering and management software does exactly this, bringing Tarde's critique and positive program for economics back to life. See Bruno Latour and Vincent Lépinay, *The Science of Passionate Interests: An Introduction to Gabriel Tarde's Economic Anthropology* (Chicago: Prickly Paradigm Press, 2009).

10. H. Thomas Johnson and Robert Kaplan, *Relevance Lost: The Rise and Fall of Management Accounting* (Boston: Harvard Business School Press, 1987).

11. H. Thomas Johnson, "Relevance Regained," *Critical Perspectives on Accounting* 5 (1994): 259–67, quotes from 262. Johnson's earlier coauthor Robert Kaplan has long been involved in creating and redesigning a riposte to reductionism, a "balanced scorecard" approach to business planning that deals with financial and nonfinancial elements of strategic decision-making, which should be different at each enterprise. Despite this flexibility, it too

seems to rely on data-centered assessments, but it does include consideration of "customers, suppliers, employees, processes, technology and innovation." Quote from
www.brefigroup.co.uk/consultancy/balanced_business_scorecard.html (accessed 25 Apr. 2011).

12. See Thomas Eriksen and Finn Nielsen, *A History of Anthropology* (London: Pluto, 2001).

13. From France, see Nicolas Flamant, *Une anthropologie des managers* (Paris: PUF, 2002). In English, see Melissa Fisher and Brian Downey, *Frontiers of Capital: Ethnographic Reflections on the New Economy* (Durham, NC: Duke University Press, 2006); Brian Moeran, *Ethnography at Work* (New York: Berg, 2007)—a participant's analysis of an advertising firm; Ellen Hertz, *The Trading Crowd: An Ethnography of the Shanghai Stock Market* (Cambridge, UK: Cambridge University Press, 1998); Melissa Cafkin, ed., *Ethnography and the Corporate Encounter* (New York: Berghahn, 2010); and Karen Z. Ho, *Liquidated: An Ethnography of Wall Street* (Durham, NC: Duke University Press, 2009). For a methods and examples overview, see Sierk Ybema, Dvora Yanow, Harry Wels, and Frans H Kamsteeg., eds., *Organizational Ethnography: Studying the Complexity of Everyday Life* (Thousand Oaks, CA: Sage, 2009).

8. Taking Discourse at Face Value and Numbers for Granted

Every historical methods primer tells students to adopt a critical stance to sources—toward discursive traces, the preserved utterances and texts of actors, documents from institutions, toward quantitative evidence, and even toward landscapes, images, and artifacts. The trap here is not that we fail to do this, after solemnly intending to. That does often happen—we become enchanted with our sources, and our initial critical distance narrows as familiarity with and reliance on them grows. (A radically critical position toward sources would entail writing nothing, as nothing can be wholly trustworthy.) Nor does this trap concern the need for contextualization and our concomitant aversion to anachronism, as in general, historians are alert to this. Rather, the trap we face with discourse and numbers is that they encode practices while concealing them and provide apparent unity and clarity while setting aside conflict and contradiction.

As important as texts, images, and quantitative evidence are for historical understanding, we must appreciate that there is no unpositioned utterance, no image without an image maker, and no number without a calculating intelligence. Facts and data are constituted by someone for a purpose, using practices that slip behind the stage curtains—unless we persist critically, thereby creating a second-order contextualization. Basic contextualization involves a systematic "looking around," establishing the milieux for institutional, economic, and technological actions and for political settings and trends, as well as the rules and routines of social performance. But the second-order version echoes classic paleographical questions: Why was this text crafted, this phenomenon measured, this tabulation published? By whom, with what tools, to what ends, with what assumptions and omissions?[1] For business historians, recognizing that a now-archived market analysis may well have been a tool for a boardroom coup may alter our perspective on it, not so much discrediting the analysis as locating it in time, space, and process. Using this document without inquiry as to its provenance and purpose, however, would be a risky strategy.

Reading detailed company overviews published in century-old trade journals without exploring their advertising pages could grant such material a higher evidentiary status than is appropriate. Not uncommonly, company profiles paraded major advertisers' virtues, bypassing labor troubles, lawsuits, or battles among owners or heirs. (Here's another reason to regret the frequent omission of advertising sections from serials microfilming projects). Conversely, when "reading" ads, decoding their symbolism and cultural meanings, scholars can too easily overlook the ads' contemporary viewers, the ad-makers' concept, design, and production processes, their publication costs or circulations, and evidence about their effectiveness. Ads can offer a gateway to multiple dimensions of business, particularly if a critical contextualization is undertaken,[2] yet they can also fuel evidence-free speculation about culture, meaning, and intention without such contextualization.

Equally important, counting derives from intentions, notably in making populations and economic activities "legible" to authorities, as James Scott has observed, or in generating order and confidence through quantitative portraits, as Ted Porter has documented.[3] A series of political, institutional, tactical, or individual decisions determined what got counted, and for those of us who later strive to analyze behavior, structure, or process through recourse to such data or statistics, the second-order contextualization remains necessary. Decades ago, Joan Scott explored the political context and foundations for mid-nineteenth-century French industrial statistics, gathered and classified not as ordinary facts and information but so as to frame authorities' understandings of the "dangerous classes" in the wake of Parisian riots and uprisings. Scott pointed out that scholars "in a sense . . . have accepted at face value and perpetrated the terms of the 19th century debate according to which numbers are somehow purer and less susceptible to subjective influence than other sorts of information." Instead, statistics and number-laden reports "are ways of establishing the authority of certain visions of social order, of organizing perceptions of 'experience.'"[4] Hence, in this environment, it is critical for business historians to appreciate that counting is a form of argumentation, as is classification, both of which have bases in efforts by those defining, analyzing, and presenting the data "to persuade readers of the necessity of accepting their interpretations."[5]

Institutionally, the temptation to tailor "the numbers" to actors' needs and plans can be compelling. In consequence, supervisory institutions have been created to review, qualify, and certify counts and reports from other institutions. This is what circulation agencies do in relation to newspaper and magazine publishing, what viewer monitors do for television audiences,[6] and what credit ratings firms do to rank buyers or borrowers by likelihood of default.[7] An obvious example of recent interest is bond rating, a letter-based classification of risk based on extensive and ostensibly rigorous data collection and analysis, which combines textual hierarchies (AAA) and quantitative assessments, while obscuring the power relations and alliances of interests that have informed assignment of securities to categories. Purchasers taking ratings for granted, failing to imagine that organizational pressures, reputation effects, and policy compromises could well induce distortions, suffered disastrously when values dipped sharply as tradability and liquidity eroded.[8]

As historians our task is to ask whence came these categories, what ends do their linked assertions and explanations sustain, and what were the interests of those who undertook gathering and arranging this quantitative evidence in the first place? When and why did businesses start to rely on numerical data, beyond their own accounts? What concerns did they have about the producers of such information? Did firms seek and trust government-generated statistics or dismiss them?[9] Again, where and why? What sorts of enterprises commenced generating their own counts, series, and quantitative analyses, particularly in monitoring their external environments? What tests to assure liability were initiated, and how were they validated? When and where did critiques of seeing the world through numbers surface, and how were such critiques met, engaged, or deflected? How did special institutions for monitoring the data supply achieve legitimacy? Again, as both qualitative and quantitative discourses are positioned, calibrating that positioning and grounding its locations in time and space is essential to effective historical scholarship.

NOTES

1. See Martha Howell and Walter Prevenier, *From Reliable Sources: An Introduction to Historical Methods* (Ithaca: Cornell University Press, 2001), chap. 3.

2. Roland Marchand, *Advertising the American Dream: Making Way for Modernity, 1920–1940* (Berkeley: University of California Press, 1986).

3. James Scott, *Seeing Like a State* (New Haven: Yale University Press, 1999), and Theodore Porter, *Trust in Numbers* (Princeton: Princeton University Press, 1995).

4. Joan Wallach Scott, *Gender and the Politics of History* (New York: Columbia University Press, 1999), 114–15.

5. Ibid., 115.

6. Pierre Bourdieu, "Television," *European Review* 9 (2001): 245–56.

7. See Richard Levich and Giovanni Majnoni, eds., *Ratings, Rating Agencies and the Global Financial System* (Norwell, MA: Kluwer, 2002). For consumers, see Louis Hyman, *Debtor Nation: The History of America in Red Ink* (Princeton: Princeton University Press, 2011).

8. John Patrick Hunt, "Credit Rating Agencies and the 'Worldwide Credit Crisis,'" Berkeley Center for Law, Business and the Economy, Jan. 2009, available at www2.wiwi.huberlin.de /finanz/skript_semfin/t12.pdf (accessed 12 Apr. 2011).

9. On this point, see Giovanni Favero, "Business Attitudes toward Statistical Investigation in Late 19th-Century Italy," *Enterprise and Society* 12 (2011): 265–316.

9. Taking the United States (or the West) as Normal and Normative

Business history as a discipline has arguably been chiefly an Anglo-Saxon creation, with origin stories that highlight the Harvard Business School during the 1930s and 1940s. That business history did not start out as a subdivision of general history "proper," but rather as an outgrowth from economic history, seems clear, although it long participated in the durable conventions of US historical culture. Put simply, for decades business historians took the United States as the anchor point in conceptualizing research programs and in assessing the significance of their results. Studies of America's great corporations defined the templates for research into Europe's or Japan's great corporations; visions of the state, of capital markets, or of accounting, derived from American institutions and policies, became ready benchmarks against which to assess practices elsewhere, which hopefully were progressing, however unevenly, toward echoing US models. The chilly reception afforded Alfred Chandler's *Scale and Scope*, which contrasted the performances of the largest American, British, and German industrials across six decades, underscores the problem. Whether Chandler intended it or not, his analysis set US benchmarks for achievement and coded the shortcomings of British and German enterprises as due to managerial or marketing insufficiencies or state policies encouraging cartels, stepping around what, in others' eyes, may have been American big business's blind spots and emergent deficiencies.[1]

Regrettably, other branches of history in English-speaking domains were equally blinkered in evaluating the practices of other nations as deviant or deficient, given American institutions and practices. For the most part, historians of the United States long ignored the rest of the world, except insofar as immigration or foreign policy impinged on their narratives.[2] Hence American benchmarks for democracy, innovation, or family relations reliably provided Whiggish demonstrations that America's mid-twentieth-century triumphs derived from superior values, virtues, institutions, capabilities, and resources. This view could not last, but the legacy of such assumptions remains an element of business history's environment.

Consider the history of Foreign Direct Investment (FDI). Distinguished US business historians have charted overseas capital spending by leading American firms, dismissing the concerns of non-US enterprises and states that limiting (or even blocking) such influxes of capital could support national-level development, which in turn has implications for growth. Such restrictions plainly signified deviance from proper business principles, as Marcelo Bucheli documented in his review of Chilean responses to external investments from the 1930s through 1990s, the most brutal phase of which yielded a CIA-led coup in 1973, following controls on incoming FDI, the murder of Chile's elected president, and a generation of foreign capital–friendly military rule.[3] Yet why should states not try legitimately to defend their firms, workers, and institutional arrangements in the face of extranational capital flows? The great smash of 2008–9 has revived such discussions as policy matters, as even IMF economists presently are reconsidering foreign investment controls as a means to

stem short-term traders' crisis-induced (and crisis-deepening) surges of liquidation and capital flight.[4] Indeed, it is relatively rare that such investments are
analyzed from the perspective of the "receiving" country, and when this is
done, investors' assertive manipulations of local law, custom, and institutions
stand out. For example, V. Necla Geyikdagi's study of French investment in
Ottoman territories illuminates the ways in which business interests worked to
undermine the imperial state and to carve up opportunities in "sectors like
banking, insurance, mining, seaports, trade, and railway construction (and operations)." Rather than simply investing to build regional capabilities and long-
term profit potential, French enterprises built railroads, for example, only if
governments guaranteed a minimum annual return for each kilometer constructed, while maneuvering in other fields to eliminate competition from non-
French firms.[5] On another, more contemporary front, the evident failure of US
accounting rules to generalize globally suggests a substantive turn away from
convergence toward US models, along with recognition that diverse interests
generate diverse practices.[6] So one key question for business historians is, How
best can we define and implement, from alternative standpoints, regionally or
transnationally framed concepts and expectations with which to interrogate
historical actions and patterns, including North American ones?

More broadly, taking Western industrialized practices as normative is
so frequently done and so irregularly acknowledged that one business- and
technology-based challenge is worth highlighting. In late- and postcolonial
sub-Saharan Africa, initial business and economic emphases focused on promoting urbanization and industrialization, in part through building infrastructure ("good roads") using state-of-the-art Western machinery. This approach proved grossly inefficient and insufficient; far from parts suppliers, road
graders and related machinery operated erratically and at low efficiencies, unless "parachute" companies from abroad handled all segments of the process.
Postconstruction maintenance was problematic, insofar as incoming engineers and skilled workers did little to train locals in machine operation and repair. Given widespread criticism, in the early 1970s the World Bank sponsored a
sharply different exploration of civil construction: the reverse substitution of
labor for machinery. Kenya pioneered with a state-directed "rural access roads"
program, employing fifteen thousand people at its peak to construct eight
thousand kilometers of roadways in the decade after 1976. Budget overrun was
just 11 percent, and nearly 70 percent of all spending stayed within Kenya versus
less than 30 percent when using mechanical equipment and foreign managers.
Locally earned wages accounted for more than 60 percent of expenditures,

rather than 10 percent with the machine-based approach. Copied by Botswana and other nations, labor-intensive construction involved using high-quality small tools and generated sharp increases in productivity, even while providing employment and skills ladders to supervision and engineering training for outstanding workers.[7] Conceivably, Western "advanced" states, in crisis or with rising structural unemployment, could profit from reviewing such innovations, with their inversion of efficiency standards and search for extensive rather than intensive solutions to both infrastructure and training challenges. Business historians, for their part, may need to unlearn received notions like "the one best way" and "technological progress" if they are to perceive innovation closer to the ground, past and present.

NOTES

1. Alfred Chandler, *Scale and Scope: The Dynamics of Industrial Capitalism* (Cambridge, MA: Harvard University Press, 1990). Critics argued as well that Chandler had misgauged the contexts for and dynamics within Britain's imperial business environment and both nations' war-blasted economies, major elements conditioning the configuration of "organizational capabilities," Chandler's core metric. American problems included commoditization in heavy industry and hence global competition with declining profits, mobile shares facilitating often ill-conceived mergers and acquisitions, and a regulatory incoherence (national, state, local) quite different from the unified system in Britain or from the Cold War collaborations that revived industry in the Federal Republic of Germany.

2. Of course, American scholars exploring European, Asian, African, or Latin American history did not ignore other nations and cultures, though they frequently did view practices and processes in the light of American expectations or interests.

3. Marcelo Bucheli, "Multinational Corporations, Business Groups, and Economic Nationalism: Standard Oil (New Jersey), Royal Dutch-Shell, and Energy Politics in Chile 1913–2005," *Enterprise and Society* 11 (2010): 350–99.

4. "Controls on Capital Part of the Policy Mix, Says IMF Staff," 19 Feb. 2010, available at www.imf.org/external/pubs/ft/survey/so/2010/POL021910A.htm (accessed 14 Apr. 2011).

5. V. Necla Geyikdagi, "French Direct Investments in the Ottoman Empire before World War I," *Enterprise and Society* 12 (2011): 525–61.

6. See, for example, Ronald Dye and Shyam Sunder, "Why Not Allow FASB and IASB Standards to Compete in the US?," *Accounting Horizons* 15 (2001): 257–71.

7. Robert T. McCutcheon, "Labour Intensive Road Construction in Africa," *Habitat International* 13.4 (1989): 109–23, and McCutcheon, "Employment Creation in Public Works," *Habitat International* 19.3 (1994): 331–55. See also Bent Thagesen, ed., *Highway and Traffic Engineering in Developing Countries* (London: Spon Press, 2001), for the generalization of these approaches beyond Africa.

10. The Rush to the Recent

Over the last decade, we have noted what seems to be a substantial drift in research time frames toward the quite recent past, the final segments of the twentieth century. In submissions to the journals we edit (*Enterprise and Society* and *Entreprises et Histoire*) and in annual meeting programs for the Business History Conference, the Association of Business Historians, and the European Business History Association, studies of business-government relations, international marketing, product development, and the like increasingly address contemporary issues with evidence from the near past.

One source of this pattern may well be business school expectations about the shape and utility of history, a substantive matter given that roughly half of all business historians work in such institutions. Classically, forward-looking research in management or strategy has drawn on enterprise experiences over, say, the preceding five or ten years, with occasional references to earlier times. The social scientific urge to predict, extrapolate trends, and generate testable hypotheses and theories underlies such approaches and their associated methods. However, this can condition a certain "presentism" and an "instrumentalism" that view history centrally through the lens of current challenges and that mine the past for useful contrasts, examples, or guidance. Presentism too readily leads to teleological narratives anchored by progressive or declinist logics, as if history had a goal: us, our nations, our time. Moreover, unfortunately, whatever seems off the track to the present simply gets omitted, along three dimensions—the deep past, the near past's contexts, and the elements of the near past that derive from deeper, long-term dynamics. Instrumentalism presumes that we can reliably link past practice to present problems, knowing (somehow) what it is from "there" that is germane to what we face "here." Indeed, from this angle, the past has value only insofar as its experiences bear relevance to ours, almost as if people and institutions "then" acted so as to produce our "now." This is the terrain of history's "lessons," which is swampy ground. Multiple histories of the same situation, phenomenon, or process are feasible, all using the same bodies of evidence and pointing in different directions. Choosing by what rule we select one interpretation over others involves a second-order instrumentalism whose justification is contestable, though rarely assessed.

The farther into the past we go, the greater the differences between then and now that we have to acknowledge and contend with as analysts and interpreters. This matters intensely because the strangeness of the deep past can restructure our perceptions of the present, helping us to visualize both continuities and shifts.[1] Meanwhile, the near past rarely gives inquirers sufficient scope or clarity to determine either the reach or depth of continuities, nor does it provide a means to assess the significance of apparent shifts. Indeed, we may have appreciably more evidence about institutions and events fifty or a hundred years ago than about more recent happenings, for which document files remain closed (if not cleansed). Alternatively, we may have vast and contradictory reams of information on recent events and as yet no metrics (other than ideology or an uninterrogated notion of "usefulness") to help us sift the chaff from the wheat. Those seeking a past germane to business purposes err when strip-mining recent decades for trends, analogies, or cautionary tales, as clever or foolish management or regulatory schemes arose from dynamics different from those now in motion—differences that vanish when practices are extracted from context. Examples (or data) plucked from recent history have their own histories, which get lost as we try to persuade them to be sufficiently similar to current circumstances to influence decision-making.

For example, automobile makers now are preparing electrical vehicles as the successors to gasoline and hybrid cars, even as veteran power companies (and some new firms) are experimenting with systems of widely scattered electricity recharge points. All have certainly explored the failed early-twentieth-century efforts to build and maintain electrical vehicles,[2] yet many unknowns and substantial gaps remain. After all, early electrics depended on sets of heavy batteries with limited reliability, which reduced speed and scope, in a context where electrical "filling stations" were implausible given the unevenness of US electrification. Twenty-first-century electrics are expected to be "go-anywhere" vehicles, creating infrastructure problems that historical experiences can highlight but hardly address. Conversely, mergers and acquisitions often fail in part because the investing entity looked only to the last few years of their prospects' histories, failing to gather information on its longer-term trends, resources, and weaknesses.[3] Laws regarding businesses or labor are usually quite old and many times modified. Looking at current forms cannot show whether the law will be a constraint on or a resource for action, much less the trajectories of its interpretation and litigation. Precedents of use, both successful and dismal, can create contexts for present interpretation, but again, choosing which precedents to rely on is itself an interpretive act, warrant for which is frequently unspecified.[4] History, then, is more of an asset than we are generally disposed to admit, though it rarely points unambiguously toward tactics in present contexts.

What bringing the deeper past into play can do for scholars of management or strategy (and for business historians in general) is to help us all decipher durable legacies, understand the roots of practices that now seem burdensome or irrelevant, and think beyond conventional forms and boundaries. On the first count, scholars exploring European transnational corporations' relations with developing countries will find colonial-era practices and policies that remain in place and in effect.[5] Marketers suddenly discovering the moral dimensions (and moral hazards) of housing markets could profit from probing the historical ambivalence of Christian theologies and societies regarding striving for worldly goods. On the second, bankers and legislators eager in the 1990s to revoke the Glass-Steagall Act, which separated commercial and investment banking in the United States, surely needed a closer understanding of the financial risks that mingling household deposits and speculative bets entailed in the 1920s. With Glass-Steagall in place, for half a century banking became one of the United States' least exciting sectors, no place for highfliers chasing big profits. This changed dramatically after 2000, leading in part to the great meltdown of 2007–8. We have now rediscovered an old truth—that, as economist Paul Krugman noted recently, "when it comes to banking, boring is good."[6]

Thinking "outside the box" has become a cliché, but for managers, thinking differently is an enormous asset, especially in steadily shifting or crisis environments. And here a long-term view can be arresting. For example, like Jesse Livermore in 1907 and again in 1929, the antiheroes of the recent global smash were those few speculators who called the turn and acted against conventional thinking by shorting a market about to experience a major crisis.[7] As William Deresiewicz observes: "We have a crisis of leadership . . . because our overwhelming power and wealth, earned under earlier generations of leaders, made us complacent, and for too long we have been training leaders who only know how to keep the routine going."[8] Relying on the recent, for managers and for business historians, is a recipe for keeping the routine going, one that pushing deeper into the past will disrupt, usefully, not by calling on us to identify salient precedents, but rather by leading us toward recognizing historical difference as a category of analysis. Asking "how was it then, what worked or not, and why?" for businesses and other organizations is a key step toward thinking clearly about what is conventional now and imaginatively about what could be different today and tomorrow, both in our search for understanding the past and in our present practice.

NOTES

1. As David Lowenthal, quoting from L. P. Hartley's *The Go-Between*, memorably put it: "The past is a foreign country. They do things differently there." See Lowenthal, *The Past Is a Foreign Country* (Cambridge, UK: Cambridge University Press, 1985), xvi.

2. David Kirsch, *The Electric Vehicle and the Burden of History* (New Brunswick, NJ: Rutgers University Press, 2000), and Michael Brian Schiffer, *Taking Charge: The Electric Automobile in America* (Washington, DC: Smithsonian Institution Press, 2010).

3. For a management perspective on this problem, see Mike Schrader and Dennis Self, "Enhancing the Success of Mergers and Acquisitions: An Organizational Culture Perspective," *Management Decision* 41 (2003): 511–22. For a review of recent history, see Patrick Gaughan, "Failed Merger: Failed Corporate Governance?," *Journal of Corporate Accounting and Finance* 16.2 (Jan.–Feb. 2005): 3–7.

4. On the significance of warrants in scholarly argumentation, see Wayne Booth and Gregory Colomb, *The Craft of Research*, 3rd ed. (Chicago: University of Chicago Press, 2008), chap. 7, "Making Good Arguments: An Overview."

5. For a careful analysis, see Alexander Lee and Kenneth Schultz, "Comparing British and French Colonial Legacies: A Discontinuity Analysis of Cameroon" (unpublished paper, Stanford University, 2009), available at www.sscnet.ucla.edu/polisci/wgape/papers/17_Lee .pdf (accessed 10 Apr. 2011).

6. Paul Krugman, "Good and Boring," *New York Times*, 31 Jan. 31, 2010.

7. Richard Smitten, *Jesse Livermore: World's Greatest Stock Trader* (New York: Wiley, 2001), and Michael Lewis, *The Big Short: Inside the Doomsday Machine* (New York: Norton, 2010). Livermore reportedly made $3 million shorting stocks in 1907 and much larger sums doing the same in 1929–30, but he kept playing markets and lost most or all of his gains both times. Lewis's 2007–9 short sellers reaped hundreds of millions by betting against the viability of collateralized debt obligations. For the details of short selling, see www.investopedia.com/university/shortselling/shortselling1.asp (accessed 18 May 2010).

8. William Dercsiewicz, "Solitude and Leadership," *American Scholar* 79 (Spring 2010): 20–31, quote from 24. On this point re labor unions in the United States, see also Jefferson Cowie, *Stayin' Alive: The 1970s and the Last Days of the Working Class* (New York: New Press, 2010).

PART TWO

OPPORTUNITIES

Thematic Domains

1. Artifacts

From museums to flea markets to junkyards, business-generated and business-related artifacts provide raw materials for historical interpretation. Marketing giveaways, fine and plain products (porcelain to matchboxes), designer desks, and steel cabinets for blueprints—all represent physical, not textual, documentation of making, managing, and consuming. Artifacts from industrial worksites are also ubiquitous in the material world of production, even in abandoned plants, mines, ports, and workshops. Machines are clearly important here, but tools, badges, and signs (re safety, location, function) also testify to the physicalities of enterprise. Moreover, from an industrial archeology perspective, buildings, roadways, landscapes, and ruins represent histories of economic initiative and exhaustion. Artifacts are evidence. They have stories worth telling: about fine or sloppy workmanship, skillful or casual design, and use, reappropriation, or improvisation. Yet effective interpretation depends on thoughtfully formulated questions, for we need to determine what these stories are about and why they are significant.[1] Thus a series of questions may help organize this section.

1. What constitutes the material culture of business, how has this changed over time, and why? What artifacts capture an enterprise's cultural commitments or serve as a sector's iconic referents (the auto hood ornament, the stock ticker, the blast furnace)? How do external shifts affect business artifacts: the arrival of electricity or of warfare; the displacement of the horse or the steam locomotive, perhaps? How do artifacts reflect or initiate historical processes? What artifacts differentiate an office from a library or a classroom; how and where were these separations made, and with what intentions? How do business artifacts express emotional sentiments (whose?), class positions, or intentionalities of control? How do they reflect the gendering of space and process?

On the last point, Delphine Gardey has recently analyzed the regendering of office skills and objects in Third Republic France. She notes that "technologies and artifacts are decisive in configuring relationships of domination and act according to certain processes whose mechanisms need to be elucidated." For example, unlike the standard story that typewriters brought women into office positions, Gardey found both that women's entry preceded typing machines and that men were "the first typists." So how were women attached to these machines? In part the answer lay in the cultural deskilling of typing work, initially regarded as quite difficult and hence a male domain, and in time recoded as routine and unchallenging, thus shifted to women. Hence "it is crucial to recall that objects are enrolled in organizational design" and exemplify the ways in which expertise is defined and brought to bear on the integration of artifacts, procedures, and people. Moreover, in the 1920s, when this work was feminized, "the furniture (typing chairs, special tables and later desks, adjustable lamps, and document holders) [was] used to dictate the position of the body, the appropriateness of the gestures and the correct way of using the object."[2] Thus in Latour's sense, objects become actors in work-life dramas, encapsulating managerial intentions and enforcing them on humans.

2. Next, where have the relied-upon furnishings, equipment, designs, communications systems, and technologies for information exchange and storage enterprises come from? For the moment, we are focusing on offices, commercial agencies, exchanges, and the like. How and why did this array become reconfigured, and at whose insistence or recommendation? More concretely, what is the history of the desk, and how did it become a cubicle? What JoAnne Yates has done in unpacking the history of telegraph messages and memos, of filing and document retrieval,[3] begs for attention in other dimensions of office practices mediated by artifacts. Does telephony, for example, follow a gendering pattern comparable to Gardey's typewriters, and how does the introduction of spatially extended systems change power and access relations? Is there a deflection of gendering consequent on the widespread adoption of cellular phones, for surely the first generation of them was once again heavy, complicated, and hence labeled male (or was it?)? In revisiting David Edgerton's concern for not overstressing the significance of innovation, so as to make room for considering everyday artifacts crucial to daily life,[4] what durable artifacts significantly conditioned business activities, and why did they *not* change when much around them was shifting? Here we may begin to recognize the transgenerational powers of paper and pencils, forms and receipts, particular desks, chairs, or windows (along with workers' expectations of occupancy and access), plus the struggles triggered when those who would improve design and workflow or promote efficiency strive to displace them.

3. How can we analyze and historicize the workplace as an artifact—a site, designed or assembled—a peopled place that actors occupy and alter in complex

and unexpected ways? What methods are promising for reconstituting the interacting agencies of managers, designers, foremen, and workers in such places? How did that world's inhabitants reorganize, subvert, and repurpose settings or configurations that managers, engineers, and consultants had arranged for efficiency, surveillance, and confinement?[5] How did assembly lines, toilets, and washrooms articulate power and resistance, for example?[6] In this vein, what about lighting? Ventilation? Cafeterias? All have histories in which artifacts, culture, and enterprise are interlaced and about which we know next to nothing.[7]

4. How can we unpack and interpret the relationships between executives and architects in constituting workspaces at factories, docks, or company headquarters or their symbolic assertions through skyscrapers and "corporate campuses"? In the United States, perhaps starting with Ford's River Rouge plant, how did enterprises come to visualize production and managerial spaces as emblems, utopias, even tourist destinations, shifting from the cloistered counting room to the flamboyant, multistory atrium or the corner office? What transnational flows and contrasts can be documented and assessed across the past two centuries in the articulation of enterprise spaces?

5. In the wide world of work outside offices, what cultural messages have enterprises and agencies sent through the materiality of buildings, the organization of production spaces, and the flows of people and objects through hospitals, waterworks, and public transit systems? To whom are these messages significant, in what ways, at what points in time, and with what institutional and interpersonal effects? What, in this environment, is an "effect," and what surplus effects are generated, in addition to or instead of those intended? Given that infrastructures are artifacts, as well, how can they figure in business histories? Consider the Paris Metro as an artifact of urbanization mediated through business interests and state capacities or, as Donald Reid has emphasized, the Paris sewers as concretizing a highly conflictual set of social and economic relationships.[8] How were business enterprises and activists involved in designing and financing each of these? Who pushed for (or against) what forms and formats, when, and why? What was the sequence of underground lines (and for the Metro, stations), and how did both unfolding construction patterns correlate with economic dimensions of Parisian growth? (NB: questions worth repeating for other major cities).

6. Last, thinking about particular artifacts and their histories, wasn't the cell phone an object with military antecedents in "walkie-talkies," later designed for construction supervisors, movie directors, and globally-mobile entrepreneurs? Isn't there room in business history for reconstructing the histories of

artifacts, genealogies of a sort, with their designers, promoters, investors, and producers all integrated into narratives of exploration, replete with dead ends and redesigns? Consider vending machines, our daily partners in securing thin coffee and packaged sandwiches. Their histories link to both consumerism and automation,[9] yet business historians have not yet moved in this direction (interestingly, in 1980s Berlin, vending machine initiatives focused on making clean, cheap syringes available for drug addicts).[10] Though Italian and Japanese vending machine makers are virtuoso designers, historical accounts of their prowess (and failures) seem to be scarce. Similarly, America's ever-present jukeboxes (coin-operated music players) are the subject of memoirs, collectors' evaluations, and popular studies but not substantive historical analyses (or for that matter, technical and engineering analyses, as these were complicated devices, prone to failures in use). Thinking closely about artifacts that integrate business, technology, and consumption could be an illuminating vector for business history.[11]

In these and surely other areas, exploring the material culture of business offers promising venues for imaginative reconstructions of work life and its tensions, the exercise of authority and initiative at multiple locations in organizational hierarchies, and the relationships between artifacts and the history of both production and consumption.

NOTES

1. Arjun Appadurai, ed., *The Social Life of Things: Commodities in Cultural Perspective* (Cambridge, UK: Cambridge University Press, 1986), and Bill Brown, ed., *Things* (Chicago: University of Chicago Press, 2004).

2. Delphine Gardey, "Culture of Gender, Culture of Technology," in *Cultures of Technology and the Quest for Innovation*, ed. Helga Nowotny (New York: Berghahn, 2006), 73–94.

3. JoAnne Yates, *Control through Communication: The Rise of System in American Management* (Baltimore: Johns Hopkins University Press, 1993).

4. David Edgerton, *The Shock of the Old: Technology and Global History since 1900* (New York: Oxford University Press, 2007).

5. For the "architecture of surveillance" in late-nineteenth- and twentieth-century America, see Anna Andrzejewski, *Building Power: Architecture and Surveillance in Victorian America* (Knoxville: University of Tennessee Press, 2008).

6. For vivid examples, see Stephen Meyer, "Rough Manhood: The Aggressive and Confrontational Shop Culture of U.S. Auto Workers during World War Two," *Journal of Social History* 36 (Fall 2002): 125–47.

7. Peter-Paul Verbeek, *What Things Do: Philosophical Reflections on Technology, Agency, and Design* (University Park, PA: Penn State University Press, 2005).

8. Donald Reid, *Paris Sewers and Sewermen: Realities and Representations* (Cambridge, MA: Harvard University Press, 1993).

9. Kerry Seagrave, *Vending Machines: An American Social History* (Jefferson, NC: MacFaland, 2002), is a popular historical account. Seagrave also wrote a comparable survey of jukeboxes for the same press. Scholarly attention to both is culturally oriented and quite scattered, at least in English.

10. Klaus Stark, Astrid Leicht, and Reinhold Muller, "Characteristics of Users of Syringe Vending Machines in Berlin," *Social and Preventative Medicine* 39 (1994): 209–16.

11. One intriguing starting point could be Paul Ormerod's *Why Most Things Fail: Evolution, Extinction, and Economics* (New York: Random House, 2005).

2. Creation and Creativity

Throughout this book we encourage business historians to draw inspiration from other historical fields and from the (other) social sciences. One underappreciated dimension of business practice is surely creativity. Many business activities, including negative ones, involve creativity—from patenting, R&D, marketing, and providing service to industrial espionage, stock fraud, aggressive downsizing, and hostile takeovers. We should not presume that the intellectual center of creativity is located in R&D units or among consultants. Instead, all entrepreneurs, engineers, managers, and workers have the potential to solve problems in an original way and to contribute ideas to such processes. Creativity arises from multiple sources, including science, social needs, dreams, literature, films, and popular culture (e.g., science fiction) and from repeated problem-solving and the learning this engenders.

What conditions foster creativity? We suggest that short-term goals, temporary assignments, and concreteness (rule-bounded sites) may be less effective than longer-term commitments and an emphasis on process. Urgency, personnel shortages, incomplete knowledge, and financial constraints can also stimulate the technical and organizational imagination.[1] However, many obstacles to creativity exist. Creating is a loose and ungovernable dynamic that can offend or confuse traditional managers. Many creative ideas prove worthless and thus are rejected, which can offend or confuse those being creative. It is also essential to identify false creativity, that is, environments or processes that are labeled "creative" but that are tightly controlled, if not routinized. For example, financial actors often present corporate mergers or spinoffs as creatively blending the assets and interests of several firms or as setting talented people free, but the only creativity here is in public relations. After all, takeovers and spinoffs are repetitive, task-like projects, many of which fail because they are underdetermined or underspecified by the actors, who judge that they are involved in a mechanical process, not a creative one. Mergers and divestitures are also difficult in ways that actors fail to recognize, involving downsizing, new logos and budgets, or entering unfamiliar markets, which introduces unanticipated complexities in blending practices, expectations, visions, and people. Rarely is a spinoff as creative as that at Dassault Systems (1982), where these challenges were recognized and workers at all ranks became involved in fashioning a new set of operating conditions, design vectors, and emergent capabilities.[2]

Inquiring further about the resources for creation is worthwhile. Some efforts involve managing scarce resources. In 1999, two Paris schools of business facing financial straits were forced to merge by the city's Chamber of Commerce. ESCP, active in Paris since 1819, and EAP, operating since 1972 at a number of European sites, joined to initiate ESCP-Europe, creating the continent's only fully international management education unit. This surely was an unanticipated, creative outcome, given the serious difficulties the institutions confronted; even the Chamber of Commerce had no idea that ESCP-Europe could be successful.[3] One outcome is development of a new culture, not simply a new set of quantitative conditions (such and such a budget, so many students and faculty). Other creative ventures need new funding, not just reorienting scarce resources. Yet given how unpredictable return on such investments can be, funding is generally uncertain and may be terminated at just the worst moment. Thus creativity depends on committed people and on reliable money flows.

Researching creation has to take into account the life cycle of goods and services. Some consumables face obsolescence; others enjoy permanence, which triggers questions for business historians. Consider the time horizons of two types of "permanent" goods: the Filofax (UK), which has been produced in the same form for generations, and electrical power stations, which are expected to produce the same output for generations. In contrast, fashions in clothing and home decorating change steadily, though at different speeds. Danish modern living rooms, which were revolutionary in the 1950s, are now sold as antiques. Meanwhile, Japanese wedding kimonos are used from one generation to another, whereas Western wedding dresses go rapidly through cycles of style. The point here is, when you are creating, for how long is what is created expected to be effective, relevant, profitable? For business historians one query could be: Are the actors concerned in creativity alert to the time envelopes into which their products are proceeding?

One perhaps surprising aspect of creation is that it cannot be accomplished without waste. As noted earlier, many ideas are offered and most do not succeed.[4] Advertising campaigns famously go through multiple trial slogans, images, and color schemes before clients settle on a final version. In technical fields, multiple designs are routinely evaluated by engineers as they seek solutions to complex problems, and when prototypes are tested, performance shortcomings trigger redesigns, sometimes by the dozen. All this work is expensive, as rejected efforts still use time and resources, physical and intellectual. Still, the first insight is rarely correct, the first draft is rarely adequate, although in management and politics this necessity is just as rarely understood. Waste, then, is inherent in creativity, but managers frequently distrust the "creatives" because they are different, they cannot be controlled, and they often fail. As a result, following the management literature's directives, enterprises seek to secure creativity without "unproductive" spending, often through planning innovation, sometimes through budget-cutting and intensive oversight. Ironically, on occasion constraints spur creativity—but not reliably.

When Google, following its venture capitalists' suggestions, hired Eric Schmidt in 2001, he introduced a hierarchical managerial structure, replacing a more amorphous framework. The result was a sharp decline in creativity in a firm noted for its imaginative solutions to technical challenges. Recognizing this, Schmidt and the founders chose to allow engineers to take 20 percent of their working time to develop their own ideas and projects.[5] Creative momentum resumed, not least because management confirmed the autonomy of the "creatives," at least in part.

Start-ups are built for creativity (unless they are McDonald's franchises), with capital that is running higher-than-average risk (unless they are McDonald's franchises). So the key question for creativity-oriented new enterprises is, What environments foster their blossoming? Start-ups will need a supportive tax regime and legal provisions, which will set rules that assist new firms in securing patents and intellectual property. Their time horizons for generating innovative products must be consistent with the complexity of the projects undertaken and the state of research and understanding in the field. Experimental development and market exploration cannot be rushed, which is hard on investors. (Google earned nothing in its first three years, for example, and Skype, purchased by Microsoft for $8.5 billion in 2011, has yet to turn a profit.) Prospects also depend on the knowledgeability of rivals. As the dot-com surge showed, many start-ups were one-idea companies; many failed due to this narrowness, yet some ideas propelled small firms into the ranks of leading corporations (Vodafone, Skype).[6] In other cases, success with one idea did not lead to further productive insights, and founders sold out their interests to investors. This was what Louis Renault attempted less than a year after he crafted his first automobile (1898), but failing to find any willing buyers, he reluctantly continued to run the business.[7] Not every creative entrepreneur is continuously creative; few Thomas Edisons appear in any generation.

One central insight can also provoke a series of product ideas, reframing a business sector. In France, Paul Rivier, a CNRS engineer who liked to fish on Sundays, designed an improved fishing rod and patented it, but the market ignored him. When his wife complained about how poorly her frying pans performed, he used ideas from his fishing rod development to solve the no-stick pan problem. Again a patent and again no commercial interest, but word of mouth about the innovation circulated, eventually drawing investors and setting off the T-Fal no-stick kitchen tool boom in the mid-1950s. Looking critically at other household and daily-use items, Rivier discovered that many designs had stagnated, leaving room for radical innovations using new materials and production processes. Researchers at the Ecole des Mines termed this reassessment of standard designs "intensive innovation"; it has stimulated other new starts reimagining mundane tools for contemporary markets.[8]

Second, how can sponsors get start-ups to do what they want done? First, as shareholding members of the board, investors have the authority to direct managers to follow their leads. This is difficult at arm's length, however, so directors may need to develop routines to learn about work in process, so as to guide policy. Sponsors also clearly need to develop their own competences in relation to the technical and market domains start-up leaders inhabit, as substantial asymmetries of information usually exist. Overseeing creativity-based start-ups from a distance, reviewing reports and "the numbers," is a recipe for trouble. Alternatively, investors can negotiate contracts with start-up leaders, a useful step as long as they recognize the need for informed governance and flexibility. Both approaches can be traced back well into the nineteenth century; these issues did not just arise with the information economy.

How do mature firms discover that they need an infusion of creativity? Signals may arrive from the external environment: decaying sales of the firm's product or service line, an increasing cost for raising funds in capital markets, or critical assessments by financial or industrial analysts. Similarly, the appearance of substitutes for a firm's core competences is also a warning sign. Internally, key personnel may defect to competitors, or planned new products may fail in the prototype or testing phase, as has frequently happened to pharmaceutical firms.

What, then, to do? Two strategies have proven effective. Managers may configure a new unit inside the firm to foster creativity, identifying actors who are in charge. The challenge for executives here is classic—staying out of the way is difficult, as is providing the specialists with resources and time enough to find a creative solution. Alternatively, management may seek a joint venture or a joint project with another enterprise or foster a project start-up tasked to break out of conventional practices. Here the challenge is a reduction of authority and control. For example, by the 1960s Fujitsu Corporation, itself a 1935 spinoff of Fuji Electric, made telephones and computers. The firm recognized the possible application of electronic devices to robotics and machine control. Realizing that this potential was too emergent to be adequately supported inside a mass-production enterprise, in 1972, executives spun off a wholly owned start-up, FANUC, which became world dominant in robotics and computer numerical control. FANUC has also entered into numerous joint ventures to explore technical opportunities, becoming wholly independent of Fujitsu only in 2009.[9]

Finally, serial entrepreneurs transform creativity into a craft skill, something that evidently can be learned through experience but not from textbooks. These individuals, like inventors, repeatedly launch firms, sell off the successful ones, close the failures, and move on to new projects.[10] Individuals like Stewart Skorman and Judy Johnston personify this capability, which involves handing off an expanding business to managers. Skorman has recently been active in launching "the ultimate movie recommendation engine," his sixth start-up over a twenty-five-year span. A former executive at what is now Whole Foods, he sold Real.com to Hollywood Video for $100 million, while dot-com bust HungryMinds.com lost $20 million. "I'm the creative guy you want to start with, but not the management guy you want to run it," he observed. Johnston left a corporate position at Hewlett-Packard to start a firm producing a children's printing kit that HP had rejected. She sold this firm to Mattell for $26 million and is now heading her third enterprise, a children's magazine. "It helps for entrepreneurs to be addicted to productivity," she noted, "including their own, but I'm not qualified to run a big company."[11] Not all serial start-ups are in creativity-based areas; rather, in the United States, Europe, and Japan, restaurateurs regularly start bistros and bars, run them for a few years, take a break, then start another.

Like many aspects of creativity, serial entrepreneurship has a history, not least going back to nineteenth-century family firm patriarchs who created new firms for their sons. Philadelphia's Bromley textile mill family was notable in this regard, generating lace, yarn, and knitting firms out of the profits of its original woolen-carpet business.[12] Hence, for business historians, researching creativity is not simply a means to stay current with enterprise trends but is also a means to reconstitute a rich and varied tapestry of business experience in the past.

NOTES

1. Michael Gibbert and Philip Scranton, "Constraints as Sources of Radical Innovation? Insights from Jet Propulsion Development," *Management and Organizational History* 4 (2009): 385–99.

2. Benoît Weil, Patrick Fridenson, and Pascal Le Masson, "Interview with Pascal Daloz: Concevoir les outils du bureau d'études: Dassault Systèmes; une firme innovante au service des concepteurs," *Entreprises et Histoire*, no. 58 (Apr. 2010): 150–64.

3. Arnoud de Mayer, "Strategic Issues Facing Business Schools," *Decision Line*, Mar. 2003, 4–9.

4. See Bruno Latour, *Aramis, or the Love of Technology* (Cambridge, MA: Harvard University Press, 1997), and Vincent Guigueno, "Building a High-Speed Society: France and the Aerotrain, 1962–1974," *Technology and Culture* 49 (2008): 21–40.

5. Eric Schmidt and Hal Varian, "Google: Ten Golden Rules," *Newsweek*, 2 Dec. 2005, available at http://analytics.typepad.com/files/2005_google_10_golden_rules.pdf (accessed 5 July 2011).

6. Syed Tariq Anwar, "Vodafone and the Wireless Industry: A Case in Market Expansion and Global Strategy," *Journal of Business and Industrial Marketing* 18 (2003): 270–88.

7. Patrick Fridenson, *Histoire des usines Renault*, 2nd ed., vol. 1 (Paris: Le Seuil, 1998), 46.

8. Vincent Chapel, "La poêle magique, ou la genèse d'une firme innovante," *Entreprises et Histoire*, no. 23 (Nov. 1999): 63–76, and Pascal Le Masson, Benoit Weil, and Armand Hatchuel, *Strategic Management of Innovation and Design* (Cambridge, UK: Cambridge University Press, 2010).

9. Seiuemon Inaba, *The FANUC Story: Walking the Narrow Path* (n.p.: n.p, 1992); Tomoatsu Shibata and Mitsuru Kodama, "Managing Technological Transition from Old to New Technology: Case of Fanuc's Successful Transition," *Business Strategy Series* 9 (2008): 157–62.

10. Ari Hyytinen and Pekka Ilmakunnas, "What Distinguishes a Serial Entrepreneur?," *Industrial and Corporate Change* 16 (2007): 793–821.

11. Jennifer Wang, "Confessions of Serial Entrepreneurs," 8 Jan. 2009, available at www.entrepreneur.com (accessed 17 May 2011).

12. Philip Scranton, *Figured Tapestry* (Cambridge, UK: Cambridge University Press, 1989).

3. Complexity

> Complexity makes definition problematic. . . . Starting in the
> middle, accepting that complexity is important and intrinsic
> is the beginning of wisdom. . . . For any complex form of
> human activity, there are likely to be aspects of context that
> bind it, interpret it, control it, and invest it with significance
> according to given, existing orders of rules, examples, other
> historical circumstances, and above all, in all likelihood, an
> institutional history.
>
> —*John Kelly*, The American Game

Complexity studies came of age in the 1990s,[1] not least because they undertook to bring together aspects of physics, biology, systems theory, and economics through attention to questions of dynamic systems, emergent properties, feedback loops, self-organizing phenomena, and nonlinear processes. Becoming familiar with this field can hold considerable value for business historians because economics, nations, markets, and enterprises represent, at different scales, space-time complexities having distinctive forms, all available for research investigation. In this section, we offer first a review of complexes and complex systems, then a short discussion of the difference between complex and complicated, followed by a sketch of how an economy exemplifies complexity, a review of some varieties of complexity, and closing remarks on historical issues and possibilities for research this line of analysis offers.

In contributing to a recent management essay collection, two Belgian scholars offered a helpful framing statement:

> [In a complex,] the components are mutually entangled, so that a change in one
> component will propagate through a tissue of interactions to other components
> which in turn will affect even further components, including the one that initially started the process. This makes the global behavior of the system very hard
> to track in terms of its elements. Unlike the simple "billiard ball" systems studied
> by classical mechanics, complex systems are the rule rather than the exception.
> Typical examples are a living cell, a society, an economy, an ecosystem, the Internet, the weather, a brain or a city.[2]

No quantitative measure of complexity has been devised; instead, "good enough" understandings and a "partial ordering" arise from experience, such that generally, one "firm will be more complex than another one if it has more divisions, if its divisions have more employees, if the divisions have more channels of interaction, and/or if its channels of interaction involve more person-to-person [exchanges]." Hence, in themselves workforce numbers, assets, or returns on investment do not document complexity. Moreover, complex systems have "intrinsic unpredictability" and do not trend toward states of equilibrium; indeed, equilibrium-based theories like classical mechanics or neoclassical economics are helpless on this terrain. Managers who pretend that their firms are stable, rational, and hierarchical fail to see them realistically, "as a constantly evolving network of *associations between circumstances and actions*," and thus "rarely have procedures to learn from experience."[3] In this light, it may be that the more personalized visions often found within family firms assist their operators in more adequately appreciating such evolving associations.

To undertake research engaging the complex, it is helpful to differentiate the concept from a near cousin, the complicated. It is an error to see complex as the inverse of simple, for "complex is the opposite of independent, while complicated is the opposite of simple."[4] Why should this be the case? Paul Cilliers explains: "If a system . . . can be given a complete description in terms of its individual components, such a system is merely complicated. . . . In a complex system . . . the interaction among the constituents of the system and the interaction between the system and its environment are of such a nature that the system as a whole cannot be fully understood simply by analyzing its components."[5] Blogger Flemming Funch fleshes out the difference skillfully:

> *Complicated* is when something contains many intricately combined parts. It is something that is hard to figure out. Even if you do figure it out, there's no guarantee that things are put together in a sensible way. *Complex* is when something acts as a system, and it is exhibiting systemic properties that aren't obvious. It is something more and different than simply a sum of its parts. There might or might not be many parts, but the result is something not very transparent, which takes on a life of its own in some fashion. An Airbus A380 is complicated. A jellyfish is complex. The Paris Metro network is complicated. How people use it is complex. Your skeleton is complicated. You are complex. A building is complicated. A city is complex.[6]

An astute online commentator added: "It seems this is comparing things that can be understood by reductionism vs. things that need to be understood by emergence."[7] Precisely so; some complicated entities can be understood, at least as artifacts, by identifying their essential components and structure (as in an engine schematic), whereas dynamic systems cannot be analyzed without centering on processes, feedback, restructuring, and adaptive change, hence time and transformation.

A complex system displays at least the following ten aspects: (1) a large number of elements; (2) elements interacting dynamically; (3) elements influencing many other elements and being influenced by them in turn; (4) nonlinear interactions, such that small causes can have large effects, and "large" events can have minimal effects; (5) interaction paths usually involving just a few steps; (6) pervasive feedback loops; (7) system interactions with the environment (it is open); (8) complex systems in equilibrium are dead, defunct; (9) system history is "co-responsible" for present behavior; and (10) elements act in response to the limited information available; no actor "knows" the system as a whole. This perspective provides a refreshing way of exploring a firm, a sector, or an economy. As Cillier explains, step by step, for economies: (1) they have large numbers of economically active people (and organizations, we might add); (2) these elements interact by lending, borrowing, exchanging (and producing); (3) interactions are diverse but do not directly indicate actors' relative influence on the system; (4) nonlinearity is everywhere; (5) usually, agents interact with regular sets of partners (even online);[8] (6) feedback is fundamental to actors' ongoing decisions; (7) its openness makes it just about "impossible" to draw the economy's borders; (8) the economy never stands still, and when it freezes, as with a credit crisis, disaster looms; (9) both distant and recent history impinges on actors' preferences and choices; and (10) no superagent has all the economy's information in hand; decisions must be made with available and incomplete information.

Thus an economy is a complex system, which provides for both cooperation and rivalry; yet it is at base unpredictable and only partly comprehensible. Discarding elegance in the reduction of economic action to core principles or algorithms, this approach's realism about action and decision-making surely provides multiple entry points for historical research. For example, as Alessandro Stanziani has shown,[9] the nineteenth-century wine trade was almost impenetrably complex. Exporters had incomplete and often misleading information about markets abroad, and uncertainties about the composition and qualities of vineyard products flowing into ports were constantly a problem. Labels could be (and were) faked, origins and districts were not well defined. Vendors also added adulterants (usually sugar) to enhance alcohol levels, with unknowable effects on flavor and durability. Collaborative and state regulation reduced complexity to a degree, but this process took generations.

Moreover, complexity is not just one thing. It materializes as a condition underlying perception and action in three principal ways, each of which can be inverted to indicate a converse condition. The candidates here are cognitive, generative, and material (or environmental) complexities, and their converses (opposite in sequence, action, or direction) are historical, regressive, and intellectual complexities. Cognitive complexity involves the multiple dimensions, or "scales," used when an actor is assessing a situation, a problem, or a "stimulus" (differentiation) or taken into account when considering "producing an output" (integration). Both involve core social activities for making sense and making meaning and thus are far more complex than decision-making rules, which are subject to logical sequencing. Moreover, the challenges of cognitive complexity are aggravated by "data smog"—an excess of available information of unknown quality and uneven or uncertain relevance to the situation at hand.[10] Cognitive complexity is thus forward looking: What have we here? What shall I/ we do and how? Historical complexity works in the other direction, from the present into the past, undertaking to derive meaning and sense from the residues, traces, or fragments of actions taken by others (and by us). In efforts to make sense of trends, patterns, or events, usually in relation to contemporary questions, historical complexity has to deal with the inverse of data smog, the "great forgetting," which entails that memories are partial, combined, and intentional (not just recordings) and that documentation has been doubly selected, by those creating texts and images and by the nonlinear processes that nonrandomly destroy historical evidence. This variety of complexity then confronts analogous problems of unevenness and uncertainty, while recognizing that there are always unknown and unknowable sources beyond the researcher's grasp.

Generative complexity involves "dealing with possible futures which are still emerging, largely unknown, non-determined, and not yet enacted" with "not-yet-defined alternatives" for action.[11] As organizational learning theorists Peter Senge and Otto Scharmer noted: "Generative complexity is about how to involve multiple players in processes of collaborative co-creation. . . . It clearly links to the blurring boundaries between self-knowledge and reality. Generative complexity inheres in all processes that deal with emergent and not-yet-enacted realities."[12] Whereas cognitive complexity stretches to comprehend current conditions, the generative variant is about building and defining futures, clearly drawing on progress motifs. Inverting this leads to regressive complexity, which configures the dynamics of decay and failure, emergent certainly, but in the sense of unfolding, underdetermined disasters (think Bhopal and *Challenger*). Finally, structural complexity concerns the material dimensions of an environment, both the constraints on action and institutional openings for initiatives (money, materials, climate, infrastructure). If cognition is complex and creativity is contingent, structure and environment represent context, an insistent presence of the real that cannot be set aside without hazard. Inverting the material to frame the ideational context, moving from outside to inside, we acknowledge the welter of competing, intersecting, and contradictory ideas, techniques, and frameworks available to those who seek guidance for action. These characteristics define intellectual complexity, the last variant noted here, but surely not the last variant.

Where are there venues for business historians to take up threads from this elaborate fabric? Perhaps we could explore means developed by managers, organizations, professions, and states to deal with increasing complexities in the economy, technical environment, work processes, social relations of production and consumption, and so on. These actors use reductionist tactics, on the one hand, as within the firm, efforts surface for simplification and for gathering statistics, refining accounting, and formalizing reporting. Initiatives for standardization within enterprises and sectors also fit well here. On the other hand, we expect that emergence-centered approaches may well be less studied. Complexity is anticipated in many large construction projects, but it emerges as a dimension of unfolding practices, which trigger unexpected challenges. A century ago (and perhaps still) within firms, managing by walking about was surely a complexity-engaging technique, just as installing flexible and adaptive equipment acknowledged the emergent character of both demand and technology.[13] Seeking news from all fronts as well as sustaining versatility recognizes the unpredictability of trends and the limits to control. Asking historical questions that can document and analyze such work can bring business historians opportunities for creative research.

NOTES

Epigraph. John Kelly, *The American Game: Capitalism, Decolonization, Global Domination, and Baseball* (Chicago: Prickly Paradigm Press, 2006), 37.

1. Notably in relation to the Santa Fe Institute, whose motto is "complexity research expanding the boundaries of science." For the Institute's early years (it began in 1984), see M. Mitchell Waldrop, *Complexity: The Emerging Science at the Edge of Order and Chaos* (New

York: Simon & Schuster, 1992). The Institute has published hundreds of working papers, a subset of which offers insights on history and to historians. See, for example, Samuel Bowles, "The Co-evolution of Institutions and Preferences: History and Theory" (working paper, 09-04-008), or Frank Schweitzer, Giorgio Fagiolo, Dider Sornette, Fernando Vega-Redondo, and Douglas White, "Economic Networks: What Do We Know and What Do We Need to Know?" (working paper 09-09-038, both accessible at the Institute's website: www.santafe.edu/research/working-papers/year/2009/. For French perspectives, see Edgar Morin, *On Complexity* (New York: Hampton Press, 2008), and Edgar Morin et Patrick Viveret, *Comment vivre en temps de crise?* (Paris: Bayard, 2010).

2. Carlos Gershenson and Francis Heylighen, "How Can We Think the Complex?," in *Managing Organizational Complexity*, ed. Kurt Richardson (n.p.: Information Age Publishing, 2005), 49.

3. Ibid, 49–51, 55, emphasis added.

4. http://en.wikipedia.org/wiki/Complexity/ (accessed 8 June 2010).

5. Paul Cilliers, *Complexity and Postmodernism: Understanding Complex Systems* (London: Routledge, 1998), vii.

6. "Ming the Mechanic: Complicated and Complex," 29 June 2008, http://ming.tv/flemming2.php/__show_article/_a000010-001928.htm (accessed 8 June 2010).

7. Mike, 4 July 2008, at ibid.

8. This transition away from face-to-face encounters—distanciation—is one of modernity's core features, according to Anthony Giddens. See his *Condition of Modernity* (Stanford: Stanford University Press, 1992).

9. Alessandro Stanziani, "Negotiating Innovation in a Market Economy: Foodstuffs and Beverage Adulteration in 19th-Century France," *Enterprise and Society* 8 (2007): 375–412, and "Information, Quality, and Legal Rules: Wine Adulteration in 19th-Century France," *Business History* 51 (2009): 268–91.

10. Quotes from George Por, "Collective Intelligence and Collective Leadership: Twin Paths to Beyond Chaos," *Sprouts: Working Papers on Information Systems* 8 (2008), no. 2, available at http://sprouts.aisnet.org/8-2 (accessed 8 June 2010).

11. Ibid.

12. Senge and Scharmer, quoted in Bolko von Oetinger, "From Idea to Innovation: Making Creativity Real," *Journal of Business Strategy* 25.5 (2004): 38.

13. MIT designers of early computer controls for machine tools recognized this, announcing their goals of creating "flexible machines" for diverse metalworking tasks. See William Pease, "An Automatic Machine Tool," *Scientific American* 187 (Sept. 1952): 101–15.

4. Improvisation

Business historians have been fascinated by innovation for generations.[1] *Improvisation* is a far less familiar term, more likely to be thought of as a capacity some musicians or comedians possess than as a tool in a manager's or an organization's kit. Our lack of interest in improvisation may in part be traced to business history's long tradition of focusing on rationalization and on rule-centered hierarchies, environments in which responsibility and routine are prized and in which change is incremental, often planned, and usually well bounded. By contrast, improvisation may be significant in ambiguous situations, in crises, in one-off projects through which multiple actors collaborate (and contend), or in decision spaces where knowledgeability and time are both in short supply. For one analyst, improvisation represents " 'on-the-spot . . . criticizing, restructuring, and testing of intuitive understandings of experienced phenomena' while the ongoing action can still make a difference."[2] Projects are especially promising sites, as they involve unknowns not recognized at the outset, unexpected events that generate sudden costs, delays, or failures, and unplanned participants whose numbers and specialties expand with the difficulties encountered. (See Prospects, 6: Projects.)

To proceed, let us first offer several examples of improvisational practices, followed by an effort to link improvisation with a cluster of user-driven categories regarding knowledgeability, and closing with some suggestions about how this concept can be of value to business historians. On 15 January 2009, USAirways pilot Chesley Sullenberger, in an Airbus 320 carrying 155 passengers and crew, departed from New York for Charlotte, North Carolina, and two minutes into the flight, struck a flock of geese, destination unknown. The plane's turbofan engines sucked in a number of birds and lost virtually all their thrust at an altitude of roughly 1,000 meters (3,200 ft). With no chance of reaching any airfield, Sullenberger safely landed the plane in/on the Hudson River; a flotilla of boats rescued all those aboard. Sullenberger's response to a crisis represented what one aviation commentator termed "heroic improvisation," an imaginative individual response to an unexpected situation.[3] Such responses may fall short more often than they succeed, as pilots of planes that did crash disastrously were surely trying to improvise their way out of life-threatening failures. Still, Sullenberger's totally "outside the box" notion of landing an 85-ton aircraft descending at 150 miles per hour (240 km/h) on a river surface proved inspired.[4]

Crisis improvisation is very difficult, more so for groups than individuals, it seems. As B. A. Turner observed of teams schooled to deal with emergencies: "An unprecedented crisis will challenge the expectations and everyday procedures of the staff of an emergency organization. They will find it necessary to adjust their understanding of what is going on before they can take any useful action. And since improvisation called for different attitudes and work practices from those of a routine response, it may be difficult for staff accustomed to working in one fashion to shift readily into a more flexible mode."[5] Truly, some working groups deal so routinely with crises and unprecedented situations (firemen, combat military forces, market makers in stock and commodity exchanges) that they devise informal protocols and shared expectations for engaging them. The Xerox copier repairmen observed by Julian Orr in the 1980s offer a classic example of what we might call "sustained improvisation." Their assignment was to maintain complicated machines under service contracts; of course, a wide variety of troubles arose. Xerox had provided repair workers with extensive documentation for each model and manuals with explicit directions for fixing deficiencies, replacing components, and testing the results. Of course as well, like online sets of "frequently asked questions" (FAQs), the manuals proved inadequate to deal with the extraordinary variety of things gone wrong. Hence repairmen improvised, enacting just that "on-the-spot criticizing, restructuring, and testing of intuitive understandings" mentioned above, and moved on to sharing their insights and novel diagnostics over morning coffee before starting the next day's rounds. Through serial improvisation the repair community gathered a body of testable knowledge about both machine quirks and their users that transcended the manuals' frozen information.[6]

Management theorist Karl Weick offers a variety of propositions about improvisational situations that resonate with business history issues. First, "if events are improvised and intention is loosely coupled to execution, the [actor] has little choice but to wade in and see what happens." That is, if your operational model doesn't work and you're not sure what outcomes any action will precipitate, you need to try something outside the handbook and watch for results. Second, "what will actually happen won't be known until it is too late to do anything about it." This is a basic point, simply because you wouldn't be improvising if you knew what you were doing, so when unexpected outcomes arise, your lack of understanding makes rationally taking corrective steps implausible. Improvising is high-risk, high-reward action. Third, "all the person can do is justify and make sensible, after the fact, whatever is visible in hindsight." Here we can get better at improvising by reflecting on process and results at the end of an action sequence, provided that later situations bear a dynamic resemblance to experiences compelling improvisation—which was the case for the Xerox repair workers. Thus there can be both learning about patterns and practices through improvisation and a rising sophistication in improvisatory skills,[7] but it's not likely that codified, reliable, or predictive knowledge will emerge.

If this is so, we can locate both crisis and sustained improvisation in relation to another category familiar to business history: research and development, and R&D's less often noticed inverse, development and research. Ideally, R&D starts with searching for foundational, scientific knowledge, which may or may not yield guidelines for innovations in artifacts and practices. This was the Bell Labs model, echoed in the chemical and pharmaceutical industries and, in a social science mode, at RAND. Research at RAND concerned systematic attempts to build reliable understandings of natural and social conditions. By contrast, a great deal of what is labeled R&D in industry is really D&R, which starts with a developmental goal (a new product or capability) facing a situation of inadequate knowledge. Focused scientific (and technical) research follows from encountering obstacles in the development process, as occurred with plastics and jet propulsion repeatedly, given the fragmentary scientific bases for polymer chemistry, metallurgy, combustion, and fluid dynamics in the 1940s. Both are formal approaches to generating explicit knowledge and control, and in some models this is where innovation arises. Crisis and sustained improvisation are instead informal approaches to devising situational solutions to immediate troubles. The resulting understandings may prove to be tacit, operational, and subject to considerable revision through iteration, but they are crucial to moving the enterprise through choppy waters.[8]

Why should any of this be valuable to business historians? Precisely because the universe of enterprise problem-solving contains R&D/D&R opportunities for systematic study, as do emergency or repeated challenges to address failing units, defective products, or inconsistent services. The routines and rules viable for the first pair are hopeless when actors confront the truly unexpected. Hence, how businesses have dealt with such fogs of confusion and swamps of unknowing offers a gauge of their flexibility and creativity.[9] One need only consider the managerial floundering by the US automobile industry in the 1970s to appreciate that using routine approaches in an unprecedented situation represents a recipe for misallocation of resources, reproduction of error, and competitive reverses. Improvisation also had a featured role in the responses of financial enterprises to the near meltdown of the global economy in 2008, sometimes intensifying rather than reducing pressures on institutions.[10] Business historians, who are familiar with finance, R&D, and innovation, could well profit from greater alertness to the nonlinearity, uncertainty, and creativity that prompt improvisation, whether actors using it prove successful or not.

NOTES

1. We are fascinated, too, but the theme has been so much discussed that we chose not to devote an entry to it.

2. Donald A. Schön, *Educating the Reflective Practitioner* (San Francisco: Jossey-Bass, 1987), 26–27, quoted at Karl Weick, "Improvisation as a Mindset for Organizational Analysis," in Weick, ed., *Making Sense of the Organization* (Oxford: Blackwell, 2001), 285.

3. James Reason, "Heroic Compensations," in *Innovation and Consolidation in Aviation*, ed. Graham Edkins and Peter Pfister (Aldershot, UK: Ashgate, 2000), 1–6, quote from 2.

4. For details see the thorough Wikipedia site: http://en.wikipedia.org/wiki/US_Air ways_Flight_1549.

5. B. A. Turner, "The Role of Flexibility and Improvisation in Emergency Response," in *Natural Risk and Civil Protection,* ed. Aniello Amendola, Tom Horlick-Jones, and Riccardo Casale (London: Chapman & Hall, 1995), 463–75, quote from 466. This essay, published six years before the 9/11 World Trade Center disaster, profiles fundamental issues of uncertainty and coordination that arise when unprecedented emergencies occur that were salient when the towers burned and disintegrated.

6. Julian Orr, *Talking about Machines: An Ethnography of a Modern Job* (Ithaca: Cornell University Press, 1996). Eventually cell phones made collective problem-finding and -solving feasible, but the machines always seemed to find new ways to break down, even as users initiated new ways to disable them.

7. As with musicians, for which see Paul Berliner, *Thinking in Jazz: The Infinite Art of Improvisation* (Chicago: University of Chicago Press, 1994). The propositions are derived from the Weick essay cited at note 1. See also Karl Weick and Kathleen Sutcliffe, *Managing the Unexpected* (San Francisco: Jossey-Bass, 2001).

8. Claudio Cibarra, "Notes on Improvisation and Time in Organizations," *Accounting, Management, and Information Technologies* 9 (Apr. 1999): 77–94; Dusya Vera and Mary Crossan, "Theatrical Improvisation: Lessons for Organizations," *Organization Studies* 25 (2004): 727–49; and Christine Jaeger, "Bureaux, micros, réseaux: Des entreprises aventureuses," *Réseaux* 4.18 (1986): 19–44.

9. Paul Adler and Clara Xiaoling Chen, "Combining Creativity and Control: Understanding Individual Motivation in Large-Scale Collaborative Creativity," *Accounting, Organizations and Society* 36 (2011): 63–85.

10. Andrew Ross Sorkin, *Too Big to Fail* (New York: Viking, 2009), and Michael Lewis, *The Big Short* (New York: Norton, 2010).

5. Microbusiness

Business historians have usually explored large-scale and middling enterprises, with the term *small business* marking an occasionally interesting residual. Indeed, in US law, "small" firms are all those with zero to five hundred employees, a class devised for reasons of policy, not clarity or analytical utility.[1] Microbusinesses are the smallest of the small, having up to nine employees (or by another definition, five or fewer, no access to commercial banking, and start-up costs below $35,000). Together employing an estimated 32 million people (ca. 2003—about one-sixth of all jobs), micros account for 98 percent of the United States' 24 million firms, three-quarters of these self-employed individuals. In addition, the US Department of Labor found that "new microbusiness start-ups from 1992 to 2005 generated more that 67 percent of gross job gains." Three-fifths of them are concentrated in four service sectors: real estate, construction and home repair, retail trade, and professional, technical, and scientific services. In addition, their owners, particularly in small towns and rural districts, "provide human capital in terms of local leadership."[2] This is a non-trivial phenomenon, and indeed it has a history, a global history. Tiny firms are and have been everywhere, yet how to conceptualize, research, and understand their diverse courses?

We address four topics here: historicizing self-employment; financing the smallest businesses; microbusinesses and households; and micros and the law/the state, especially in relation to the informal economy. (For resonances and contrasts between developed and emerging economies, see Prospects, 3: From Empires to Emergent Nations.) Self-employment sounds simple, but it is inordinately complicated. A technician assembling computer components on contract in his basement is both self-employed and a dependent subcontractor; a therapist providing counseling from her rented office is both self-employed and an independent professional; whereas a business school professor, serving as a $3,000 per day consultant, is both self-employed and tenured. Self-employment can be a temporary defense against economic turmoil, a lifetime economic role, or a part-time adjunct to a permanent job, just from these examples. It occurs at all class and income levels: studies of the very poor find self-employment one part of clustered strategies for "getting by," given the uncertainties of working for others.[3]

A century or more ago, the self-employed included many physicians and attorneys, shop owners, and architects, as well as farmers, itinerant peddlers and millwrights, saloon and boardinghouse keepers, and repairmen of shoes or machines. All segments of the class structure were present, as were women, in far greater numbers than we had suspected.[4] The ambiguities of the category stand out as soon as we recognize that in the past, as is true today, some of the self-employed brought family members into their work processes, often without compensation other than sustenance, some recruited ill-paid trainees, assistants, and apprentices, and yet others hired clerks or took on partners. Several things seem plausible across the generations: the spaces for self-employed professionals have narrowed; the desire to be one's own boss continues; and poor people's involuntary self-employment remains, given their dearth of experience, education, and capital. The Internet has opened new spaces for self-employment, through blogs that generate advertising revenue (and consulting opportunities) and journalism sites owned by an editor who contracts out writing assignments to freelancers (who, curiously, are also self-employed). These phenomena suggest that an intricate net of relationships among tasks, owners, clients, and actors has been deployed in the spatially stretched world of online production. Exploring historically the relationships of such microbusinesses to subcontracting and outsourcing is overdue.

How do micros get start-up and expansion funds? They are too small scale in their planning to attract the attention of banks; indeed, few of their proprietors qualify as entrepreneurs on this count, as they are just trying to make a living, not a fortune, just trying to work, not innovate.[5] Hence, most commonly, funding comes from family, friends, savings, or small-time moneylenders, or through social connections. Recently, state agencies, at least in the United States and Britain, have undertaken to assist beginners. An Oregon program identified this as public service, noting that 60 percent of its clients were women, half from ethnic or racial minorities. In Portland, a New York artist fleeing the city after 9/11 secured a $7,000 loan to open a flower stand and soon became self-supporting. More generally, "microenterprise may be a particularly strong option for those living in areas where wage jobs are very scarce," for the disabled, and "for those [with] child care needs."[6]

Such tentative maneuvers in the industrialized West, whose policy mismatches merit historians' attention, have been far outpaced by microlending/microsavings initiatives in emergent economies beset by deep poverty. Postindependence programs to fight Bangladesh's rural deprivation yielded three, now-huge banks for the poor (Grameen, ASA, and BRAC), which led "a global 'microfinance' movement dedicated to expanding access to small-scale loans, savings accounts, insurance, and broader financial services." This surge followed the failures of state-sponsored or state-subsidized rural credit banks in India, the Philippines, and dozens of other nations, recording loan default rates from 40 to 95 percent. By contrast, market-oriented microfinance institutions have consistently recorded payback rates above 95 percent (until recently). In India notably, investors jumped into microcredit operations, imagining profits that failed to materialize from "retail" banking.[7] Historically, research on sources of credit for tiny businesses is relatively rare, though Claire Zalc explored this issue for immigrant start-ups in interwar France, and Ivan Light and Edna Bonacich documented Korean *kye* circles to fund postwar immigrant businesses in Los Angeles.[8] Geographer Jane Pollard has analyzed financing and spatial dynamics among recent Birmingham (UK) designer-centered jewelry microbusinesses.[9] These works can all provide inspiration for historians' projects.

Households are much entangled with microbusinesses, in what Balihar Sanghera calls "domestic embedding . . . a mixture of competition, domination, negotiation, and custom." Among immigrants to the United Kingdom, though husbands are usually treated as sole proprietors at retail shops and restaurants, wives are uniformly involved, either by assisting directly or, when women "working" in public places is deemed culturally inappropriate, by maintaining family and home life single-handed (and in many cases doing both). Children's labor is also "negotiated and contested," reflecting "the power relations and different interests of family members." Such operators conduct business "as a way of 'making ends meet' rather than as an opportunity to accumulate capital." They do enjoy "a measure of social prestige," because having a microbusiness lets them "escape the employment relation and provides a better alternative to casual and low-pay work." In consequence, owners' goals center on business survival and "making enough for the family."[10] Historians, thanks to Susan Ingalls Lewis, now realize that female-owned microbusinesses were hardly unusual; she discovered two thousand of them in New York State's capital city, Albany, during the half century after 1830, many operated from homes.[11] A century later, Avon and other direct-selling organizations encouraged tens of thousands to become female microentrepreneurs, using house parties to sell cosmetics to their acquaintances as well as making door-to-door sales visits. Thus utilizing Sanghera's findings, business historians could well investigate how domestic embedding worked for both male- and female-headed microfirms in other eras and locations and the degree to which its components' relative significance changed over time.

Microbusinesses intersect with few major institutions, but they do confront the law and engage the state in two opposed ways. From nineteenth-century Philadelphia to contemporary Hanoi, the state's policing institutions "have a long history of trying to drive vendors from the streets or to restrict their access."[12] Indeed, the suicide of an unlicensed Tunisian fruit vendor, after repeated beatings by "municipal inspectors," reportedly triggered the first phases of the Arab Spring revolution that toppled President Zine el-Abidine Ben Ali.[13] Control, inspection, suppression: these are frequent state responses to unwelcome microbusinesses, particularly in what has become known as the "informal economy."[14] France had a long tradition of freedom of commerce, dating to the 1790s, but in a World War One panic about "foreigners," the Third Republic established a commercial registry, drawing immigrant-owned firms into its administrative net, a process that would culminate in the orderly dispossession of noncitizen Jewish businesses, as Vichy contributed to creating the Holocaust.[15] These lawful victimizations surely provide food for thought and foundations for research.

By contrast, state efforts to foster other microbusinesses anchor the assistance and funding schemes noted above in the United States and Britain. In France, the last generation's changes in journalism employment have led to a proliferation of freelancing by reporters laid off due to downsizings and bankruptcies. In response to appeals from labor and employers' associations, the government developed legislation especially for individuals contracting with multiple enterprises, providing them with access to the benefits of the welfare state (health care, social security).[16] Clearly, in the "right" contexts and for the "right" people, hostility to and control over microbusinesses can be recalibrated as support and provision. Exploring these different vectors could enlarge and enrich business history.

NOTES

1. This is the Small Business Administration's black box, identifying those eligible for advice, loans, and special programs.

2. Michael Woods and Glenn Muske, "Economic Development via Understanding and Growing a Community's Microbusiness Segment," in *Entrepreneurship and Economic Development*, ed. Norman Walzer (Lanham, MD: Lexington, 2007), 187–209. Local leadership here refers to service on school or charity boards, planning groups, or in government positions, elected or appointed.

3. Denise Anthony, "The Promise of Micro-Enterprise: Understanding Individual and Organizational Impacts," *Contemporary Sociology* 35 (2006): 231–34.

4. Susan Ingalls Lewis, *Unexceptional Women: Female Proprietors in Mid-19th-Century Albany, New York, 1830–1885* (Columbus: Ohio State University Press, 2009). This accomplished study of ostensibly ordinary women secured the 2010 Hagley Prize for the outstanding book in business history—recognition of imaginative research skillfully executed.

5. Balihan Sanghera, "Microbusiness, Household, and Class Dynamics: The Embedding of Minority Ethnic Petty Commerce," *Sociological Review* 50 (2002): 241–57.

6. Valerie Plummer, "Microbusiness, Macro-impact," Community Investments, Spring 2006, 10–14, 22, and Jeffrey Ashe, "Microfinance in the United States: The *Working Capital* Experience," *Journal of Microfinance* 2.2 (2000): 22–58; for the UK, see Bernard Offerle, "Innovation, Micro-Business, and UK Government Support, *Revue LISA* 4 (2006): 171–188, available at http://lisa.revues.org/2237 (accessed 7 June 2011).

7. Beatriz Armendaniz and Jonathan Mordrich, *The Economics of Microfinance*, 2nd ed. (Cambridge, MA: MIT Press, 2011), chap. 1, and David Roodman, "Grameen Bank, Which Pioneered Loans for the Poor, Has Hit a Repayment Snag," *D.R.'s Microfinance Open Book Blog*, 9 Feb. 2010 available at http://blogs.cgdev.org/open_book/2010/02/grameen-bank-which -pioneered-loans-for-the-poor-has-hit-a-repayment-snag.php (accessed 9 June 2011). Hundreds of small competing microlenders emerged in Bangladesh, leading to families taking multiple loans they could not pay back (the analogy to Westerners running up balances on multiple credit cards is noted). Collapses of the small fry in the global economic smash and eventual pressure on the major MFI's in some cases yielded state takeovers. Roodman's in-depth study of microfinance, *Due Diligence*, will be published in 2012 by the Center for Global Development. See also James Brau and Gary Waller, "Microfinance: A Comprehensive Review of the Existing Literature," *Journal of Entrepreneurial Finance and Business Ventures* 9.1 (2004): 1–26.

8. Claire Zalc, *Meeting Shops: Une histoire des commerçants étrangers en France* (Paris: Perrin, 2010), and Ivan Light and Edna Bonacich, *Immigrant Entrepreneurs: Koreans in Los Angeles, 1965–1982* (Berkeley: University of California Press, 1991). *Kyes* are donor clubs in which prospective owners contribute regularly and which distribute start-up funds through a lottery. The cycle continues until all members have received their cash-out payments. It is dishonorable for early winners to stop contributing. Credit has long been entwined with moral rules and judgments, and it is worth inquiring whether, how, and where this has eroded.

9. Jane Pollard, "Making Money, (Re)making Firms: Microbusiness Financial Networks in Birmingham's Jewellery Quarter," *Environment and Planning A* 39 (2007): 378–97.

10. Sanghera, "Microbusiness," 242, 247–49.

11. Lewis, *Unexceptional Women*, chap. 1. Lewis excluded self-employed teachers (music, dance, languages), nurses, midwives, physicians, writers, women who took in boarders but were not listed as boardinghouse keepers, dressmakers/laundresses/milliners for whom no place of business was recorded, and female capitalists who invested in enterprises but did not participate in them.

12. Martha Lincoln, "Report from the Field: Street Vendors and the Informal Sector in Hanoi," *Dialectical Anthropology* 32 (2008): 261–65. For Philadelphia, see also Regina Austin, "'An honest living': Street Vendors, Municipal Regulation, and the Black Public Sphere," *Yale Law Journal* 103 (1994): 2119–31.

13. Kareem Fahim, "Slap to a Man's Pride Set Off Tumult in Tunisia," *New York Times*, 21 Jan. 2011, available at www.nytimes.com/2011/01/22/world/africa/22sidi.html (accessed 9 June 2011).

14. Alejandro Portes and William Haller, "The Informal Economy," in *The Handbook of Economic Sociology*, ed. Neil Smelser and Richard Swedberg (Princeton: Princeton University Press, 2005), 403–27.

15. Claire Zalc, *Meeting Shops*, and Zalc, "De la liberté du commerce pour tous à la carte de commerçant étrangère, 19ème siècle–1938," in *Petits entreprises et petits entrepreneurs en France (19e–20e siècles)*, ed. Anne-Sophie Bruno and Claire Zalc (Paris: Publibook, 2006), 29–48.

16. Simone Sandier, Valérie Paris, and Dominique Polton, *Health Care Systems in Transition: France* (Copenhagen: WHO Regional Office for Europe, 2004). In addition, very small enterprises in France (*très petites entreprises*) have taken to reclassifying their few employees as self-employed contractors (*auto-entreprises*), which swells the nominal number of microbusinesses and lowers state revenues, as employers then no longer pay their shares of health and pension taxes.

6. The Military and War

Conceptualizing military institutions as enterprises with training and warfare practices opens the way for business historians to analyze their budgets, hierarchies, priorities, and failures across time and space. Like businesses, military organizations have lively internal political struggles over the sources and uses of funds, the development of innovations (material, logistical, strategic), and the allocation of resources. Like firms, they buy goods and services, seek the advice of consultants and experts, and scramble to recover from poor preparation for or defeat in competition. Particularly during World War Two and the Cold War, rival armies, navies, and air forces sponsored cutting-edge technological ventures that transformed communications, information management, and transport as well as the conduct of warfare. On another front, business historians could research combatants' strategic and tactical maneuvering as varieties of management under conditions of uncertainty—involving decision-making with incomplete information, iterative feedback loops from practice, and improvisation in the face of inadequate resources, sudden crises, or unanticipated opportunities for victory. (See Opportunities, 4: Improvisation.)

Forty years ago, a wave of critical US scholarship focused on the military-industrial complex, a key dimension of the Cold War's global arms race, generally arguing that expansive military spending wasted resources needed for other social tasks and distorted economic incentives, hindering growth. Perhaps it is time to reexplore the linkages between public and private institutions through which warfare capabilities were created and sustained and to look back to earlier eras, reassessing the two-way exchanges between military and civilian sectors. Clearly a militarization of society and business arises on the demand side, as the maintenance of substantial peacetime forces involves both vast spending of public monies and a widespread presence of military bases, personnel, and activities across the landscape. Yet a civilianization of the military may also be fashioned in parallel, as serving in the armed forces becomes framed as a "career" (and not just for staff officers and specialists) and as reserve units slide back and forth between everyday life and combat or support duties.

Moreover, a subset of military technical innovations have had dual-use outcomes, spilling over into the general economy, being adopted and developed commercially (e.g., a great deal of modern instrumentation and measurement technologies, including optronics,[1] followed such a course). Civilian appropriation of military innovations for market-centered uses has been underinvestigated, outside the realm of computing. We know, for example, that military specifications for communications equipment or jet engines reflected expectations of use in far harsher conditions than versions of the "same" technologies for private use. So how were such devices reconfigured for civilian applications—redesigned, priced, marketed, and serviced? How were such transformations managed and funded? In Britain, Germany, and France, how was—is—military R&D related to corporate R&D? Are they complementary domains with considerable interaction or separate spheres, and in either case, why? How have relations between the two changed over time? To what degree do military organizations respond to changing fads in business management and accounting practices? What selectivity is evident in adopting and adapting practices, and why? Does the flow ever reverse, and if so, under what conditions (one possibility would be Cold War military project-management practices spilling over into civilian terrains)?[2] Going back a century or more, how was the business of supply managed, with what evidence of waste and corruption and with what creativity or innovation?[3] Business historical research into these patterns and trajectories could be revelatory, particularly in revising simplified diffusion notions of technological and organizational change.

During wars, how do industries, trade associations, and financial enterprises interact to address military necessities? What varieties of negotiations take place, and with what consequences for mobilizing and redirecting production and capital?[4] After all, the state is not a typical client, in that its agencies can in effect set prices, demand quantities, punish ineffectual partners or contractors, and at the limit, seize control over enterprises or transport systems and militarize their managements. Transitions from peace to war and from warfare into peacetime economies also deserve close study. In the US experience, entrepreneurial resistance to being enlisted in military provision was notable in both world wars, as were massive logistical problems in moving war-related goods across continents and oceans. In the UK, imperial institutions and a robust shipping sector resolved such concerns, despite Nazi submarine forces.[5] Mobilizations also shatter existing labor markets and labor relations, displacing company- or industry-wide policies and bringing into plants both unfamiliar workers (women, minorities, prisoners, forced laborers [in Japan, Germany, and the USSR]), and workers unfamiliar with the tasks at hand.

A critical related issue is what happens to a war machine's "acquired" workers when the fighting ends, well or badly. Moving to the nineteenth century, in demobilizing after the American Civil War, with Union military forces shrinking over 90 percent, what disposition was made concerning surplus small arms, horses, wagons, uniforms, and other impedimenta no longer needed? What provisions did the state (or the states) make for war veterans?[6] After World War Two, the United States found itself with several million surplus machines and tools and thousands of purpose-built factories. How were these reallocated to private hands, through what channels, for what uses, and with what returns to public coffers? In situations of military occupation, how is business restarted, reoriented, or reinvigorated, given the collapse or defeat of the prior regime? In recent years, the Laboratoire de recherche historique Rhone-Alpes undertook a substantial CNRS project studying the course of French businesses under the German occupation (1940–44), which we believe could serve as a model for similar inquiries.[7]

Finally, military organizations gather intelligence on businesses and economic capabilities in their own nations and in those of potential enemies, much of which could be valuable for business historians, once declassified. For example, the US Department of Defense sponsored research into the machinery and tool industries of other nations during the Cold War,[8] whereas the Air Force supported inquiries about economic dynamics by RAND analysts that remain richly informative long after the policy debates they influenced have faded.[9] Armed forces engineering groups also pioneered work on devising standard units and artifacts and operational protocols in many fields, another set of initiatives with implications for business practice over the generations. (See Prospects, 8: Standards.) It is equally essential to recognize that modern military procurement itself is very big business, contracting that is too rarely examined from military actors' points of view.[10] In preparing for innovations, military agencies seek competitive prototypes for testing and upgrading (or rejection). Here the setting and renegotiation of requirements and specifications exposes insufficiencies of knowledge, uncertainties about performance and pricing, and frequently revised expectations among all the parties. In the urgency of hot war and the intensity of the Cold War, orderly behavior may well be suspended as radical ideas, sketches for "winning weapons," and novel persons and institutions crowd onstage. The detailed, precise specifications that characterize careful peacetime projects can give way to experimental developments pushed forward to deployment as speedily as possible, with uncertain consequences.

In war and peace national variations are evident, as well. For the United States, competitive bidding represented a politically sensible and ostensibly economically rational strategy long after the complexity and indeterminacy of weapons and communications systems had made it archaic. This yielded to a Cold War–era transfer of responsibility to corporate contractors, whose self-interests may well have overwhelmed patriotic motives as the Soviet threat diminished. Meanwhile, the French military sought out small, technically expert companies they could dominate and control or monopolies that were favorites of the state apparatus. Results, not the virtues of competition, were at stake, alongside power and knowledge. Such contrasts beg for comparative study.

NOTES

1. Larry Masten, *Understanding Optronics* (Dallas: Texas Instruments, 1981), and; J. P. Fouilloy and Michel Siriex, "History of Infrared Optronics in France," *Proceedings SPIE 2552* (1995): 804–14. These authors trace French optronics back to jet engine instrumentation, starting in the late 1940s.

2. Harvey Sapolsky, *The Polaris System Development: Bureaucratic and Programmatic Success in Government* (Cambridge, MA: Harvard University Press, 1972). Sapolsky notes both that the project's management and control techniques (e.g., PERT) were widely influential and that they were often bypassed so as to get Polaris missile submarines into operational status.

3. A solid example of research in this vein is Mark Wilson, *The Business of Civil War: Military Mobilization and the State, 1861–1865* (Baltimore: Johns Hopkins University Press, 2006). For the transformation from military purchasing to prototyping and the procurement of complex weapons, see Kate Epstein, "Inventing the Military Industrial Complex: Torpedo Development, Property Rights, and Naval Warfare in the United States and Great Britain before World War I" (PhD diss., The Ohio State University, 2010).

4. Though concerned with broader questions and a longer time period, Adam Tooze, in *The Wages of Destruction: The Making and Breaking of the Nazi Economy* (New York: Viking, 2007), explores these issues in depth.

5. Nelson Lichtenstein, *Labor's War at Home* (New York: Cambridge University Press, 1983), and Robert Cuff, "United States Mobilization and Railroad Transportation: Lessons in Coordination and Control, 1917–1945," *Journal of Military History* 53 (1989): 33–50. See also David Edgerton, *Britain's War Machine: Weapons, Resources, and Experts in the Second World War* (London: Penguin, 2011).

6. Theda Skocpol, "America's First Social Security System: The Expansion of Benefits for Civil War Veterans," *Political Science Quarterly* 108 (1993): 85–116.

7. "Les entreprises françaises sous l'Occupation," Groupement de recherche, no. 2539 (GDR CNRS, 2002–9). See the website at http://gdr2539.ish-lyon.cnrs.fr/index_fr.php (ac-

cessed 19 May 2010). The group published three valuable essay collections: on overseas French enterprises, on cultural and media firms, and on consumer goods makers. In addition, following a conference at the Copenhagen Business School, Joachim Lund edited a comparable volume: *Working for the New Order: European Business under German Domination* (Copenhagen: Copenhagen Business School Press, 2006), which addresses the Netherlands, Scandinavia, Belgium, Byelorussia, and Greece.

8. Some of these studies are now available online through the Defense Technical Information Center: www.dtic.mil/dtic/ (accessed 19 May 2010).

9. Hundreds of RAND reports are downloadable from www.rand.org/ (accessed 19 May 19, 2010). For an overview, see Alex Abella, *Soldiers of Reason: The RAND Corporation and the Rise of American Empire* (Boston: Houghton Mifflin, 2008).

10. Thomas McNaugher, *New Weapons, Old Politics: America's Military Procurement Muddle* (Washington, DC: Brookings Institution Press, 1989), and John Alic, *Trillions for Military Technology: How the Pentagon Innovates and Why It Costs So Much* (New York: Palgrave Macmillan, 2007).

7. Nonprofits and Quasi Enterprises

How can nonprofits be a subject for business history, given that the profit motive is central to what we understand as business? First, nonprofits are and have long been a significant part of economies, capitalist and precapitalist. One estimate indicates that more than 10 percent of the US workforce is active in nonprofit work.[1] Moreover, centuries earlier, in early modern times, religious institutions and communities undertook many roles that were also handled by profit-seeking businesses. For example, monasteries produced wine, foodstuffs, and cloth, sold artifacts (holy objects), and provided health care to the poor, to travelers, and to penitents. They also served as regional financial institutions.[2] In both periods, nonprofits helped the business system by creating jobs, facilitating money flows, assisting those experiencing hardships, and attending to needs and opportunities ignored by the profit system. We often forget that today in many nations, nonprofits operate colleges, universities, and schools (including religious educational institutions), hospitals (though some in the United

States are reconfiguring themselves as profit-oriented), mutual insurance companies, and cooperatives. Specific examples include the British clothing store chain John Lewis and the Cooperative Society, which together represent a substantial segment of UK retailing.[3]

That the development of capitalism made major inroads into nonprofit activities cannot be overlooked, however. The commodification process has narrowed their workable domains.[4] Consider blood transfusions. A century ago scientists, charitable organizations, and medical institutions researched and handled transfusions. Originally, providing blood was a moral or patriotic duty, and donors were thanked, not paid. Since the 1970s profit-making firms have intervened in this process, creating a market for blood that has in turn generated a series of deadly problems.[5] The national basis for blood supplies shifted to a global market, chiefly supplied by innovative American firms, with blood becoming a disembedded commodity, often provided by poverty-class, compensated volunteers. The rising cost and complications of using American-branded blood brought French nonprofits and hospitals to attempt reliance on "free" local blood supplies, yielding a tragic outcome when AIDS-tainted supplies were fed into the health system.[6]

In our view, it is worth inquiring into nonprofits' management practices along three dimensions. First, how are they operated within the larger business system? Questions include: How is decision-making distinctive from or similar to that in "regular" businesses? What happens to value added (the nonprofits' "profits")? Who are their stakeholders, and what voice do they have? Fundamentally, what does management mean for nonprofits (and by extension, religious organizations), and what is its history? For example, corporations have often created their own nonprofits; in Japan every leading firm has its own foundation. How did such institutions come into being? Second, what are the business dimensions of care for the ill, aged, poor, orphaned, handicapped, and excluded between the early modern era and the last century? The state and private enterprise have never proven adequate to these needs; hence a third type of institution has persisted in many variations, as states lose political will and private firms recognize that profit opportunities are slim among such clients.[7] One case from France's postwar history is particularly noteworthy. Homelessness was a significant challenge in the later 1940s (individuals displaced by war, veterans unable to adjust to peacetime society), but neither the state nor companies took adequate initiatives to deal with it. Instead, Abbé Pierre created an organization, Les Compagnons d'Emmaus, a nonprofit focusing on homelessness, finding shelters or jobs and recruiting funds from the public. The early managers were poor people attracted to the mission; later this kind of social work became a new field for entrepreneurship. It offered second careers for private sector managers, accountants, or engineers who abandoned their jobs for public service, a religious vocation, or a fundamental life change. Nowadays this and similar organizations have found it essential to hire certified professionals as managers, employing specialists to avoid errors, litigation, and possible failure, yet this work remains outside commodification.[8]

Third, how are cultural and educational nonprofits operated, and what business histories might they have? Museums, orchestras, historic sites and heritage organizations (think of Britain's National Trust), and archives and conserving institutions generally are nonprofits, as are many educational institutions, though this differs from nation to nation. What economic issues are entwined with the creation of such institutions? For example, the Philadelphia Orchestra arose from the cultural interests of local financiers and industrialists in the early twentieth century but needed substantial private subsidies every year for decades.[9] That it has recently declared bankruptcy likely says as much about the changing character of the regional wealthy as it does about budgeting for labor and concert hall expenses. How have other such institutions been funded? Increasingly, in the last generation or two, fundraising has become almost as important as core missions, so what does this tell us about pricing and marketing cultural experiences?

The innovative performances and prospects of nonprofits can too easily be overlooked. Nonprofits are willing to take risks that neither the state nor the market will accept. For example, starting in the late 1960s,[10] Médecins Sans Frontières has sent physicians and nurses into war-torn regions where no other institutions can see their way to helping injured and threatened people. Equally, nonprofits strive to educate immigrants and assist them with integrating into unfamiliar societies, as was classically undertaken by urban settlement houses in the US cities, starting in the 1890s.[11] Nonprofits have been at the cutting edge of historic preservation in multiple nations, as well.

Both private interests and public institutions are closely linked to nonprofits, at times in conflicting ways. In some cases, families contest the donation of patriarchs' legacies to foundations, arguing that this denies them assets they had the right to anticipate would be theirs. Indeed, aging wealthy individuals at times come into contact with reformers needing funds for public services and agree to provide bequests, as did Carnegie and Rockefeller in the United States.[12] On the other hand, state regulations govern the lawful extent of donations, their uses, and their tax standing (i.e., whether they are deductible from income or estates). In consequence, nonprofits have a direct interest in every change in such laws and are, at least in the United States, known to lobby legislators on behalf of their interests, just as corporations do.

Nonprofits are active at every spatial scale, but they commonly begin with strong local roots. In Lyon, a group formed to take account of the educational needs of handicapped children. It expanded to national scale, but with enlargement had difficulty dealing with finances, especially given the increasing flow of donations. State controls and efforts to bring in qualified accountants did not work. Instead, one parent of a handicapped child, also a middle manager at a chemical producing corporation who was worried about his daughter, got onto the organization's board. He recruited more parents from the firm, in similar situations; when managers constituted a third of the board, they instituted a successful financial reorganization.[13] This is important because a nonprofit can be reorganized most effectively when its members take a matter into their own hands—outsiders lack commitment and vision. Though one person may have a vision, a collective is needed to move institutions forward.[14]

In a different vein, it is well known that American executives find it important to join the boards of key charities and foundations in their area, be it New York, Chicago, or Los Angeles. Historically, how has this community membership been managed through nonprofit participation in the United States, with the Rotary, Boy Scouts and Girl Scouts, and Community Chests (1890s–1950s)? What is the long-term pattern in other industrialized nations, as nonprofit board memberships are evidently coming to Europe? Nonprofits also become international organizations, just like MNCs (multinational corporations). From the Red Cross and Red Crescent to NGOs of all stripes, these institutions have realized their missions on a global scale. In consequence, they, along with their smaller brethren, are vulnerable to political and economic crises, to regime changes that alter their working environments, and to market crashes, which shrink their endowments and their fundraising results. Equally, foundations like the one created by Bill and Melinda Gates act locally and globally by consciously supporting initiatives from the bottom up. This strategy departs from a tradition in which funding reinforced personal or political priorities, as with the US oil industry's quite conservative Pew Family Foundation's early decades. Whereas the Pews' support for Rev. Billy Graham's evangelical campaigns reflected American provincialism, the Gates's philanthropy evidently springs from a broad cosmopolitanism. In light of these considerations, nonprofits can be seen as an evolving field of enterprise, and thus business historians may wish to explore their long-term development.[15]

NOTES

1. Molly Sherlock and Jane Gravelle, *An Overview of the Non-Profit and Charitable Sector* (Washington, DC: Congressional Research Service, 2009), available at www.fas.org/sgp/crs/misc/R40919.pdf (accessed 5 July 2011).

2. Adrian Bell and Richard Dale, "The Medieval Pilgrimage Business," *Enterprise and Society* 12 (2011): 601–27, and Kathryn Burns, *Colonial Habits: Convents and the Spiritual Economy of Cuzco, Peru* (Durham, NC: Duke University Press, 1999).

3. John Wilson and Rachel Vorberg-Rugh, "Management and Organization of the Cooperative Wholesale Society, 1863–2010" (paper presented at the Association of Business Historians annual conference, Reading, UK, July 2011).

4. Susan Strasser, ed., *Commodifying Everything: Relationships of the Market* (New York: Routledge, 2003).

5. Sophie Chauveau, "De la transfusion à l'industrie: Une histoire des produits sanguins en France (1950–fin des années 1970), *Entreprises et Histoire*, no. 36 (Oct. 2004): 103–19.

6. Jane Kramer, "Bad Blood," *New Yorker*, 11 Oct. 11, 1993, 74–95; Philippe Steiner, "Gifts of Blood and Organs: The Market and "Fictitious" Commodities," *Revue française de sociologie* 44.5 (2003): 147–62; and Kieran Healy, *Last Best Gifts: Altruism and the Market for Human Blood and Organs* (Chicago: University of Chicago Press, 2006).

7. Helmut Anheier and Wolfgang Seibel, eds., *The Third Sector: Comparative Studies of Non-Profit Organizations* (Berlin: De Gruyter, 1990).

8. Axelle Brodiez, "Entre social et humanitaire: Générations militantes à Emmaus (1949–2009)," *Le Mouvement Social*, no. 227 (2009): 85–100.

9. Hannah Kim, "Funding Practices and Strategies of the Philadelphia Orchestra: 1900–1940" (master's thesis, Rutgers University, Camden, NJ, 2000).

10. Corina Gregoire, Georgeta Nae, and Gheorghe Grigoire, "Private Actors' Involvement in International Public Policy Making," *Transactions MIBES* [Management of International Business and Economic Systems], 2008, 684–93, available at http://mibes.teilar.gr/conferences/MMIBES_CD_2008/POSTER/Grigore%20C_Nae_Grigore%20G.pdf (accessed 5 July 2011).

11. John Ehrenreich, *The Altruistic Imagination: A History of Social Work and Social Policy in the United States* (Ithaca: Cornell University Press, 1985).

12. For a transnational perspective, with views of the UK, Germany, Eastern Europe, Japan, and the Philippines, see Helmut Anheier and Jeremy Kendall, eds., *Third Sector Policy at the Crossroads: An International Non-Profit Analysis* (London: Routledge, 2001).

13. Magali Robelet, David Piovesan, Jean-Pierre Claveranne, and Guillaume Jobert, "Secteur du handicap: Les métamorphoses d'une gestion associative," *Entreprises et Histoire*, no. 56 (Sept. 2009): 85–97.

14. Magali Robelet, "Secteur de handicap: Les métamorphoses d'une gestion associative," *Entreprises et Histoire*, no. 56 (Sept. 2009): 85–97.

15. A substantive recent study on one element in nonprofits' activities is Olivier Zunz, *Philanthropy in America: A History* (Princeton: Princeton University Press, 2011), which deals with the Pews and many others.

8. Public-Private Boundaries

It is no longer possible to imagine the public and private spheres as decisively separate, if ever they were.[1] Some governments are in business, some businesses perform government functions for profit (in the United States, commercial prisons), and there are many boundary cases in which an enterprise or agency operates on both sides of a porous divide. Hence, given the waves of nationalizations and privatizations in the West and in the East, business historians need to acknowledge the temporary character of any attribution or claim about public versus private property, enterprise, or policy. Recognizing this can spark diverse research inquiries. Our discussion will be in two parts: first, an assessment of porosities and overlaps between public and private, and second, comments on exchanges and appropriations.

Historically, the boundary has been full of holes. Moreover, at times dual public-private claims or shared authorities have been established, which is what we mean by overlapping. The borderline is often unstable, ambiguous, or both; and these need not be deficiencies, for a lack of specificity can facilitate initiatives. Key historical questions concern the actors involved, their interests and negotiations, the financial dimensions, definitions of public and private interests, and of course, creativity in problem-solving. These phenomena may involve appropriating private capabilities for public purposes or devoting public facilities to private interests. In addition, given that there arguably are dual technologies, serving both military and civilian uses, are there not also dual enterprises, which serve both public and private needs? Military-industrial corporations are obvious members of this club, but so too were the Rothschild bankers who vetted and marketed bonds for governments and companies alike. The modern military itself constantly disregards its border with the private world: it recruits members of the public, else it would have no forces, even as it cannot exist without private enterprises or relationships with state enterprises. Military-business interactions are negotiable, involving economic and political issues and creating an equivocal dynamic that can be energizing, debilitating, or both by turns, to all parties. (See Opportunities, 6: The Military and War.)

Public concessions to private firms, licensing business monopolies at particular places, date to the ancien régime, continue through colonial railways, French coal mining, and international oil exploration, and are present in today's airport management and sports arena retailing.[2] They have been extended and refined into public-private partnerships, which originated in Britain and have multiplied globally,[3] currently including augmenting the TGV fast-train network in France. Given the immense costs of adding lines, the public railway agency chose a construction and operations partner, VINCI, which is securing finance, providing the workforce, and building the facilities, in exchange for a permanent share of the revenue stream.[4] Such partnerships may lead to privatization,[5] as with water authorities globally in the late twentieth century, a process that continues to be unsettled, given the reluctance of private owners to make major, often overdue capital investments.[6] These relationships may begin without establishing rules for behavior or performance, which can lead to corruption, abuse of trust, and conflicts of interest.[7]

Another clear example of the porous boundary is the higher-education system in France, which trains thousands of engineers and administrators in the *grandes écoles* at public expense (no tuition) for state jobs. These students receive a salary while learning. Many, after perhaps a decade as civil servants, are hired away by private-sector firms. At this point French corporations compensate the government for their past salaries (a practice anathema in the United States), thereby acquiring mid-career managers or engineers with considerable experience and developed networks. This system, called *pantouflage,* has been criticized for fostering departures of the best and brightest public servants, leaving agencies with a less talented, even if long-serving, staff.[8] In Japan, companies recruit talented civil servants in their fifties, which contributes to the rising gerontocracy of Japanese management. That process creates second careers and is termed "descent from heaven," because "heaven" is the Ministry of Finance, and state agency leaders are the functional equivalent of the former nobility or aristocracy.[9]

In the United States and the United Kingdom, by contrast, except at the very top, the divide between managers, engineers, and scientists in public agencies and private corporations is much firmer. Governments pay high-skill employees far less than leading corporations, but the attraction of public service, and perhaps influence on policy, is substantial. Meanwhile, prominent politicians and military officers do retire from administrative positions to take senior jobs in lobbying and management, notably in defense-supply sectors. This has occasionally happened in France, as retired generals have become heads of human resource departments at Peugeot, Dassault, and other firms. The American revolving door also moves senior federal administrators, when their parties lose an election, into law firms and think tanks—holding zones where they bide their time until later electoral success facilitates their return to heading agencies and commissions.[10]

Overlaps are situations in which private and public institutions compete or share similar responsibilities.[11] French public and private hospitals exemplify this phenomenon. Politicians see health care as a public good and thus hospitals are important, but the critical issue is cost. Public hospitals provide slow service and are not individualized, not responsive to patients, whereas private hospitals focus both on areas that are profitable and on well-fixed clients. In the 1990s, the government planned a rationalization process, which would replace competition with a division of labor. Public hospitals would provide high-tech devices that private clinics couldn't afford, for example. Local health care advocates resisted, as this approach would produce a lack of proximity and accessibility for most citizens, creating private clinics for the rich and public hospitals for the rest. That was indeed the outcome. As clinics multiplied, however, hospitals for workers and the poor began closing. Income from using sophisticated, high-tech devices could not cover deficits for primary care, while state funding shrank.[12]

In the United States, public health became a state priority in the nineteenth-century immigration decades, generating the establishment of large public hospitals and health clinics in major cities and community hospitals in small towns and rural areas. Religious groups and medical schools also built hospitals, many of which were operated privately by nonprofits. In the 1970s many American public hospitals collapsed (except those for military veterans) as governments at all levels began dropping the subsidies necessary for acquiring new technologies and for serving the poor. Thus American medical care has become heavily privatized, though funded through a maze of public agencies (Veteran's services, Medicare, Medicaid, state-level plans) and private, for-profit insurance companies. In consequence, tens of millions of the uninsured have no regular care and crowd emergency wards when illness arrives, even as profit-seeking high-tech medical corporations nationwide are consolidating chains of hospitals for the privileged. Pricing medical services has, in consequence, become chaotic, with item-by-item negotiations between providers and insurers metastasizing as searches intensify for strategies to overcome growing losses. [13]

Critics have argued that state-business competition stimulates inefficiencies and creates a crowding out of private initiatives, given the differential resources and power of the two parties. Yet any close look at the American health care system might suggest that such competition could instead provide ample public benefits and yield efficiencies instead. After all, no public policy benefits every stakeholder; reconfiguring US health care could injure private enterprise, but that could be a worthwhile outcome if public health improved. On another front, postwar state overseers of French financial markets stipulated that bonds be issued only with government permission. When agencies certified bonds solely for government and state enterprises' purposes, another crowding-out effect materialized, which arguably was far from positive. Large-scale military contracting has generated more mixed reviews, for though it deflects enterprises from their own interests and plans, it does commit the state to paying the bill for potentially transformative innovations.

In banking, though private institutions have high visibility, public banks are not trivial. Consider the Bank of England and the Federal Reserve, or the Banque de France, a private bank nationalized in the 1930s. Closer to the people, in 2007, the French postal system transformed its savings and checking account unit (started in 1918) into a full-service but public bank, which competes with commercial banks throughout the nation. By law, La Banque Postale cannot ignore the poor, but it is not clear that it can simultaneously serve them and seek clients among the rich, who can provide sizable deposits for placement as loans. Small account holders now face high fees for overdrafts and services, an unexpected consequence of public-private competition.[14] We also note that, in a world of privatization and globalization, many states have started sovereign investment funds, using government funds to purchase ownership shares in national and international enterprises. The roots of this phenomenon bear investigation, as do comparative and transnational histories of public-private partnerships, movements of personnel across the boundary, and the dualities of health care, banking, and other services, between states and markets.

Finally, a line is also crossed when private organizations appropriate public property and vice versa, in mobilizations of public assets for private gain and in state nationalizations, confiscations, or reorientations of private property and its uses. Historically in the United States, private developers have licensed public lands to extract timber, develop oil reserves, and recently, to exploit natural gas formations in shale geologies. Along America's Atlantic seashore, ocean-side home owners have routinely blocked public access to beaches, and only in some cases have state governments acted to reverse this seizure.[15] In France, the government had to pass a special law (1986) to regulate similar beach sei-zures, confirming citizens' access and the state's right to establish littoral parks as a preservation step. However, the costs of maintaining such reserves became so substantial that the managing authority recently moved to establish public-private partnerships to secure funding, including concessions for commercial retail operations.[16]

Nationalizations and confiscations do not put an end to business history; in-stead, they raise important questions about the reasons for state takeovers and the organizational changes that follow and how these affect the future courses of the agencies and enterprises involved. How are such actions distributed among sectors and regions? Not uncommonly, enterprises in Europe and Asia have completed a cycle from private to public to private again, and recently, threatened in the financial crisis, have sought substantial public support, though not supervision. These trajectories offer exciting possibilities for long-term historical studies. On the local level, governments can intervene in property uses through planning and restrictions, moves that some observers also call confiscations. In the 1970s, on a New England island, Martha's Vineyard, a county commission established land conservancies to limit tourism and hous-ing development, and it instituted a real estate transaction fee, dedicated to purchasing farm and forest land, removing such terrain permanently from the market.[17] The double irony was that land and home buyers thereby reduced the future stock of available land, and in so doing, they increased the value of all property on the island. Extended to the limit, this practice would destroy land development there. In a sharply different era and place, from the seventeenth century the French monarchy subjected privately held salt marshes and water lands to royal control, in order to assure supply for the state's salt extraction monopoly; thus such impositions are hardly modern, which reinforces our sense of both the value and the complexity of exploring public-private borderlines across the centuries.[18]

NOTES

1. Morton J. Horwitz, "The History of the Public/Private Distinction," *University of Penn-sylvania Law Review* 130 (1982): 1423–28, and Jeff Weintraub, "The Theory and Politics of the

Public/Private Distinction," in *Public and Private in Thought and Practice*, ed. Jeff Weintraub and Krishan Kumar (Chicago: University of Chicago Press, 1997), 1–42.

2. See Dena Goodman, "Public Sphere and Private Life: Toward a Synthesis of Current Historiographical Approaches to the Old Regime," *History and Theory* 31(1992): 1–20.

3. Roger Wettenhall, "The Rhetoric and Reality of Public-Private Partnerships," *Public Organization Review* 3 (2003): 77–107. An influential management analysis is James Perry and Hal Rainey, "The Public-Private Distinction in Organizational Theory: A Critique and Research Strategy," *Academy of Management Review* 13 (1998): 182–201.

4. Stéphanie Leheis, *Profil du projet: France–TGV Méditerranée* (Paris: Laboratoire Techniques, Territoires, et Sociétés, Université de Paris-Est, July 2009), available at: http://halshs .archives-ouvertes.fr/docs/oo/55/o1/87/PDF/case_study_report_tgv_med_part_5_1_ project_profile.pdf (accessed 6 July 2011).

5. George Pagoulatos, "The Politics of Privatization [in Greece]: Redrawing the Public-Private Boundary," *West European Politics* 28 (2005): 358–80. On the partnerships' history, see Martha Minow, "Private and Public Partnerships: Accounting for the New Religion," *Harvard Law Review* 116 (2003): 1229–70, and E. S. Savas, *Privatization in the City: Successes, Failures, Lessons* (Washington, DC: Congressional Quarterly Press, 2005).

6. Karen Bakker, "A Political Ecology of Water Privatization," *Studies in Political Economy* 70 (Spring 2003): 35–58, and Bakker, *Privatizing Water: Governance Failure and the World's Urban Water Crisis* (Ithaca: Cornell University Press, 2010).

7. Sven-Olof Collin, "In the Twilight Zone: A Survey of Public-Private Partnerships in Sweden," *Public Productivity and Management Review* 21 (1998): 272–83; Graeme Hodge, "The Risky Business of Public-Private Partnerships," *Australian Journal of Public Administration* 63.4 (2004): 37–49; and Hodge and Carsten Greve, "PPPs: The Passage of Time Permits a Sober Reflection," *Public Administration Review* 69 (Mar. 2009): 32–39.

8. Christophe Charle, "Le Pantouflage en France (vers 1880–vers 1980)," *Annales: Economies, Sociétés, Civilisations* 42 (1987): 1115–37.

9. Chalmers Johnson, "The Reemployment of Retired Government Bureaucrats in Japanese Big Business," *Asian Survey* 14 (1974): 963–75. See also Kent Calder, *Strategic Capitalism: Private Business and Public Purpose in Japanese Industrial Finance* (Princeton: Princeton University Press, 1993).

10. Toni Makai and John Braithwaite, "In and Out of the Revolving Door: Making Sense of Regulatory Capture," *Journal of Public Policy* 12 (1992): 51–78 (on Australia), and Thomas Susman, "Lobbying in the 21st Century: Reciprocity and the Need for Reform," *Administrative Law Review* 56 (2006): 738–52.

11. David Ammons and Debra Hill, "The Viability of Public-Private Competition as a Long-Term Service Delivery Strategy," *Public Productivity and Management Review* 19 (1995): 12–24.

12. Rosemary Stevens, *In Sickness and in Wealth: American Hospitals in the Twentieth Century* (Baltimore: Johns Hopkins University Press, 1999).

13. Philip Mangrove, *Public and Private Roles in Health* (Washington, DC: World Bank, 1996), and Jacob Hacker, *The Divided Welfare State: The Battle over Public and Private Social Benefits in the United States* (Cambridge, UK: Cambridge University Press, 2002).

14. Marc Milet, "La Banque Postale 'pas comme les autres': Entre identité postale et rhétorique du marché," *Revue française d'administration publique*, no. 119 (2006): 427–38.

15. Mark Poirer, "Environmental Justice and the Beach Access Movements of the 1970s in Connecticut and New Jersey: Stories of Property and Civil Rights," *Connecticut Law Review* 28 (1996): 719–812.

16. Gérard Bellan, Jean-Claude Dauvin, and Denise Bellan-Santini, "Knowledge, Protection, Conservation, and Management in the Marine Domain: The Example of the Mainland French Coast," *Open Conservation Biology Journal* 4 (2010): 9–18.

17. Carla Rabinowitz, "Martha's Vineyard: The Development of a Legislative Strategy for Preservation," *Environmental Affairs Law Review* 3 (1974): 396–431.

18. Yannis Suire, "L'homme et l'evironnement dans la Marais poitevin (seconde moitié du XVIe siècle–debut du XXe siècle) (doctoral thesis, Sorbonne, Paris, 2006), available at http://theses.enc.sorbonne.fr/2002/suire (accessed 6 July 2011).

9. Reflexivity

Reflexivity (active learning amid the ongoing flux of change) has become a fundamental issue in contemporary social theory,[1] financial management,[2] and historical analysis. This is the case, first, because it invites us to contemplate and reconstruct environments in which cause and effect proves to be a two-way street and hence ambiguous both in organizations and the material world. Second, reflexivity emphasizes serial feedback loops in which outcomes affect agents' understandings and decision-making going forward, shifting their priorities or intcrests, sometimes at lightning speed, thus changing later behavior. Further, reflexivity signals processes in which actors (including scholars) become increasingly alert over time to their own positions, contexts, assumptions, and attitudes regarding the objects of their interest and hence reflect on their practices, reappraising and altering them. This last loop also includes the "internal conversations" of individuals as they quietly determine "future courses of action," a dynamic Margaret Archer has identified.[3] A central corollary is that the "human sciences" cannot become "hard sciences," precisely because no universal generalizations are possible when the objects of analysis have agency and can reconfigure both meaning and process through learning and action.[4] In this section, we discuss these varied learning dynamics and their significance for business history: first, reflexivity as an adaptive process, and second, reflexivity as a venue for critical thinking.

The central questions: How do businesses, managers, regulators, or investors change by learning? How is such learning triggered, mediated, and stored? What historical patterns contrast with contemporary practices or perhaps resonate with them? What types of organizations need learning cycles more than others, and why? Learning often involves conflict with present protocols and habits, so how do actors become open to such conflict and move toward integrating new knowledge into existing activities? Equally and historically, when and where is *un*learning called for, and how was this facilitated? Businesses actors are constantly scanning their environments and processing incoming information in relation to goals and practices, so how have actors identified the useful and the tangential in these flows, and how might environmental shifts have altered the notion of what's useful?

It's easy to say that the world changes and we change with it, but focusing on reflexivity emphasizes the complexity of this dynamic. Our actions trigger changes that, once perceived, recalibrate the grounds for our next round of actions. Being able to recognize that such loops exist and that feedback information may necessitate reorientations on our part is a key element of survival in competitive contexts like workplaces or markets. Moreover, our reflexive actions may alter the environment for others' choices and routines. Determining what reorientations to make and when and how to implement them is one key to successful action. Such repositionings are not automatic in organizations; rather, they result from discussion and debate, which hierarchical organizations frequently shun. For example, European firms commonly use management tools like ERP (software for information control), which is said to be efficient, yet employ it mechanically to gauge corporate capabilities rather than reflexively so as to revise assessments based on feedback and unanticipated inputs. Consultants are supposed to generate an interactive, reflective process to enhance their clients' decision-making, but we know that too often they are either well-paid yes-men, telling executives what they want to hear, or one-size-fits-all vendors, who bring similar recipes to varied situations. Plainly, it is the role of the historian to distinguish between such practices and the analytics of reflexivity and critical learning.[5]

So where are or were there places in businesses for debate, for the influx of novel and unexpected information? Enterprises are not monarchies, we know, and hierarchies are notoriously leaky. Business historians thus could look for staff reports at interfaces between the firm and "the world"—marketing studies showing demand morphing in unanticipated ways, human relations documents noting shifts in job applicants' demographics, user surveys providing surprises that managers ignored, technical analyses exploring new materials (or new services) that augmented (or undermined) capabilities. In a broader vein, scholars could seek out professional forums on the state of the trade or the art (likely published in technical journals) or conference papers and consultants' analyses assessing trends, missed opportunities, and rivals in other regions or nations.

As one target for researchers, we have often wondered whether, when, and why shifts in corporate policy followed contracts with consulting teams, and when and why their recommendations were ignored or rejected. What categories of feedback are understood and perhaps accepted, and what types of information are brushed off, discarded? (Think perhaps of a quant-heavy firm's efforts to deal with shifting cultural norms.) After all, sham exercises in reflexivity can be mounted, then used to reinforce current strategies and commitments, value orientations, and resource allocations, instead of charting new paths. The RAND Corporation's long and contested relationship with the US Air Force illuminates the pressures involved and their consequences for both enterprise and public policy.[6] At a metalevel, what routines can organizations create and propagate so as to learn to pay attention to particular elements within the information flow? Routinizing alertness and flexibility is surely difficult, so where has it been done well or badly (for badly, consider Parmalat, GM, and Chrysler)?[7]

Taking in possibly unwelcome news from outside (that is, outside the person, firm, sector, region, or country) entails costs. At stake are the autonomy, reputation, and knowledgeability of key actors when relying on financial advisers, government regulators, or even the *Harvard Business Review*. So how are insertions from the outside reflexively mediated on the inside? The options are multiple, surely—authority claims, crisis rhetoric, progressive talk about "learning organizations"—but the process through which the French aircraft industry determined by about 1970 that it would have to work in transnational partnerships thereafter, ending a cherished autonomy, would be fascinating to reconstruct.[8] Indeed, exploring how reflexivity works in crises, in times of resource scarcity, intensified competition, war, or technological transition (steam to electricity, land lines to cell phones) could be instructive.[9] Arguments for delay or inaction, for deepening investment in current practices, for incremental reorientation, and for radical change may inform sectorwide discussions or those in one planning team. After all, what reflexivity, in this adaptive-process form, can and ought to do is to spotlight alternatives to current practice.

In another mode, reflexivity represents a critical "interior" resource for actors. As Giddens explained:

> The reflexivity of modern social life consists in the fact that social practices are constantly examined and reformed in the light of incoming information about those very practices, thus constitutively altering their character. . . . All forms of social life are partly constituted by actors' knowledge of them. Knowing "how to go on" in Wittgenstein's sense is intrinsic to the conventions which are drawn upon and reproduced by human activity. . . . But only in the era of modernity is the revision of convention radicalized to apply (in principle) to all aspects of human life. . . . What is characteristic of modernity is . . . the presumption of wholesale reflexivity—which of course includes reflection on the nature of reflection itself.[10]

Thus actors, including historians, are in a position to become increasingly self-aware about their conventions for gathering and assessing information, including the information that fuels research, and they may be expected to reflect on the ways in which these conventions can be altered as the character and quality of information shifts. Sorting out how to approach such fundamental reorderings is an ongoing collective process, of course. In business history, already largely a qualitative discipline, diminishing returns from traditional approaches, along with its marginalization in history faculties and instrumentalization in business schools, could lead to a comparable reflexive process, to which this small volume hopes to contribute.

NOTES

1. Anthony Giddens, Ulrich Beck and Scott Lash, *Reflexive Modernization: Politics, Tradition, and Aesthetics in the Modern Social Order* (Stanford: Stanford University Press, 1994); Pierre Bourdieu and Loic Wacquant, *An Invitation to Reflexive Sociology* (Chicago: University of Chicago Press, 1992), and Pierre Bourdieu, *Science of Science and Reflexivity* (Chicago: University of Chicago Press, 2004).

2. George Soros, "General Theory of Reflexivity" (a lecture at the Central European University, Budapest, 26 Oct. 2009): www.soros.org/resources/multimedia/sorosceu_20091112/reflexivity_transcript (accessed 11 June 2010).

3. Margaret Archer, *Structure, Agency and the Internal Conversation* (Cambridge, UK: Cambridge University Press, 2003).

4. Hence, neither economics nor management can become a science, other than in meta-phorical references.

5. For a key and critical analysis of US consulting, see Christopher McKenna, *The World's Newest Profession: Management Consulting in the Twentieth Century* (Cambridge, UK: Cambridge University Press, 2006).

6. Alex Abella, *Soldiers of Reason: The RAND Corporate and the Rise of the American Empire* (New York: Houghton Mifflin, 2008).

7. On the US auto industry's deafness to looming challenges and crises, see the classics, Stanley Aronowitz, *False Promises* rev. ed. (1973; Durham, NC: Duke University Press, 1991), and J. Patrick Wright, *On A Clear Day You Can See General Motors* (New York: Wright, 1979), and more recently, Paul Ingrassia, *Crash Course: The American Auto Industry's Road from Glory to Disaster* (New York: Random House, 2010), Alex Taylor III and Mike Jackson, *Sixty to Zero: An Inside Look at the Collapse of General Motors* (New Haven: Yale University Press, 2010), and Richard Gall, *General Motors: Life Inside the Factory* (Bloomington, IN: Author-House, 2010).

8. The redoubtable Bill Gunston provides a foundation in his *Airbus: The Complete Story*, 2nd ed. (Sparkford, UK: Haynes, 2010). Gunston has offered high-quality technical analysis of aircraft and engines for at least a quarter-century.

9. For a provocative analysis of the run-up to the 2008 crisis, centered on Lehman Brothers and anchored in flows of information and reflexive strategizing, see Michael Lewis, *The Big Short: Inside the Doomsday Machine* (New York: Norton, 2010).

10. Anthony Giddens, *The Consequences of Modernity* (Stanford: Stanford University Press, 1990), 38–39.

10. Ritual and Symbolic Practices

The range of ritual and symbolic business practices available for historical analysis is remarkably broad. Consider the ways in which plants and shops initially open for business, with banners and balloons, giveaways and ribbon cuttings, and droning speeches by politicians and managers. In offices and foundries alike, co-workers and managers regularly mark births, anniversaries, engagements, marriages, and deaths, formally and informally.[1] Companies give out prizes and honors, bonuses and promotions at ceremonies (or they did so once, but perhaps no longer, immediately prompting historical questions). Like holidays, bonus awards highlight annual calendars, at year's end in American finance, in June and November for Japanese managers. Contract signings, merger agreements, product rollouts at conventions, trade fairs, and fashion shows are loaded with symbolic behaviors and artifacts (pens with logos, embossed programs, T-shirts, coffee mugs, key chains).

At the individual level, new workers regularly find themselves "initiated" to their jobs through jokes and tricks ("get me the left-handed monkey wrench")[2] but also through standardized introductory tours, training sessions (safety rules, computer use, confidentiality), or information transfers concerning benefits or vacation time. Not uncommonly, veteran employees also school the newbies about whom not to argue with, what procedures are customarily skipped, and how to get things done quickly and quietly through bypassing offices notorious for delays. At work, coffee and tea breaks can express core expectations among employees (working through breaks is disruptive), as can lunchtime or lunchroom performances (or withdrawal from them).[3] So too does overtime (in emergencies or as a routine means for management to avoid adding staff) both catalyze and symbolize relationships within organizations. Performance reviews are rituals, being face-to-face exchanges about one's past and future in the organization. Unsurprisingly, firings have become ritualized as well: in US firms, they include the dreaded visit to the Human Resources center, a brisk notification of separation (and perhaps the reason), revisiting one's desk or shop floor for a few minutes, accompanied by security personnel, to gather personal items and to return keys and access cards (if any), the whole ceremony closing with an escorted walk to the parking lot.[4] How this came to be is, naturally, a historical matter, as are its variations by period and place.

History, too, must be invoked to understand the spectrum of patron saints for trades and occupations, the related artifacts and observations, and their links to collective identities. For example, St. Catherine of Alexandria is the holy overseer of milliners and haute couture,[5] and St. Augustine the patron saint of both printers and brewers (which may account for printers taking the saint's day off to drink). Yet what did these rituals mean, to whom, when, and why, including workers, employers, and the clients of firms? What other religious rituals had durable relevance to business operations, even as twentieth-century secularization proceeded globally? What comparable patterns arose among non-Christian believers and in non-Christian territories?

Dress and demeanor in enterprises can be highly ritualized, and has been, far into the past. As Richard Sennett explained: "The streets of London and Paris two centuries ago [featured] precise indicators of social standing.

Servants were easily distinguishable from laborers. The kind of labor performed could be read from the peculiar clothes adopted by each trade, as could the status of a laborer within his craft, by glancing at certain ribbons and buttons he wore. In the middle ranks of society, barristers, accountants, and merchants each wore distinctive decorations, wigs, or ribbons."[6] The transformation of this diversity into business dress (the sack suit, the blue serge, the double-breasted pinstripe)[7] and factory garb (overalls, twill pants, solid color shirts with company emblems and embroidered worker names) represents the uneven advance of a new array of uniforms, designating class and status rather than craft or occupation. Gender issues are readily entwined with clothing expectations—refined versus rough masculinity (above) or the emergence of the shirtwaist as a modest yet feminine style for early twentieth-century American office workers, followed by the matching jacket and skirt and the pants suit in the 1960s.[8]

Dress can as well be oppositional and defiant,[9] not least in firms and among individuals active in nontraditional or creative businesses: theaters, film-making sets, art galleries, fashion boutiques, advertising suites. In traditional settings nonconforming dress can announce independence and creativity or, equally, resentment and withdrawal. In Albert O. Hirschman's terms, it embodies "voice," withholding "loyalty," and can lead to "exit."[10] The gradual death of men's ties as artifacts of managerial status deserves research in a related vein, as does the highly ritualized formality of those environments where tie wearing persists: courtrooms, law offices, medical consultation units, executive suites. Perhaps the casualization of dress in mid- and lower-level administration goes hand in hand with the casualization of employment, as symbolic badges of authority are tangential for temporary or part-time employees.

Three examples may give texture and context to the preceding observations. Calor, a French family firm making consumer electrical goods since 1917, sold out to a managerial enterprise, SEB, in the 1960s. The new owners eliminated what they considered wasteful, even if long-observed, rituals and symbolic practices, streamlining workplace activity, in the expectation of enhanced productivity. No luck; under the new administrative regime, turnover increased and productivity cratered. Management brought in a group of consulting anthropologists and followed their advice to restore key elements of the previous cultural apparatus. In short order, the crisis ended and the firm sailed forward again on an even keel.[11] By contrast, at the newly started Microsoft, "Business rituals and symbols were incorporated early into 'backstage' operations, . . . motivated by the explicitly-stated goal of winning the market 'game.'" As David Goss relates the story:

In 1980, apparently under the impression that [Bill] Gates could supply them with an operating system and a programming language, IBM approached Microsoft to help develop their own PC—a prospect that hugely excited Gates. . . . However, Microsoft . . . used CPM [an operating system] under license from [Gary] Kildall's company [Intergalactic Digital Research]. . . . Gates, anxious to secure the deal for his software, arranged for the IBM representatives to meet Kildall with a view to securing a jointly-owned product. Kildall, unlike Gates, seemed unwilling and uninterested in engaging in IBM's rituals of corporate power. Gates and his Microsoft managers appeared to show due deference and enthusiasm for the rituals of corporate business dealing—signing non-disclosure agreements, treating IBM as a valued client, even putting on suits and ties! Kildall, in contrast, seems deliberately to have displayed disdain and indifference towards these conventions, canceling a pre-arranged meeting to indulge his flying hobby, keeping the IBM delegates waiting all day and finally, entering into a hostile dispute over the non-disclosure agreement. The result was the IBM team's refusal to deal with [him].[12]

Gates bought another operating system, excluded Kildall, cut the deal with IBM, and moved on and up.

Finally, at the micro level, Tomoko Connolly narrates a retirement party for Mike O'Casey, an "Irish-American from rural Virginia," after nearly twenty years of work as human resources director at a Japanese high-tech corporation's US plant. Operations manager Mike Clark directed the proceedings, which were overseen by the generally silent plant manager, Mr. Sakai. After drinks and appetizers, Clark "told the restaurant staff to rearrange the dining tables so that the top seats, closest to the back wall, would go to Plant Manager Sakai, Vice Plant Manager Tabata, and Procurement Manager Ishibashi. He then told Mr. O'Casey to take a seat in the middle of a very long dining table,"[13] surrounded by his family. Here two rituals were interlaced: the spatial recognition of top management's privileges, which the restaurant staff had not appreciated, and the centrality of the honoree to the room's organization. After further drinking (a Japanese corporate ritual):

At the top end of the table, Procurement Manager Ishibashi started fidgeting with his video camera. He pointed the camera at Plant Manager Sakai and jokingly said in Japanese that he had just called up the [company] headquarters by Skype. He then pretended he was talking with the head office, saying "this is Virginia calling. We are starting our dinner. Honorable Chairman Asayama, please give us your wise opening remarks." Vice Plant Manager Tabata frowned and said to Ishibashi in Japanese: "What you have just said will be formally recorded in the official log, and I will report this back to Mr. Asayama. Ha, ha, ha!" Every Japanese who heard the conversation burst out laughing. Mitsui translated it to the rest of the crowd. They all laughed. The little skit reminded everyone of Tokyo's enormous power over the entire Virginia outpost.[14]

Here the language barrier prevented local employees' immediate access to the byplay among the Japanese managers, even as the "little skit" dramatized the managers' closeness to, and the locals' distance from (and subordination to) Tokyo's power. The interior exchange between Tabata and Ishibashi illuminated a ceremonially suspended boundary between the formal and the carnivalesque, for inside the plant, Ishibashi's impudence would indeed have been recorded, damaging his career prospects. Rituals matter, but you have to know how to execute them and how to read them.

A range of questions for research derives from this overview. How do business rituals and symbolic practices or artifacts serve as means for inclusion and exclusion, and with what implications? What are the responsibilities of firms toward the people who take part in these practices and how and why does this change? Surely such practices are different across borders, so why might this matter to business prospects? What do symbolic rewards reward? Does recognizing rituals and symbols alter existing academic notions of corporate culture, and if so, how? To what degree do these practices and artifacts actually matter, and to whom? How can we document or measure this? How have symbolic practices emerged historically, and what are their boundaries? For example, are the industrial sports teams sponsored by corporations, starting in the late nineteenth century in North America, Europe, and later, Japan, elements within ritual and symbolic arrays? Why or why not? What shifts does sports professionalization induce? Plainly, these are fruitful arenas for contemporary business analysts; exploring their historical dimensions and significance for business actors and institutions in the past awaits research by energetic and imaginative scholars.

NOTES

1. Now even electronically, as e-mail circulation of such notices has become routine.

2. See Benjamin Botkin, *A Treasury of American Folklore* (New York: Crown, 1944), chap. 5, pt. 3, "Jesters." Botkin notes: "In almost every occupation, part of the education or initiation of the new hand consists in sending him on foolish errands, usually in search of a mythical or impossible object, such as a left-handed monkey wrench, a bottle stretcher, a four-foot yard stick, or a sky-hook."

3. For insight into the complexities of the lunchroom, see Nicolas Hatzfeld, "La pause casse-croute: Quand les chaines s'arrêt à Peugeot-Sochaux," *Terrain*, no. 39 (2002): 33–49. See also Jean-Pierre Durand and Nicolas Hatzfeld, *Living Labour: Life on the Line at Peugeot France* (London: Palgrave Macmillan, 2003).

4. For current approaches, see Linda Magoon and Donna de St. Aubin, *Tips When Hiring and Firing Employees: 50 Plus One* (Chicago: Encouragement Press, 2006).

5. For background, see Ali Basye, "Happy St. Catherine's Day," 25 Nov. 2010, available at http://onthisdayinfashion.com/?p=8171 (accessed 27 Apr. 2011). This saint's day has been removed from the official calendar, due to the lack of evidence that this saint ever existed. For St. Augustine, see www.scborromeo.org/saints/hippo.htm (accessed 27 Apr. 2011).

6. Richard Sennett, *The Fall of Public Man: On the Social Psychology of Capitalism* (New York: Knopf, 1977), 65.

7. See Christopher Breward, *Fashioning London: Clothing and the Modern Metropolis* (Oxford: Berg, 2004). For a glimpse of the suit's reconfiguration in recent Japanese stylings, see Dorinne Kondo, "Fabricating Masculinity: Gender, Race, and Nation in a Transnational Frame," in *Between Woman and Nation: Nationalisms, Transnational Feminisms, and the State*, ed. Caren Kaplan, Norma Alarcon, and Minoo Moallem (Durham, NC: Duke University Press, 1999), 296–319. A compelling study is Anne Hollander, *Sex and Suits: The Evolution of Modern Dress* (New York: Knopf, 1994).

8. Heather Vaughn, "Icon: Tracing the Path of the 1950s Shirtwaist Dress," *Journal of American Culture* 32 (2009): 29–37.

9. For a famous US case, see Kathy Peiss, *Zoot Suit: The Enigmatic Career of an Extreme Style* (Philadelphia: University of Pennsylvania Press, 2011).

10. Albert O. Hirschman, *Exit, Voice, and Loyalty: Responses to Decline in Firms, Organizations, and States* (Cambridge, MA: Harvard University Press, 1970). Helpful also along these lines is Mary Douglas, *How Institutions Think* (Syracuse, NY: Syracuse University Press, 1986).

11. Dominique Claudet and Dominique Pierzo, "Culture interne et recyclage de mémoire dans une société de fabrication d'appareils ménagers," in *Mémoire d'avenir, l'histoire dans l'entreprise*, ed. Maurice Hamon et Félix Torres (Paris: Economica, 1987), 99–105.

12. David Goss, "Reconsidering Schumpeterian opportunities: the contribution of interaction ritual chain theory," *International Journal of Entrepreneurial Behaviour and Research* 13.1 (2007): 3–18, quote from 12.

13. Tomoko Connolly, "Business Ritual Studies: Corporate Ceremony and Sacred Space," *International Journal of Business Anthropology* 1.2 (2010): 32–47, quote from 36–37.

14. Ibid., 37.

11. The Centrality of Failure

Arguing that failure is a central experience and process in business may seem totally counterproductive. But without failure, business history could have a constricted value, contrary to the expectations of success-driven groups like the military, consultants, entrepreneurs, journalists, and even business administration scholars. The prestige or relevance of failure studies will likely be less than that of works emphasizing performance and success. Still, one case worth revisiting is the 1994 book by consultants James Collins and Jerry Porras, *Built to Last: Successful Habits of Visionary Companies.* Ten years later this book, a bestseller, had sold 3.5 million copies worldwide. Yet in its 2004 edition, careful readers could observe that "almost half of the visionary companies on the list have slipped dramatically in performance and reputation, and their vision currently seems more blurred than clairvoyant."[1] These firms included Motorola, Ford, Sony, Disney, Boeing, Nordstrom, and Merck. Collins qualified his message in the title of a later book: *Good to Great: Why Some Companies Make the Leap . . . and Others Don't,* and even more so in its sequel: *How the Mighty Fall,* released fifteen years after his initial celebration of corporate visions.[2]

By insisting on both the possibility and the reality of failure, a fully realized business history would mirror historians of international relations who confidently proclaim: "Every empire will perish."[3] Economic organizations, like all others, cannot ignore their intrinsic fragility, and thus an international relations perspective can be much more realistic than many business policy guides. Business history shows that enterprises operate in an atmosphere of uncertainty, risk, and ambiguity (often while facing information asymmetries when dealing with other actors) and that the temptation to discard business ethics in extreme circumstances can be great. It also takes into account phenomena appreciated by both historians and economists: business cycles, booms and busts, bubbles. Not continuity but survival is of the essence, and no one, inside or outside a firm, should ever dismiss the chances for company death. This explains the intensity of emotions that, in crises, may inspire heroic or pyrrhic actions not only by entrepreneurs and executives but also by other members of an organization.

In America, a 2005 estimate indicated that "more than 10 per cent of all companies fail every year, with more than 10,000 closing every week."[4] To be sure, small commercial and industrial firms are more prone to failure because many enterprisers lack knowledge, experience, resources, connections, or networks, yielding a high rate of attrition and, for the majority, a short life expectancy. Still, large organizations are also vulnerable, at home and abroad, often at the project or product level. In the United States, a major industrial technology program, the VideoDisc, developed between 1964 and the 1970s, failed at Radio Corporation of America. Worldwide, Sony's charismatic leader Norio Ohga launched the Betamax format for video cassette recorders (1975), expecting that by being first and delivering high quality, it would lead the market through lock-in and path dependence. Yet Betamax failed against JVC's VHS format, with its lower retail price and compatibility with other brands. Also, Sony and JVC "were both developing technologies that were unproven. As a result of the desire to get into the marketplace faster, both firms spent little time on research and development and tried to save money by picking a version of the technology they thought would do best, without really exploring all the options."[5] Even less urgent and less adventurous behavior may prove dangerous. Economies of scope, a feature of most multinationals, are not permanent. In 2005, France's Carrefour had to sell its eight stores in Japan, closing additional South East Asia sites by 2010,[6] and the next year American world leader Walmart shut eighty-eight stores in Germany: neither had adapted to local consumers' expectations. Economic concentration, although regularly promoted by banks, consultants, and governments, is not much safer. Since the beginning of the twentieth century, a majority of mergers and acquisitions have failed. Clearly, innovations are not the only source of failure. Alternately, continuity, inaction, or passivity in strategy or routines may lead to similar crises. Once this is understood, three major questions arise: When a failure process materializes, what is immediately at stake? What are the possible consequences? What are the longer-term legacies?

Monographs on individual failures and quantitative surveys illuminate a variety of triggering economic issues: shocks in prices or market outlets, insufficiency of credit networks, accumulation of minor tensions, broadening of risks taken, limits to internal controls, and technological obsolescence. These all put into question actors' behavior and values. Hence we need to search for the reasons why farmers, merchants, industrialists, bankers, department stores, and even insurance companies fail. *Crucially, failure is a social process.*

Failing debtors maneuver to stay active or to make a comeback. Creditors attempt to keep the debtor going so as to recover their capital, even though they may use threats of assignment, of bankruptcy, of foreclosure. Intermediaries often intervene, notably certified accountants, audit firms, lawyers, receivers, financial advisers, and banking institutions. Rumors are denied, draining confidence, or explode, leading to panics. Self-regulation within the business system provides another option: a failure may lead to a negotiation. As Philip Ollerenshaw noted: "We need to explain the process of receivership, what transactions take place during that period when a firm 'navigates' failure, and what role is played by internal or external stakeholders."[7] Other bodies, such as chambers of commerce or trade associations, may play mediating roles. Additional collective examples of business self-regulation have appeared. In America, from the late 1890s through the 1920s,

> a new set of nonprofit, business-funded organizations spearheaded [a] campaign against commercial duplicity. [They] shaped the legal terrain of fraud, built massive public-education campaigns, and created a private law-enforcement capacity to rival that of the federal government. Largely born out of a desire among business elites to fend off proposals for extensive regulatory oversight of commercial speech, the antifraud crusade grew into a social movement that was influenced by prevailing ideas about social hygiene and emerging techniques of private governance. This initiative highlighted some enduring strengths of business self-regulation, such as agility in responding to regulatory problems; it also revealed a key weakness, which was the tendency to overlook deceptive marketing when practiced by firms that were members of the business establishment.[8]

In many more cases this is not enough, and the courts deal with failure. Judges interpret the legal procedures that have been developed across centuries. This is frequent for small and medium-size businesses, for which bankruptcy is a commonplace legal procedure, applied annually to thousands of firms in a standardized manner.[9] In a limited number of cases, failures become politicized. Entrepreneurs, small shareholders, and wage-earners try to develop leverage on public opinion. Then the scandal, the panic, or the potential consequences of the failure process may force policymakers' direct intervention at local, regional, national, or international levels. Purely political factors may also be key determinants of governments' responses to failures. Like all other actors, state agencies try to determine who wins and who loses in the process.

What are the consequences of failures? To be sure, they usually destroy capital and jobs, but historical research also documents revivals. Despite Sony's VCR disaster, the Betamax format secured a durable base among professional media users. Indeed, a prominent Japanese engineer invented the camcorder in 1989 so as to use Betamax plants and machines left behind after its mass-market defeat. Some failures may lead to recovery or a second life. The US Chapter 11 legislation for company reorganization has become a regular instrument in this respect. An even more important issue is what happens to failed entrepreneurs. Many end their business careers, moving to other occupations. However, others try to start anew, reinforcing a recurrent theme: the second chance.

A recent microhistory of 47 farmers and 134 merchants, manufacturers, and professionals who failed economically in post–Civil War Atchison County, Kansas (1865–96), gives a qualified answer about second chances.

> While the vast majority of the individuals studied were able to find productive employment within a relatively short period of time, many were not able to totally reverse the consequences of economic failure. They were unable to regain either the wealth or income they had enjoyed before failure or that they would have enjoyed had they continued on upward trends they had experienced before failure. Furthermore, they also faced diminished opportunities for independent farm or business ownership, particularly after 1880, as it became harder to resist economic forces that were reducing the numbers of independent farmers, retailers and wholesalers.[10]

However, trajectories may rebound in positive directions, as

> these same forces were also creating new middle-class jobs for salaried employees with larger manufacturing, wholesale and retail firms, railroads, utilities and government agencies and, over time, an increasing number of the individuals studied found employment in such positions. Together with the remaining but more rare opportunities for farm and business ownership, this was sufficient to keep the vast majority of the individuals studied out of long-term poverty.[11]

Similar research is needed for other areas and periods. A third consequence is that at various junctures in Kansas (and worldwide) "the experiences of failed debtors and their creditors . . . created an impetus for reform in the agricultural and mercantile credit systems and the legal processes set up to deal with economic failure."[12] Thus regulatory and ethical frameworks are periodically adjusted.

The legacy of failures is multifarious. Smashups alter the sense of work-related meanings among their victims, either inside or outside firms. Organizational change events such as site closure, business or project failure, downsizing, restructuring, or mergers and acquisitions provoke reactions of loss and grief.

Some firms or labor markets just ask the displaced to heal themselves by letting go and moving on. However, many employees show strong attachments to organizational location and place, a disposition with substantial implications. The termination of projects may also induce a sense of loss in temporary organizations. The importance of continuing bonds has to be taken into account when individuals or groups are challenged to recast relations between self and others.[13]

At another level, is there a collective, active-learning memory of failures? The straightforward lessons of failures can easily be forgotten. In central-bank crisis management, US Treasury Secretary Alexander Hamilton failed to codify the techniques he invented to stem the 1792 panic, America's first financial market crash. They were rediscovered eight decades later, in Britain. Memories of deceased organizations are often maintained in many ways as well, through reunions, newsletters, and websites. Broader issues should be noted, however. Despite the business world's reputation for rationality, its credulousness is without limits, even at the top. Innovation alone is not sufficient to sustain an enterprise. Product rollouts, novel sales techniques, and massive advertising fostered the rapid growth of the Cyril Lord textile group in Britain, the United States, and South Africa, which nevertheless ended in insolvency.[14] Even if it is central, innovation can be also be corrupted, as with the Enron disaster, in which innovative accounting protocols concealed a massive and criminal fraud.[15]

The sources of a failure should not be restricted to specifics: a moment, a place, or a sector, for "an organization fails when its ability to compete deteriorates as a consequence of actual or anticipated performance below a critical threshold that threatens its viability. Symptoms of organizational failure include market share erosion, persistent low or negative profitability, shrinking critical—that is financial, human, and technological—resources, and/or loss of legitimacy."[16] Yet failures can never be explained *only* by a gradual or abrupt shift in the business environment. Instead, they expose major characteristics and fracture points, such as the power and responsibility of ownership, the positive or negative effects of compensation and incentives on the relationship of managers and employees to the organization, the link between authority and the possibility of debate, or the ability to attribute causes and to implement lessons in a world of meanings which are never clear-cut.[17] When failure threatens, the whole chain of value is at stake, from suppliers to consumers. The risk of failure puts to the test the ability of actors and organizations to struggle against troubles that exceed current practices, habits, management tools, and corporate culture, and yet its essential challenge is that it offers an opening to restore or recreate social and cultural legitimacy.

NOTES

1. Rev. ed. (1994; New York: Harper Business, 2004). Quote from Jennifer Reingold and Ryan Underwood, "Was 'Built to Last' Built to Last?," *Fast Company*, 1 Nov. 2004, available at www.fastcompany.com/magazine/88/built-to-last.html.

2. Jim Collins, *Good to Great* (New York: Harper Collins, 2001), and Collins, *How the Mighty Fall* (New York: Harper Business, 2009).

3. Jean-Baptiste Duroselle, *Tout Empire périra: Une vision théorique des relations internationales* (Paris: Publications de la Sorbonne, 1981).

4. Kingsley Appiah, "Predicting Corporate Failure and Global Crisis: Theory and Implications," *Journal of Modern Accounting and Auditing* 7 (2011): 38–47.

5. Robin Cowan, "Tortoises and Hares: Choice among Technologies of Unproven Merit," *Economic Journal* 101 (1991): 801–14, and John Nathan, *Sony: The Private Life* (Boston: Houghton Mifflin, 1999).

6. Anita Davis, "Carrefour to sell off SEA stores," *Asian Venture Capital Journal*, 21 July 2010, available at www.avcj.com/avcj/official-record/1723539/carrefour-sell-sea-stores (accessed 5 July 2011), and Deutsche Welle, "World's Biggest Retailer, Wal-Mart, Closes Up Shop in Germany," 28 July 2006, available at www.dw-world.de/dw/article/0,2112746,00.html (accessed 5 July 2011).

7. Philip Ollerenshaw, "Innovation and Corporate Failure: Cyril Lord in U.K. Textiles, 1945–1968," *Enterprise and Society* 7 (2006): 777–811, quote from 778.

8. Edward J. Balleisen, "Private Cops on the Fraud Beat: The Limits of American Business Self-Regulation, 1895–1932," *Business History Review* 83 (Spring 2009): 113–60.

9. Pierre-Cyrille Hautcoeur, ed., "Justice commerciale et histoire économique: Enjeux et mesures," *Histoire et Mesure* 23.1 (2008), thematic issue.

10. David J. Vandermeulen, "The Country of the Second Chance: Economic Failure and Recovery in Atchison County, Kansas, 1865–1896" (PhD diss. in history, University of Virginia, 2007).

11. Ibid.

12. Ibid. See also Scott Sandage, *Born Losers: A History of Failure in America* (Cambridge, MA: Harvard University Press, 2005).

13. Emma Bell and Scott Taylor, "Beyond Letting Go and Moving On: New Perspectives on Organizational Death, Loss, and Grief," *Scandinavian Journal of Management* 27 (2011): 1–10.

14. Ollerenshaw, "Innovation and Corporate Failure."

15. Malcolm S. Salter, *Innovation Corrupted: The Origins and Legacy of Enron's Collapse* (Cambridge, MA: Harvard University Press, 2008).

16. Kamel Mellahi and Adrian Wilkinson, "Managing and Coping with Organizational Failure: Introduction to the Special Issue," *Group and Organization Management* 35.5 (2010): 531–41.

17. Patrick Fridenson, "Business Failure and the Agenda of Business History," *Enterprise and Society* 5 (2004): 562–82.

12. Varieties of Uncertainty

Business historians have often explored organized efforts to overcome uncertainty through routinization, hierarchy, contracts, cartels, bureaucracy, standards, controls, and quantification, among other means. Far less often have we worked to understand uncertainty as a baseline condition for business practice, as a variable in decision-making, or as a fundamental component of innovation. Critical to deploying uncertainty as a useful concept is recognizing that it occupies a variety of domains in different configurations and takes a broad range of situational forms; together these dimensions constitute the "lexicon" of uncertainty.[1] Like failure, uncertainty is always with us, and like failure, it is neither uniform nor simple.

Being uncertain means that we do not have reliable knowledge about some future state of affairs, when "reliable knowledge" in turn means a risk-adjusted confidence in outcomes. As Frank Knight pointed out nearly a century ago, uncertainty denotes situations in which risk cannot be calculated, in which insurance against negative results cannot be purchased (or in many cases, even conceptualized).[2] Of course, not everything is uncertain; we can have confidence in most of our material and social activities, but when anticipating risk, we move cautiously and/or seek insurance. Put another way, risk is complicated and subject to rationality, whereas uncertainty is complex and extrarational[3]— that is, risk involves knowable options, steps, and opportunities, whereas uncertainty deals with multiple, interactive unknowns. (See Opportunities, 3: Complexity.) Yet for all that, uncertainty does not lack form.

Let us first consider the temporal and spatial dimensions of uncertainties, then a few of their domains germane to business history, and finally some of their operational or situational forms. The duration of uncertainty may be short (whether my old car will start on this cold winter day), middling (whether a product will be accepted or ignored by consumers), or long term (how long will I live?). Given this spread, our responses are sharply different—for the uncertain auto, we keep our cell phone charged, figuring we can call a taxi as a backup. For the product, we sponsor focus groups to alleviate our anxiety or prepare a variety of novelties for the season, trusting that some will hit our vaguely visible target. For our lives, insurance is pointless (it provides for other people), but we choose (and mix) healthy and hedonistic practices, saving for a vigorous old age or spending freely, presuming that we'll never make it to being "old." Responses to the uncertain are likely to diverge, because on this terrain, *we cannot know what we are doing and what will happen* in any rational, reliable fashion. Spatially, uncertainty has similar variabilities, ranging from the local (whether traffic accidents or transit breakdowns will make us late to work today; whether recurrent commuting miseries press us to relocate our homes) to the regional and national (whether incoming branches of chain retailers will ruin local proprietors) and transnational (whether shifting global trade patterns and share or currency values will enhance or undercut capital flows and labor markets). Obviously, as all the spatial examples include time frames, and the temporal ones are situated in households, economies, and states, time and space uncertainties intersect in complex ways that are important to actors.

Thinking about domains for uncertainty in business, at least four seem worth a mention: politics, finance, technology, and authority. Considering the state is a standard twentieth- and twenty-first-century business policy item, but it was often far from enterprise agendas (avoiding anachronism is good). Either way, addressed or ignored, governments and the politics that created and surrounded them generated waves of uncertainties for enterprises: the course and character of regulation, tariffs, foreign policy, taxation, etc. When enterprises and their organizations sought to affect politics and policy, they were surely surprised by outcomes: for example, the US National Association of Manufacturers could hardly believe the New Deal's popularity and eventually mounted a long-term (and largely successful)[4] drive to undo the managerial uncertainties that labor relations law had created. Financial uncertainties, especially regarding credit and credit rating, represent indefinitely renewable sources of stress and confusion, whose significance to the larger business environment rises as the involvement of banks in incorporations (IPOs and refinancings) and stock and bond trading increases. Uncertainties about markets and clients can be crippling, but the German harmonica maker Hohner managed to penetrate the nineteenth-century US market by employing an American agency to assess the trustworthiness of local dealers before authorizing product shipments.[5] Firms entering international markets have employed comparable strategies to transcend cultural boundaries, but they have their own hazards—notably, finding trustworthy agents. Under such uncertainties actors can't predict results, and with the swelling scale of transactions and the increasing number of players, they can't even know who or what is driving the market's movements—as problematic a matter in the telegraph age as today.

Technological uncertainty is familiar to all, and its most promising locale for business historians likely concerns actors looking forward and undertaking decisions in environments in which technical knowledge is fragmentary, contradictory, or emergent. If inaction is feasible here, it can serve as a plausible strategy, yet given competition, perhaps a losing non-move, as the stakes may be substantial. Authority, culturally or within organizations, is highly vulnerable to uncertainties, both for leaders and the led. Hierarchy represents a structural move to evade uncertainty. Yet it is no substitute for presence and alertness; from the days of the early railroads to the present, hierarchy promotes shifting problems to higher levels rather than taking decisive actions lower down, as middle managers avoid taking steps that might be reversed when reviewed. This generates reciprocal uncertainties, not least because superiors rarely have the detailed familiarity with circumstances that ground-level agents possess, and because, for their part, ground-level agents are constrained not to frame broader visions of the enterprise or of the economic or political significance of *their* actions. Mission statements don't fix this problem, we argue.

Last, thoughtful observers have delineated conceptually distinctive forms of uncertainty, though they understandably do not map neatly onto a spectrum or matrix. (We should not anticipate encountering a general theory of uncertainty any time soon, for example.) Four among these merit attention here: permanent, radical, insider, and regressive uncertainties, sketched respectively by Karl Weick, John Maynard Keynes, Donald Mackensie, and Ulrich Beck. Permanent uncertainty arises through the rising complexity of technologies, "because of their poorly understood processes and raw materials, continuous revision of the design . . . and the fact that implementation often is the means by which the technology itself is designed."[6] In a sense, technology runs ahead of science; increasingly we appreciate *that* things work, but without understanding *why* or *how* they work, for how long, much less how to respond to their stochastic failures. In such circumstances, users become codesigners of artifacts and systems that will crack and crash, even as they send feedback information that fuels cycles of redesign. These characteristics intersect with Keynes's radical uncertainty, a dynamic that commences when we recognize that "the data we have is incomplete and we are also unsure as to the extent of its incompleteness." Acknowledging this shortcoming produces "a more radical type of uncertainty [where] probabilities are unknown, comparisons of probability and weight are impossible, and probable values cannot be ranked." This leads to forced decision-making through "weak rationality"—organized guesswork, which generates ostensibly practical steps to address "theoretically indeterminate" problems.[7] With probability calculations impaired, action lacks reliable foundations, defining a radically uncertain territory, where, Keynes noted, actors try "to behave in a manner which *saves our faces as rational, economic men*."[8]

Mackensie's insider uncertainty pertains to organizational projects and actors' "social distance from the production of knowledge." Those close to testing, for example, have "access to sources of uncertainty barred to others," which usually fosters caution, whereas other insiders, often managers lacking access or relevant knowledgeability, make overblown claims to certainty. Outsiders, with little information, also launch thinly based uncertainty claims (re hazards, costs, rollout timing, etc.).[9] Such uncertainty *differentials* are richly related to emergent politics of innovation, regulation, and evaluation, among other matters.

Perhaps most daunting is Ulrich Beck's notion of regressive uncertainty. Writing about mad cow disease in the UK, he noted that in the search for causes, analysts found that "the more facts we know the more uncertainty grows," a condition Anthony Giddens terms "manufactured uncertainties," in which "more knowledge can actually produce more uncertainty."[10] For example, in reviewing planning for US supersonic transport, Boeing designer Edward Wells observed: "The strange thing . . . was that the more we came to know, the less well things worked out for us. Instead of entering into a situation in which the problems began to offset one another, the problems were actually compounding."[11] Regressive uncertainty raises the issue of limits to human capabilities in the face of high-complexity phenomena and represents a quiet warning to historians about unacknowledged presumptions of rationality and progress.

NOTES

1. Richard Wenzel, "What We Learned From H1N1's First Year," *New York Times*, 12 Apr. 2010. Wenzel noted that "our public health authorities need to become clearer about the lexicon of uncertainty—what they know and don't know about a pandemic." Rod O'Donnell has described uncertainty as "multidimensional and multinatured," which resonates with the approach taken here. See O'Donnell, "Probability, Expectations, Uncertainty, and Rationality in Keynes' Conceptual Framework," *Review of Political Economy* 2 (1990): 253–66.

2. Or, as with recent credit default swaps, presented as a form of insurance, because actors failed to appreciate their circumstances as involving incalculable uncertainties, not measurable risks that could be clearly priced. See Michael Lewis, *The Big Short* (New York:

Norton, 2010), along with the classic by Frank Knight, *Risk, Uncertainty and Profit* (Boston: Houghton Mifflin, 1921).

3. Our understanding of this distinction between complicated and complex derives from Bruno Latour (*Pandora's Box* [Cambridge, MA: Harvard University Press], 1999, 304), though it has often been noted elsewhere. See, for example, www.noop.nl/2008/08/simple-vs-complicated-vs-complex-vs-chaotic.html.

4. Howell Harris, *The Right to Manage* (Madison: University of Wisconsin Press, 1982).

5. Hartmut Berghoff, "Marketing Diversity: The Making of a Global Consumer Product— Hohner's Harmonicas, 1857–1930," *Enterprise and Society* 2 (2001): 338–72.

6. Karl Weick, "Technology as Equivoque," in *Making Sense of the Organization* (Thousand Oaks, CA: Sage, 2003), 152.

7. O'Donnell, "Probability," 259, 264. A related, useful observation by Keynes is that "the market can remain irrational longer than you can remain solvent," which remains germane, given recent global financial crises. For discussion about whether Keynes did say this, see http://quoteinvestigator.com/2011/08/09/remain-solvent/ (accessed 23 Nov. 2011). Richard Langlois uses an analogous term, *structural uncertainty*, meaning "a lack of complete knowledge on the part of the economic agent about the very structure of the problem that agent faces." See Richard Langlois, "Risk and Uncertainty," in *The Elgar companion to Austrian economics*, ed. P. Boettke (Aldershot UK: Elgar, 1994).

8. J.M. Keynes, "The General Theory of Employment," *Quarterly Journal of Economics* 51 (Feb. 1937): 214, emphasis added.

9. Donald Mackensie, *Mechanizing Proof: Computing, Risk, and Trust* (Cambridge, MA: MIT Press, 2001), 333.

10. Ulrich Beck and Johannes Willms, *Conversations with Ulrich Beck* (Cambridge, UK: Polity, 2004), 124.

11. Thomas A. Heppenheimer, *Turbulent Skies: The History of Commercial Aviation* (New York, Wiley, 1998), 241.

PART THREE

PROSPECTS

Promising Themes in Developing Literatures

1. Deconstructing Property

"Property is theft," famously observed Pierre-Joseph Proudhon, who later added, "Property is freedom."[1] These paired comments set out key propositions germane to understanding property historically: that it is social, relational, and a source of conflict (theft is a taking and a claiming), valued (it's worth something), empowering (the "freedom" point), exclusive (mine, not yours; sometimes ours, not theirs), and implicitly, anchored in laws and social sanctions (otherwise, thefts proliferate, destroying security). Property may or may not be tradable; we can sell you our cars, but not our kidneys, at least under current rules. Indeed, the special character of intellectual property is that I can sell you my knowledge, yet still have it to use or sell again. Property also may or may not be gifted: a kidney, yes, a toxic-waste dump, no (you just can't give it away). Hence, regarding property as only that which can be traded or given starts from the wrong end of the process. Core questions instead are: How, historically, does property take on certain socioeconomic characteristics, how do these become naturalized, and what significance did its consequent and inevitable definitions and practical variations have for the conduct of business? Centrally, how does deconstructing our default assumptions about property enable us to develop creative business history projects?

We focus here on five issues: property rights, intellectual property, fabricating property and owner/user relationships, valuation, and states and their fates. Property rights are legally and culturally rooted, as both elements define who can hold property and what can be done with it. Consider: What property can illegal immigrants or noncitizen refugees own in nations either now or in the past? How about nonresident investors? Are their property rights different from those of citizens? What varieties of property can states own and operate, ranging from weapons factories to soft drink bottlers?[2] Do citizens have property rights in both private and state pensions? Such issues have been central to debates on and analyses of privatization efforts in neoliberal and postcommunist polities, but they were significant a century earlier as well, when states began working with private firms and inventors to create new weapons. Kate Epstein's research on the first-phase military-industrial complex, circa 1880–1910, for example, illustrates the puzzles both the British and the American militaries faced in determining who "owned" privately designed, publicly funded weapons that today we would regard as having been co-produced.[3]

Under what circumstances do states have property rights in their own currencies or in flows of funds from public enterprises? Here rests the range of concerns about sovereign funds, through which governments maneuver in markets to advance or protect state managers' domains and perhaps national interests. Legal bases for property and legal regimes for its administration and sale differ substantially between, for example, locations that rely upon a British common law foundation and those that derive practices from the Code Napoléon.[4] In addition, property rights and transactions have extended historically into areas deemed inappropriate or impious; selling religious indulgences had something to do with sparking the Reformation, after all, whereas a commercial trade in blood has surfaced in recent generations, commodifying what had once been a gift relationship.[5] Property rights are historical, time and space bound; naturalizing them erases questions of great interest.

Next, Adrian Johns has pushed scholars (and attorneys) to recognize that laws about intellectual property (IP) "do not precede, but emerge in response to a heated cultural and historical negotiation of values." Indeed, his study *Piracy* "revels in stories of how intellectual property laws (and their precursors) have been used, policed, challenged, ignored, contested, arbitraged, or abrogated in practice."[6] Johns focuses on publishing and the complex problems of owning knowledge and controlling its dissemination. Copyright, for example, had to be established by stepwise accretions; some territories (Russia, Japan, the United States) long resisted, avoided, or ignored appeals from Britain or France. Comparably, patents assert property rights, legitimized by state registrations, but their scope, as well as what can be patented, differs by political regime. Some nations, like Japan, make it difficult for foreigners to file; others, like the United States, ritualize licensing, which yields litigation over infringements.[7] In both areas, professionalization arises, as specialists in patent or copyright law advise users, help individuals or firms prepare an application, or counsel them on whether and how to patent innovations. These have joined traditional experts in the law of physical property: land, buildings, tools, and so forth. Given the dominance by economic and legal historians of these issues, their business history dimensions deserve attention.[8]

Business strategies can turn on patenting decisions, as with the long saga of hybrid corn breeding, one of the foundations of agricultural biotechnology. That US companies devised hybrid corn lines that could not be saved for starting another year's crop unseated farming traditions that conserved cash and preserved autonomy through selecting "seed corn" from each autumn's yield.[9] Unlike IP, here we have a fabrication of *material* property that is branded, traded, and legally protected. Other such fabrications abound, as with the classic privatization of European common lands, the transformation of native American or aboriginal lands into "real property," the creation of water and riparian rights, with associated rents and damage claims, and more recently, the construction of "cap and trade" units, which polluters purchase (to offset excess discharges) from firms that have cleaned up their processes and have residual units to vend.[10] In all these areas, inaugurating new forms of property or new property rights generates business and thus research topics for historians.

A variation on the fabrication theme is devising new owner/user relationships through licensing, leasing, and servicing. An alternative to alienating property once and for all, these strategies create a liaison between providers and clients. Thinking historically and comparatively about how such practices emerged would be fruitful for business historians. Certainly, as Ross Thomson showed a generation ago, the United Shoe Machinery Corporation (USMC) permitted its clients to only lease its highly effective array of devices, refusing to sell them. Antitrust suits charged USMC with monopolistic practices, but more recent observers have argued that "leasing served as an alternative to contractual warranties for assuring the quality of machines and as a way to foster the provision of a range of manufacturer services and information" to support their use.[11] Similarly, IBM and AT&T (also antitrust targets) leased mainframes and telephones for decades, providing extensive service networks, policies that arguably resonated with USMC's system and quality commitments. What might these cases tell us about juridical conceptions of property and practice in American business, about the groundwork for organizational innovations, and about how enterprises enact competition through quality and service rather than through cartels or price wars?[12] Similarly, following Thomas Dicke's effective overview,[13] deeper research into franchises as mechanisms for establishing distinctive property relationships is surely warranted.

Reconsidering property entails thinking about values, prices, and the valuation process—the means through which figures are attached to material and abstract phenomena. Property has, by turns, market value, cultural value, sentimental value, historical value, and replacement value, at a minimum. This indicates either how soft our concepts of value have been or how restrictive thinking only about pricing can be. Conflicts over valuation, we would suggest, frequently involve conflating multiple modes for assessing value, which is routine outside the domain of equations and algorithms. So historians could well inquire into how valuations of merging corporations were determined (so many millions for goodwill, more added for imaginary assets, once called "water"?), how the value of a family firm being sold was calculated, or how analysts assess the value corporations gain through mergers and acquisitions. On the last point, observers increasingly doubt that mergers add value to enterprises; stocks often fall, brutal downsizings recur, and crises sometimes explode. Even General Electric, acquisitive in the Jack Welch era, later found it necessary to spin off divisions that proved disappointing. What may be the implications of such outcomes, and are there different historical patterns related to location, sector, or market scope? In some cases, valuations are determined by hiring an outside professional—a merchant bank, a consultant, an accounting firm. How did such practices emerge, and what critiques of them followed? Valuation in bankruptcy is yet another contested dynamic, which varies with the goal: liquidation versus reorganization and rationalization (as with US railways in the Morgan era). In joint ventures and shared projects, property issues provide conflict points as well, over divisions of labor and of income.

Last, let us turn to governments. States oversee property relations and rights, whether feudal, monarchist, communist, syndicalist, parliamentary, intertribal, democratic, or dictatorial. This incomplete roster of state structures globally and historically should immediately signal that no essentialist version of optimal or basic government-business property relations can be defended. When, how, and where has to be established by researchers, along with the dimensions of these factors. States define some properties as taxable (exempting others), certify ownership, and oversee transfers while following diverse principles and practices. Still, patterns can be instructive. Do expansive, imperialistic states echo one another's conceptions of government's relation to private property and business assets? In mixed economies, how are state enterprises articulated with "private" businesses; how are contractual relations sustained and monitored between the two realms? What consequences does state failure have for property holders, domestic and foreign, and for state-owned property? On this last point, the 1999 collapse of Argentina's financial system destroyed both the nation's international credit and the property rights of its middle and working classes. The latter's small businesses, which were key employers, collapsed amid the banking crisis and the credit famine, leading to evictions and the construction of Buenos

Aires's extensive "Hoovervilles" (a term from the American Great Depression) for the displaced masses.[14] As current research into crises expands steadily, anchoring projects by learning which forms of property are erased and which preserved as states collapse can form a solid vector for business historical research.

NOTES

1. Pierre-Joseph Proudhon, *What Is Property? An Inquiry into the Principle of Right and Government* (1840, trans. 1876; (Cambridge, UK: Cambridge University Press, 1994), and Proudhon, *Les Confessions d'un Révolutionnaire pour servir à l'histoire de la Révolution de Février* (Paris: Rivière, 1929). The classic intellectual biography in English is George Woodcock, *Pierre-Joseph Proudhon: His Life and Work* (New York: Schocken, 1972; repr. London: Routledge, 2010). Proudhon also indicated that property was "impossible" and that it was "despotic," claims that bear closer consideration.

2. Milena Veenis, "Cola in the German Democratic Republic East German Fantasies on Western Consumption," *Enterprise and Society* 12 (2011): 489–524.

3. Katherine Epstein, "Inventing the Military Industrial Complex: Torpedo Development, Property Rights, and Naval Warfare in the United States and Great Britain before World War I" (PhD diss., The Ohio State University, 2010). Because of government claims about ownership of a new torpedo design, its originator left Britain to set up manufacturing in Trieste, where the Austro-Hungarian Empire was comfortable with him selling products to clients everywhere.

4. Bernard Schwartz, ed., *The Code Napoleon and the Common-Law World* (New York: NYU Press, 1956). Locales where both frameworks interpenetrate and conflict are especially interesting, for example, Louisiana in the Unites States, as a long series of *Tulane University Law Review* articles confirms.

5. Richard Titmuss, *The Gift Relationship: Human Blood and Social Policy* (New York: Vintage, 1972), and Sophie Chauveau, "De la transfusion à l'industrie: Une histoire des produits sanguins en France, 1950–fin-des-années 1970," *Entreprises et Histoire*, no. 36 (2004): 103–19.

6. Adrian Johns, *Piracy: The Intellectual Property Wars from Gutenberg to Gates* (Chicago: University of Chicago Press, 2009). Quoted matter in Christopher Kelty, "Steal This Review!" *Historical Studies in the Natural Sciences* 41 (2011): 255–64, quotes from 258.

7. Masaaki Kotabe, "A Comparative Study of US and Japanese Patent Systems," *Journal of International Business Studies* 23 (1992): 147–68.

8. Catherine Fisk, *Working Knowledge: Employee Innovation and the Rise of Corporate Intellectual Property, 1800–1930* (Chapel Hill: University of North Carolina Press, 2009).

9. See Deborah Fitzgerald, *The Business of Breeding: Hybrid Corn in Illinois, 1890–1940* (Ithaca: Cornell University Press, 1990), and Fitzgerald, "Farmers Deskilled: Hybrid Corn and Farmers' Work," *Technology and Culture* 32 (1993): 324–43. Hybrid lines would not produce the same variety and yields from saved seeds, forcing farmers to buy fresh seed each spring. See also William Lesser, "Intellectual Property Rights and Concentration in Agricultural Biotechnology," *AgBioForum* 1.2 (1998), 56–61; Mark Mikel and John Dudley, "Evolution of North American Dent Corn from Public to Private Germplasm," *Crop Science* 46 (2005): 1193–1205; and Center for Food Safety, *Monsanto vs. US Farmers* (Washington, DC:

Center for Food Safety, 2005). For a recent and compelling analysis of intersections between biology and history, see Edmund Russell, *Evolutionary History: Uniting History and Biology to Understand Life on Earth* (New York: Cambridge University Press, 2011).

10. Richard Coniff, "The Political History of Cap and Trade," *Smithsonian Magazine*, Aug. 2009, available at www.smithsonianmag.com/science-nature/Presence-of-Mind-Blue-Sky -Thinking.html (accessed 1 June 2011). The idea is that the state sets an annual limit for each firm's discharges. Those who go over must buy units from those under the limit, advantaging the latter, which have reduced emissions.

11. Ross Thomson, *The Path to Mechanized Shoe Production in the United States* (Chapel Hill: University of North Carolina Press, 1989), and Scott Masten and Edward Snyder, "U.S. v. United Shoe Machinery Corporation: On the Merits" (Working Paper No. 686, School of Business Administration, University of Michigan, 1992), 2, available at http://quod.lib.umich .edu/b/busadwp/images/b/1/5/b1586634.0001.001.pdf (accessed 1 June 2011).

12. See Richard John, *Network Nation: Inventing American Telecommunications* (Cambridge, MA: Harvard University Press, 2011).

13. Thomas Dicke, *Franchising in America: The Development of a Business Method, 1840–1980* (Chapel Hill: University of North Carolina Press, 1992). For wider, more contemporary views, see Ilan Alon, "Global Franchising and Development in Emerging and Transitioning Markets," *Journal of Macromarketing* 24 (2004): 156–67, and Deborah Burke and E. Malcolm Abel II, "Franchising Fraud: The Continuing Need for Reform," *American Business Law Journal* 40 (2002): 355–84.

14. For analysis, see Guillermo Perry and Luis Servén, "The Anatomy of a Multiple Crisis: Why Was Argentina Special and What Can We Learn From It?," Chief Economist's Office, The World Bank, 2002, available at http://econ161.berkeley.edu/Stray_Notes/perry.pdf (accessed 1 June 2011), and Ana Corbacho, Mercedes Garcia-Escribano, and Gabriela Inchauste, "Argentina: Macroeconomic Crisis and Household Vulnerability," *Review of Development Economics* 11 (2007): 92–106.

2. Fraud and Fakery

Morning newspapers and podcasts all too often bring news of business frauds unmasked. Late in 2010, Philadelphians encountered a front-page story about a construction supply firm that, for nearly twenty years, had been deceptively presenting itself as minority owned, thereby securing $119 million in illegal contracts for reinforced concrete work.[1] The report expressed no surprise at this criminal adventurism, understandable given the frequency of such opportunism. Art forgery is hardly rare, and its most notorious perpetrators have at times reached the status of folk heroes (in some circles).[2] Comparable fakery also litters the history of business, but it has not drawn business historians' attention until recently. Perhaps this lack of interest followed from the Chandlerian rehabilitation of corporations and their leaders from charges of being social menaces, as Progressive and Depression-era critics of robber barons and stock market trickery argued.[3] Still, memorable scandals generated stacks of revelatory, usually ephemeral books: from Crèdit Mobilier, Teapot Dome, and Ivar Kreuger's wooden match kingdom, to recent US corporate frauds, involving Enron, Tyco, World Com, and the now-iconic Bernard Madoff.[4]

That we have rarely attempted to take the measure of fraud and fakery as historical phenomena, assess change across time and difference across space, or conceptualize its variants may stem from the seeming uniqueness of each case and the apparent lack of theoretical resources to help frame broad questions that could identify patterns reflecting temporal and spatial complexities. We hope here to foster such questioning by outlining one theoretical view of white-collar crime, reviewing some recent research, and offering an empirically derived, speculative matrix of fraud as relational behavior among individuals, businesses, and nonbusiness agencies.

How can historians think systematically about fraud and comparable white-collar crimes? One promising response comes from Australian legal sociologist John Braithwaite, who argues for the centrality of *social and economic inequality* to crimes by both the rich and the poor. The poor can initiate crimes to satisfy unmet needs, at times framed in relation to those far more privileged. However, Braithwaite stresses that inequality also triggers crime at the top, as the vast array of goods available to "rich people (and organizations)," whose basic needs are already satisfied, leads to a search for additional "goods for exchange [and hence to] criminal opportunities to indulge greed." Moreover, rich and poor "criminal subcultures develop to communicate symbolic reassurance to those who decide to prey on others, to sustain techniques for neutralizing the evil of crime and to communicate knowledge about how to do it."[5]

Here we have two promising vectors for grasping the fraud problem: the privileged and the ambitious may well seek gain without limit, transcending social rules—a goal their privileged status makes feasible. Second, fraudsters and con artists (corporate or individual) exploit communications links and locally validated claims that justify their initiatives, not least in constituting the victim (a firm, agency, or individual) as "the sucker." Someone has to "buy in" to a cheater's game, else it's meaningless. Indeed, the relationship between the schemer and the sucker connects predation with gullibility and humiliation, not least because "inegalitarian societies are structurally humiliating."[6] Those gulled are ashamed of falling for a "con"; those executing the fraud are shameless.

Street sellers of fake Gucci bags and financial hustlers have this facilitative social dimension in common. Moreover, individuals active in both situations depend intricately on institutional suppliers—for forged DVDs, fake Polo sweaters, duplicated fashions, or "certified" mortgage loans.[7] A century or more ago, enterprises in Ottoman-era Izmir sold shiploads of oriental carpets to Europe and America, yet in any environment where authenticity is a value creator and deep knowledgeability is needed to establish authenticity, the chances for misrepresentation and fakery were high. So too with nineteenth-century wines, not uncommonly represented in export relations as having finer lineages than were actually the case.[8]

From work in progress by Edward Balleisen,[9] we can pinpoint the powerful role of information asymmetries in fraudulent performances, for routinely the faker's specialized knowledge (or assertion of same) is critical to creating suckers. Last, from Foucault, bringing in state and society, it's helpful to ask when and where frauds were treated as mere "illegalities," annoying but tolerated, and when and where they stand forth as "criminalities," threatening social order sufficiently that their suppression became a government or collective responsibility.[10] Taken together, these aspects of the deceitful transaction or relationship provide a means to ask questions about frauds and fakes historically.

This is exactly what Stephen Mihm did as he analyzed the counterfeiting of US paper currency prior to the American Civil War, an activity in which manufacturing fakes facilitated fraudulent purchases. For complex reasons, the federal government, while reserving coinage to the national state, had decentralized (to state-chartered banks) the production of private promissory bills, which lubricated commerce while being (theoretically) redeemable for specie on demand. Mihm asked, among other things, how it was possible for US fakers to produce and circulate huge quantities of bogus currency from the 1790s through the 1860s. Why were governments powerless or unwilling to challenge them? Who supported and who opposed, who profited from and who was injured by, false bills? What structural and situational conditions encouraged widespread counterfeiting, and what changed to bring this "plague" to an end?[11] In

Braithwaite's terms, inequality was central, as there was never enough specie to sustain an expanding economy or to properly support a sound paper currency. Hence enterprisers in the Midwest printed floods of paper money to buy land, underwrite purchases of materials for housing or factories, or settle accounts with distant suppliers in the East. So too were the (somewhat) wealthy eager to use unbacked paper bills in schemes to further enrich them, playing on information asymmetries. Given that hundreds of US banks issued notes, few users could determine which came from strong, weak, or completely imaginary banks. Everyone accepting a false note was a "sucker," to be sure, unless he or she could pass it along to another economic actor. The end-game losers were those who tried to deposit such currency in banks with well-trained tellers, who refused the notes or seized them.

Two situational sidebars are of interest. Counterfeiting had little relevance to southern commerce in the antebellum decades, as slave states had well-developed policing forces, harsh penalties for fakery (as in the United Kingdom), and a much slower tempo of cash transactions (governed by agricultural seasonality and merchant credit ledgers). Space and local situations mattered. Second, when the Union's Civil War government determined to issue paper "greenbacks" to fund war expenditures, eager counterfeiters met their match in a new national police force, the Secret Service, which, following arrests, confined malefactors in Washington, DC, jails until trials.[12] Once a triumphant national state took charge of the counterfeiting problem, counterfeiting receded to the margins of American fraud. Mihm's work represents a key starting point for business historians beginning to think about fakes and frauds as nasty, if imaginative, inversions of lawful economic relations.

Thus far we have noted cases in which businesses defrauded clients and in which individuals (note passers) defrauded businesses. With shaky banks printing stacks of bills, we also have examples of businesses defrauding other businesses. This set of relations leads to a preliminary effort to conceptualize the varieties of frauds in relational terms, as the table below illuminates (*actors* along the left side and *targets* across the top). Plainly, this is incomplete, as it doesn't include false certifications (education/skill) or collaborative frauds against individuals, firms, or governments (economic conspiracies). More can surely be done to improve or replace this framework, but we believe that even this version can provide a platform for framing questions, at a minimum, about: (1) historical patterns of fraud (incidence, trends), nationally and transnationally or, as the US case suggests, among regions; (2) efforts at reducing piracy and copying (an intellectual property issue from nineteenth-century books to contemporary knockoffs of fashions and software); and (3) the relation between fraud and business self-regulation (trade associations), the management of quality (through enforceable standards), the assessment of clients (through credit agencies), and the assurance of fidelity in contracts and projects. Certainly, fakery has been widespread historically (e.g., newly crafted antiquities surface century after century),[13] but its systematic investigation by business historians can yield deeper understanding, reaching beyond individual cases.

NOTES

1. "Fraud Case on the 'Cutting Edge,'" *Philadelphia Inquirer*, 12 Oct. 2010, 1, 4. US law provides "set-aside" shares of joint federal-state infrastructure construction projects for firms owned by women and ethnic minorities. The accused company set up a shadow firm, fronted by a Philippines-born, naturalized American citizen, which secured supply agreements for some 336 bridge contracts from 1991 to 2007.

2. Notably the Vermeer faker, Hans van Meergeren, whose mid-twentieth-century talent and arrogance are profiled in Edward Dolnick, *The Forger's Spell* (New York: Harper, 2008). For the more recent Drewe and Myatt fakeries in the UK, see Laney Salisbury and Ali Sujo, *Provenance* (New York: Penguin, 2009).

The Fraud Matrix: A Rough Schematic	Individuals (Consumers/Citizens)	Businesses	Government Units (and Nonprofits)
Individuals (Consumers/ Citizens)	*Interpersonal frauds* "Really, I'm divorced . . . ," loan cosigning and defaults; pretend advisers (counseling, investments)	*Individuals defraud businesses* Passing counterfeit money; credit card–insurance fraud; lawsuits for faked injuries	*Individuals defraud state agencies* Tax fraud; fake expense reports *Individuals defraud nonprofits*—gifts of counterfeit art or antiquities
Businesses	*Businesses defraud clients* Useless goods; fake medicine; fraudulent investments	*Businesses defraud other businesses* False weights; quality fakery; no-pay orders; tactical bankruptcies	*Businesses defraud governments* Bills for nonexistent or inflated goods or services; tax cheating *Businesses defraud nonprofits?*
Government Units (and Nonprofits)	*Governments defraud citizens* Acquiring private property at lowball prices; fraudulent election results	*Governments defraud businesses* Contract price "renegotiation" after delivery; bid rigging to favor friends	*Nonprofits and governments defraud other governments and nonprofits* Examples?

3. See Matthew Josephson, *The Robber Barons* (1934; New York: Harcourt, Brace, 1962). Indeed, the first Harvard professorship of business history and the creation of the *Business History Review* in the 1920s were intended as antidotes to harsh critiques of trusts and big business.

4. A recent popular overview of one vector is David E. Y. Sarna, *History of Greed: Financial Fraud from Tulip Mania to Bernie Madoff* (New York: Wiley, 2010). Oddly, Sarna was the target of an SEC securities fraud complaint in 2006; see www.sec.gov/litigation/complaints/2006/comp19798.pdf for the text of the accusation, filed in the US District Court, Southern District of New York. Its resolution is unclear.

5. John Braithwaite, "Poverty, Power, White-Collar Crime, and the Paradoxes of Criminological Theory," in *Criminological Theory*, ed. Marilyn McShane and F. P. Williams (New York: Routledge, 1997), 68, 74 (reprint of an article published in the *Australia and New Zealand Journal of Criminology* in 1991). See also Braithwaite, "Criminological Theory and Organizational Crime," *Justice Quarterly* 6 (1989): 333–58.

6. Ibid., 75.

7. Mary Lynn Stewart, "Copying and Copyrighting Haute Couture: Democratizing Fashion, 1900–1930s," *French Historical Studies* 28 (2005): 103–30. Indeed, the couture sector in time authorized simplified copies of seasonal styles: see Alexandra Palmer, *Couture and Commerce: The Transatlantic Fashion Trade in the 1950s* (Vancouver: University of British Columbia Press, 2001).

8. Donald Quataert, "Machine Breaking and the Changing Carpet Industry of Anatolia, 1860–1908," *Journal of Social History* 19 (1986): 473–89; Brian Spooner, "Weavers and Dealers: The Authenticity of an Oriental Carpet," in *The Social Life of Things*, ed. Arjun Appadurai (Cambridge, UK: Cambridge University Press, 1986), 195–235; and Alessandro Stanziani, "Wine Reputation and Quality Controls: The Origin of the AOCs in 19th-Century France," *European Journal of Law and Economics* 18 (2004): 149–67.

9. Edward Balleisen, "Business Fraud on the Entrepreneurial Margin" (unpublished paper presented at the Penn Economic History Forum, Philadelphia, 7 Oct. 2010).

10. Michel Foucault, *Discipline and Punish: The Birth of the Prison* (New York: Pantheon, 1977).

11. Stephen Mihm, *A Nation of Counterfeiters: Capitalists, Con Men, and the Making of the United States* (Cambridge, MA: Harvard University Press, 2007). Much fake money was produced by copyist engravers—"real" counterfeiters—but even more flowed from weakly capitalized western banks seeking to boom trade (land sales, building, town development) by releasing money to local entrepreneurs for which there was little or no specie reserves as backup.

12. Ibid., 199, 240–59. For European examples over a longer time span, see Gérard Béaur, Hubert Bonin, and Claire Lemercier, eds., *Fraude, contrefaçon et contrebande de l'Antiquité à nos jours* (Geneva: Droz, 2006).

13. Kenneth Lapatin points out that "Cretans had been producing fake antiquities even before the discovery of the Minoan ruins. . . . In fact their reputation for deceit dates back to antiquity." Lapatin, *Mysteries of the Snake Goddess: Art, Desire, and the Forging of History* (New York: Houghton Mifflin Harcourt, 2002), 28.

3. From Empires to Emergent Nations

We open with a framework statement by Anthony G. Hopkins: "The big issues of the post-colonial era cannot be understood without acknowledging the extent to which they are a legacy of empires that dominated the greater part of the world during the past three centuries."[1] In between empires and the postcolonial era lay the colonial world, colonizing being an imperial option, along with establishing trade routes and centers, extracting tribute, or setting up military outposts and territorial occupations. Empires, colonies, and emergent nations all have business histories, though specialists in other fields (imperial, political, economic, maritime, and national histories of former colonial areas) have written most of today's vast, provocative literature. Our goal here is quite basic: to step a few paces back from the established business history literatures on multinational enterprises and foreign direct investment in order to introduce other potentially "big issues" concerning empire, colonization, and national emergence that are deeply entwined with business institutions and actions.

In Hopkins's view:

> Empires were transnational organizations that were created to mobilize the resources of the world. Their existence and their unity were made possible by supranational connections. Their longevity was determined by their ability to extend the reach and maintain the stability of these connections.... [Moreover] empire was an act of integration involving the mobilization of *economic* resources; it required political intervention to create and protect property rights, to control transactions costs, to shape cooperative interest groups, and to manage opposition.[2]

Crucially, empire required businesses—for Britain, the London capital markets, plus commodity exchanges, merchant houses by the hundreds, shipping lines, harbors, wharfs and warehouses, and suppliers of ships, sails, engines, weapons, maps, instruments, and labor (slave, migrant, indentured, and "free"). The extensive connectedness of empires and their impulses to mobilize resources generated business incentives for both concentration and dispersion: in the first case, establishing entrepôts as intense places of encounter and entanglement, and in the second, triggering multiple sequences of shift and transfer for elites, business people, workers, knowledge, artifacts, and technology.[3] Consider Cape Town, from the 1650s through the eighteenth century the Dutch East India Company's "oceanic crossroads . . . a site within a shipping network that accommodated large numbers of people," either as settlers or as seasonal transients. Known as the "Tavern of the Seas," Cape Town provided long-distance travelers on Europe-Asia routes a halfway stopping point for rest, repairs, and provisioning. As ships usually paused for a month at Table Bay, commerce thrived there, including a slave trade that supplied much of the region's workforce.[4] Comparable imperial entrepôts included Calcutta, Timbuktu, Macau, Canton, Hong Kong, Salonica, Alexandria, Boston, and New Orleans, many of which participated in elaborate transoceanic relationships before, during, and after colonial times.

Imperial interactions generated dispersals and migrations as well. The Chinese merchant *diaspora* (a contested term) extended overseas what were ongoing internal population flows to the west and north, transformations induced "by contact with European trading empires." Urban areas became what Philip Kuhn calls Imperial China's "school for emigrants," as those exiting rural domains learned how to commercialize their skills, how to handle money, and "how to do business in an environment where political power was held by others."[5] Similar patterns emerged in the late eighteenth century, when "the rapid growth of Ottoman-European trade" stimulated the spread of "non-Muslim Ottoman subjects (Greeks, Jews, and Armenians)" across the Mediterranean world's port cities, cultivating a durable "cosmopolitanism"—an international culture "expressed by commercial elites before the shaping of national identities."[6] We suggest that cosmopolitanism would be a productive topic for business historical research.[7]

Jeffry Frieden has crisply delineated the decision to colonize and its business context:

> Cross-border investment involves an explicit or implicit contract between the host country and the investor. The arrangements developed to monitor and enforce these contracts—from gunboat diplomacy to private negotiations—are varied institutional forms responding to different characteristics of the investment and the environment. Colonialism is a particular, perhaps particularly noxious, form that the "resolution" of these quasi-contractual issues can take: the

use of force by a home government to annex the host region and so eliminate the
interjurisdictional nature of the dispute.[8]

Frieden also links the imperial installation of colonial states to these investments' characteristics, arguing that enterprises extracting primary materials
for home economies are more likely to opt for "the unilateral use of force" than
firms operating "public utilities" (railways, power plants) and that "foreign loans
should seldom be linked to military intervention." Home states will abandon
threatened owners of manufacturing facilities in far-off lands, as the value of
factories falls sharply when they are isolated from enterprise networks. Alert
host administrations will also recognize this and avoid confrontations. These
inviting propositions situate the establishment of colonialism within a wide array of investment options, delivering value to research through cross-disciplinary
conceptualization.[9]

Clearly colonies were hothouses for transplanting home country–sponsored
businesses to distant terrains, but under what assumptions and with what consequences? Entanglements with host cultures can be enlightening or befud-
dling and destructive; colonies may be fabricated for receiving emigrant settlers (Australia, Algeria) or may be organized for administrative elites to control,
then exploit or develop (India, Indochina). Business histories of these interlaced intentions will be instructive. For example, British and Dutch shipping
firms in the South Asia trade learned that they could profit substantially, not
only by transporting migrant workers from Asia "to plantations, mines or railroad construction sites" in Africa or the Americas, but also by vastly expanding
a local customary market—for pilgrimages to Mecca (the hajj). As Michael
Miller explains, from the 1850s Europeans organized steamship transit for the
Islamic faithful in vessels adapted to carry both people and goods in the pilgrimage season and goods alone at other times of the year. These efforts "evolved
out of colonial investment and practice and in fact mirrored wider imperial
business patterns, from the deployment and incorporation of indigenous networks to the business consequences of decolonization." The latter included
new states awkwardly displacing colonial-era ship operators and generating
mass confusion among stranded pilgrims, before inviting experienced local organizers to again manage transit affairs. The advent of fast and relatively inexpensive air travel by the 1960s, together with increasing wealth in the region,
brought the seaborne pilgrim trade to an end.[10] Colonization triggered other,
quite secular, touring initiatives: the durable Thomas Cook firm inaugurated
packaged international tourism in British-"protected" Egypt in the 1870s, and

an adventurous French firm extended its North Africa colonial shipping routes to Saharan tours before, but especially after, World War One.[11]

This sequence opens the way to inquiring more generally about what happens to the colonizers' companies when independence is secured and about the fate of state property following decolonization. In the French case, firms "born" or "planted" overseas achieved a high rate of conversion to financial, transport, or logistics companies in new African and Asian states, reinventing themselves rather than closing shop.[12] In South Asia, Tirthanakar Roy suggests, "it is useful to study post-war Indian business history in term of the relationship and interaction between the two worlds: modern and traditional." India's classic business towns anchored the "'bazaar' economy [which] engaged in commodity trade, produced and traded handicrafts, used boats and carts for transportation, relied heavily on caste and community for a variety of needs and used indigenous bankers for remittance and capital." "Mills, mines, and plantations," by contrast, were modern businesses, with railway access to ports and links to capital markets. Roy found that in Calcutta, where Europeans controlled the modern sector and Indians the traditional, "the relationship was unstable and antagonistic," but in Delhi and Bombay, "the modern sector had stronger bazaar roots," yielding more stable interactions. Here the colonial and the postcolonial "overlapped" in divergent ways, sounding a theme that business history has "yet to take up . . . in a serious way."[13] Similarly, crony capitalism, "characterized by personal relationships between politicians and corporate figures . . . had its antecedents in British colonialism." There, officially sanctioned "collusion with private enterprises" for "revenue farming" paved the way for the postindependence Malaysian economy's close relations between "tycoons" and "top politicians." The consequence was a politically infused system of licensing, monopolies, and state concessions, yielding "rent-seeking" behavior that evaded competition.[14]

In the aftermath of World War Two and during the decolonization process, eager actors scrambled to acquire both private and public property, whether in Central Europe, Viet Nam, or Zimbabwe, as property rights became dramatically unsettled. Business activity at these transitional nodes could exhibit defensive or creative, protective or improvisational features, just as politics and culture do in stressful times. A key question, then, would concern the degree to which the businesses of emergent nations reproduced the processes and mechanisms from earlier eras, including businesses in countries emerging from Soviet-style communism, from state-capitalist dictatorships (e.g., contemporary North Africa or 1990s Latin America, the Philippines, etc.) or from civil wars (Sri Lanka,

Sudan, the former Yugoslavia). What local or East Asian business-society and business-government relations fostered the Little Dragons' unanticipated leapfrogging of conventional development pathways?[15] How did their particular business histories condition the remarkable post-1990 expansion of BRIC (Brazil, Russia, India, China) economic prowess, and what unacknowledged shortcomings might such research expose? If arguably each state has engaged in a "rediscovery of capitalism," how was this achieved and how differently in each case?[16] Finally, how do the businesses of emerging nations actually emerge onto the postwar stage of global policymaking, in the WTO, the IMF, the GATT tariff rounds, and in associations campaigning for equitable trade relations, bilaterally and multilaterally? The agenda is broad, but thinking transnationally about empires, colonies, and emerging nations could invigorate an equally broad range of business history projects.

NOTES

1. Anthony G. Hopkins, "Back to the Future: From National History to Imperial History," *Past and Present*, no. 164 (1999): 198–243, quote from 203.

2. Ibid, 205, 215, emphasis added. Hopkins also distinguishes between predatory and developmental empires, the former being "redistributional," having "no record or expectation of cumulative economic development," whereas the latter "were committed to activating latent or underutilized resources" (206).

3. See Tirthanakar Roy, "Flourishing Branches, Wilting Core: Research in Modern Indian Economic History," *Australian Economic History Review* 44 (2004): 221–40.

4. Kerry Ward, "'Tavern of the Seas?': The Cape of Good Hope as an Oceanic Crossroads in the Seventeenth and Eighteenth Centuries" (paper presented at the Seascapes, Littoral Cultures and Tran-Oceanic Exchanges conference, Washington, DC., 2003), available at http://webdoc.sub.gwdg.de/ebook/p/2005/history_cooperative/www.historycooperative.org/proceedings/seascapes/ward.html (accessed 10 June 2011).

5. Philip Kuhn, "The Homeland: Thinking about the History of the Chinese Overseas," The Morrison Lecture in Ethnology, 1997, available at http://chinainstitute.anu.edu.au/morrison/morrison58.pdf (accessed 11 June 2011). See also Kuhn's article, "Why China Historians Should Study the Chinese Diaspora, and Vice-Versa," *Journal of Chinese Overseas* 2 (2006): 163–72.

6. Evridiki Sifneos, "Cosmopolitanism as a Feature of the Greek Commercial Diaspora," *History and Anthropology* 16 (2005): 97–111.

7. For gateways to a rich and argumentative literature, see Henk Driessen, "Mediterranean Port Cities: Cosmopolitanism Reconsidered," *History and Anthropology* 16 (2005): 129–41, and Bruno Latour, "Whose Cosmos, Which Cosmopolitics?," *Common Knowledge* 10 (2004): 450–62. Ulrich Beck has written extensively about the topic from a sociological standpoint. See Beck, *Cosmopolitan Vision* (Cambridge, UK: Polity, 2006), and Beck and Na-

tan Sznaida, eds., "Unpacking Cosmopolitanism for the Social Sciences (Special Issue)," *British Journal of Sociology* 57 (2006): 1–168.

8. Jeffry Frieden, "International Investment and Colonial Control: A New Interpretation," *International Organization* 48 (1994): 559–93, quote from 559. See also Frieden's snyoptic *Global Capitalism: Its Fall and Rise in the Twentieth Century* (New York: Norton, 2006).

9. Frieden, "International Investment," 570–73. On the economic aspects of ending colonial ventures, see Gerold Krozewski, *Money and the End of Empire: British International Economic Policy and the Colonies, 1947–1958* (London: Palgrave Macmillan, 2001).

10. Michael Miller, "The Business of the Hajj: Seaborne Commerce and the Movement of Peoples" (paper presented at the Seascapes, Littoral Cultures and Trans-Oceanic Exchanges conference, Washington, DC, 2003), available at www.historycooperative.org/proceedings/seascapes/miller.html (accessed 10 June 2011). A revised, expanded version is Miller, "Pilgrim's Progress: The Business of the Hajj," *Past and Present*, no. 191 (2006): 189–228.

11. Waleed Hazbun, "The East as Exhibit: Thomas Cook & Son and the Origins of the International Tourism Industry in Egypt," in *The Business of Tourism: Place, Faith, and History,* ed. Philip Scranton and Janet Davidson (Philadelphia: University of Pennsylvania Press, 2007), 3–33, and Kenneth Perkins, "The Compagnie Générale Transatlantique and the Development of Saharan Tourism in North Africa," in ibid., 34–55.

12. For one French postcolonial policy, see Philip Raikes, Michael Friis Jensen, and Stefano Ponte, "Global Commodity Chain Analysis and the French *filière* Approach: Comparison and Critique," *Economy and Society* 29 (2000): 390–417; for another, see Hélène d'Almeida-Topor, "French Trading Companies in Sub-Saharan Africa, 1960–1990," in *The Multinational Traders,* ed. Geoffrey Jones (London: Routledge, 1998), 173–82. A valuable overview is Bill Ashcroft, *Post-colonial Transformation* (London: Routledge, 2001).

13. Roy, "Flourishing Branches," 236.

14. Sheila Yacob, "Hidden Disciplines: in Malaysia: The Role of Business History in a Multidisciplinary Framework," *Australian Economic History Review* 45 (2009): 302–24, quote from 315–16. See also David Kang, *Crony Capitalism: Corruption and Development in South Korea and the Philippines* (Cambridge, UK: Cambridge University Press, 2002). More than a few observers have argued that such crony relationships are rising in the United States, given the increasing role of big business in funding elections and shaping policy. For two perspectives, see Owen Ullman, "Crony Capitalism American Style," *International Economy*, July–Aug. 1999, 6–11, and Paul Krugman, "Crony Capitalism, USA," *New York Times*, 15 Jan. 2002.

15. The classic brief overview is Ezra Vogel, *The Four Little Dragons: The Spread of Industrialization in East Asia* (Cambridge, MA: Harvard University Press, 1993). See also Joseph Stiglitz, "Some Lessons from the East Asian Miracle," *World Bank Research Observer* 11 (1996): 151–77. The four original dragons were Taiwan, Hong Kong, Singapore, and South Korea. Later writers have added Indonesia, Malaysia, and Thailand. Japan of course was the original Asian miracle economy.

16. Mark Beeson and Mark Berger, "The Paradoxes of Paramountcy," *Global Change, Peace, and Security* 15 (2003): 27–42.

4. Gender

Studying gender in relation to business history is not a new idea; decades ago, Mary Yeager and Angela Kwolek-Folland produced pioneering work on women in American business. However, basic explorations of gender and business have not reached far beyond the Anglo-American and French scholarly world.[1] Hence we outline a range of themes and research venues that, if developed, could provide robust connections between enterprise and society through the lens of gender—both male and female articulations of social structures, performances, and representations. In addition to bringing women into our analyses, gender studies are useful for business history because they open questions about masculinity's place in social relations within and among enterprises and associations, about gendered constructions of agency and competence, and about long-term shifts in expectations and opportunities for men and women with highly varied attributes and capabilities.[2] To this end, we discuss gender and consumers, companies and gender relations, entrepreneurship, institutions and associations, and the demographics of gender.

Consumption. What should interest business historians in the recent surge of research on gender and consumption? Consider first, the agency of women as clients for businesses, then women as household managers and activists in consumer groups, and last, the underexplored area of men as buyers of goods. Regarding agency, by the 1930s, US cosmetics companies had devised cheap, mass-market hair shampoos for use by lower-middle-class women. To their surprise, upper-class women flocked to purchase these products, leading firms to introduce a range of higher-priced versions. Women consumers had reconfigured the market, confounding corporate expectations.[3] Such feedback impacts are more common and significant than is often thought. Second, the image of women as conscientious household managers pervades domestic literatures from the eighteenth century—husbands as spendthrifts and wives as savers and budget overseers. This mythical construction has long been an organizing cultural principle; but its incompleteness is plain, for it conflicts with equally potent images of women and daughters as compulsive buyers and men moaning about wrecked budgets. A class divide may be encoded here, with the first dichotomy perhaps deriving from elite views of the nineteenth-century working class and the second presenting advertising and media fantasies about acquisitiveness and gender, chiefly among twentieth-century white-collar families.[4] Exploring ambiguous, gendered discourses about economy and family offers a promising venue for business history research.

Next, women have been leading activists in consumer associations from their beginnings before 1900, with many developing substantial expertise in household economics, a gendered scholarly field in which women were both researchers and students. These associations provided critical technical analysis of products, advocated consumer protections, and encouraged businesses to be responsive to customer needs and complaints.[5] As Matthew Hilton explained:

> In 1890, a Consumers League was formed by the Women's Trade Union League in New York, which soon inspired equivalent organizations across Western Europe, all of which campaigned against poor labor conditions behind the manufacture of goods sold in the main high-street stores. . . . As consumers movements emerged in the West, they applied notions of equitability in markets collectively as well as individually. In the latter half of the twentieth century, as the consumer movement expanded across the developing world, this theme was adopted more forcefully.[6]

The history of men as consumers, with few exceptions, remains to be written, even as our understanding of the masculine aspects of gender has deepened.[7] What sorts of businesses have men patronized? How have these patterns shifted? What can we learn about gender and society from male-only enterprises?[8] Shopping is different from paying bills; it is a cultural exercise, chiefly done in public (excepting mail order and the Internet), which demonstrates social values, personal connections, and decision-making skills.[9] Conventionally, middle-class men bought goods for women, but some men purchased women's goods for themselves, and not just cross-dressers and transgendered people. When Shiseido marketed a new line of cosmetics designed for Chinese women, Aupres, in the early 2000s, stunned managers discovered that sales to Chinese men were substantial, not as gifts but for personal use. In consequence, the company revised its product line to include items targeting both men and women seeking beauty.[10] Market researchers have documented this behavior but have had trouble mapping or analyzing it.

A recent study takes consumption by men in the nineteenth century as one of its key themes. Amy Lippert's research on the visual culture of Gold Rush San Francisco shows that eager miners patronized a dozen photography shops, having portraits made that showed them holding picks and shovels, sitting on bags of fake gold nuggets. They sent these images of masculinity triumphant to families back home, but saved for other uses the photo portraits local prostitutes distributed as *cartes-de-visite*. This practice introduces the question of pornography and vice as businesses.[11] Of course, what some regard as leisure, others regard as sin. Straddling this divide, George Chauncey's research on early-twentieth-century New York carefully outlined the range of enterprises seeking to serve clients from both poor and prosperous segments of the gay community.[12] (See Prospects, 9: The Subaltern.) Here gender, enterprise, and society were intricately entwined. Remembering that masculinity is a highly variable performance, imaginative business historians should be able to frame comparable projects for other places and periods. After all, Donald Trump and Thierry Mugler are both alpha males in business, as were Andrew Carnegie and Henry Clay Frick, but each enacted different masculinities in business and in public.

Companies. Research for the recent *Dictionnaire historique des patrons français* revealed women having far greater influence on French enterprises than had been suspected. Widows inherited businesses, many wives operated them for ill or injured husbands, and women often represented families on boards of corporations, especially after a family firm had merged with a larger enterprise.[13] Necessity compelled them to transgress the common bourgeois presumption that women should not be involved with profit-making. Though some women inheritors mastered the family trade (or learned it while their spouses declined), more commonly they relied on managers to generate steady revenues.[14] Multigenerational firms could have a number of aging female part-owners, relying on profits or dividends as their sole support. When firms encountered reverses, they suffered severely and could be wooed either to sell their shares to entrepreneurs seeking takeovers or to vote to replace family managers with outsiders promising revitalization. Thomas Mellon Evans, one of the America's early conglomerators, was adept at such maneuvers during the 1940s and 1950s.[15] Unfortunately for the former owners, Evans converted many such firms into cash cows, paying next to no dividends while using profits for further acquisitions. Wives and widows of corporate leaders, however, regularly played different and quite public roles. They started or served art museums, cultural organizations, or health- and charity-oriented nonprofits, and in some cases, created foundations. In early years, they seem to have been more prominent and active than were men, but as nonprofit professionalization crept in, by the mid-twentieth century in the United States and Europe, male managers had relegated them to stylized functions. (See Opportunities, 7: Nonprofits and Quasi Enterprises.)

Women in business long had to deal with male expectations about the exercise of power, often voiced as "No woman should have authority over men." Culturally, working for a female boss was considered demeaning, but this did change, as women managers and owners became emancipated from family and patriarchal assumptions. Generally, this historical process is opaque, so questions about how, when, where, and why it unfolded remain salient. Clearly, it is also incomplete and complex, if the recent case of Liliane Bettencourt is any evidence. Mme. Bettencourt has owned a majority stake in L'Oréal for more than forty years, constituting the third-largest personal estate in France. She bought islands in the Indian Ocean and widely funded political campaigns and medical research. However, in 2008, her daughter (breaking gender stereotypes) attempted a legal coup, arguing that her eighty-five-year-old mother was incompetent and was wasting family funds. The richest woman in France thus discovered that, however free her wealth and networks of influence had helped her become, she could neither disentwine herself from the bonds of family, nor avert being publicly labeled as an addled old woman by a family member grasping for her fortune.[16]

Entrepreneurship, institutions, associations. Each of these domains has significant gender aspects that bear on business history. Entrepreneurial women started thousands of small businesses in nineteenth-century North America and Europe, but chiefly in sectors serving bourgeois women's needs: dress and hat making or hair work. Operating boardinghouses or small retail establishments selling meals, produce, and ladies' goods was also routine, although men usually owned laundries or general stores, which sometimes had women managers.[17] Women also replaced men as department store clerks, typists, and telephone operators; what motivated managers to instigate such shifts deserves further exploration.[18]

Moving beyond these boundaries could happen through participation in associations and social movements, however. French suffragist and journalist Marguerite Durand started an activist newspaper in Paris in the 1880s, *La Fronde*. Hiring other women as writers, illustrators, and printers, she created training sites for female professionals and skilled workers.[19] However, other newspapers and printers hired women typesetters chiefly to break strikes by organized men, who for their part had refused to bring women into their unions. As this case suggests, gender relations in business history are more complex that we might imagine. Not being firms, associations provided venues for enterprising women to learn management and budgeting while advocating temperance or opposing colonialism. As all-male, all-female, and mixed-sex associations existed in industrializing nations, researchers could focus on how gender mattered to each form of organization and to what extent their work trained individuals for business or drew on individuals from businesses.

Similarly, the relationship between higher education and business emerged by the late nineteenth century, with the initiation of business, engineering, and administrative schools. At the top of France's educational system sat the Grandes Ecoles, all-male institutions that provided the Third Republic with bureaucrats, professors, engineers, and managers. Once pressure for women's admission mounted, ministries and private associations (e.g., the Paris Chamber of Commerce) created separate, second-echelon schools, whose female graduates could not secure positions comparable to those for male Grandes Ecoles alumni. Nevertheless, twentieth-century women entered academic faculties and eventually climbed university job ladders, both scholarly and administrative, reaching top positions. In business though, the glass ceiling ruled, with female engineers and managers rising to vice-presidencies but not CEO posts. These institutional exclusions only began to crack in the 1970s, when the most prestigious Ecoles dropped their male-only barriers. More recently in the United States, Wall Street firms, which traditionally recruited entry-level analysts almost exclusively from Princeton and Harvard, have added women to their rosters. Yet gendered networks and task assignments persist at investment banks, constraining women's career tracks and leading many of them to resign.[20] Thus we may ask how gender issues are linked to the development and maintenance of elite institutions in education and in business across the industrialized world. Gendered educational histories merit investigation because they present a complex backstory to gendered practices in executive suites.

Demographics. At some historical junctures, the usual population balance between men and women alters (wars, migrations), and at others, men take up activities conventionally gendered female (cooking) and vice versa (women driving cars).[21] These configurations have implications for business opportunities and practices. In mid- and late-nineteenth-century North America, bachelors and single women became notably more common in urban populations than either before or afterward, creating needs for housing, services, and meals outside families, needs that enterprises addressed profitably.[22] In the aftermath of major conflicts, like the Civil War and World War One, involuntary singleness faced hosts of women, pressing them into workforces, even as physical damage forced many men out of the same workforces or into unwished-for niches where handicapped veterans could find employment. In France and the United Kingdom, however, the 1914–18 deaths of managers and engineers created openings for other men (not women) in business, some from unconventional backgrounds. Absent such demographic disasters, other societies have been aging (Italy, Japan, China), with women living longer than men, a trend that affects marketing, retirement, and succession in firms, product innovation targets, and other enterprise policies. Differential life expectancies, plus differential risk-taking and safety practices, long produced lower insurance rates for women in the United States and Europe, though a recent European court decision revoked this practice for the European Union. In sum, even the driest population data, viewed across time, can provide points of departure for business history research exploring gender, institutions, and practices.

NOTES

1. Mary Yeager, ed., *Women in Business* (Cheltenham, UK: Edward Elgar, 1999); Yeager, "Maverick and Mavens of Business History," *Enterprise and Society* 2 (2001): 687–768; Angela Kwolek-Folland, *Engendering Business: Men and Women in the Corporate Office, 1870–1930* (Baltimore: Johns Hopkins University Press, 1994); Kwolek-Folland, *Incorporating Women: A History of Women and Business in the United States* (New York: Twayne, 1998); Kwolek-Folland, "Gender and Business History," Enterprise and Society 2 (2001): 1–10; and Annie Fouquet, Jacqueline Laufer, and Sylvie Schweitzer, "Les femmes chefs d'entreprise: La parité pour demain?," in *Dictionnaire historique des patrons français*, ed. Jean-Claude Daumas (Paris: Flammarion, 2010), 812–16.

2. Christopher McKenna, "'Better Living Through Chemistry'? Industrial Accidents and Masculinity at DuPont, 1890–1930," *Entreprises et Histoire*, no. 17 (1997): 9–21.

3. Kathy Peiss, "Culture de masse et divisions sociales: Le cas de l'industrie americaine des cosmétiques," *Le Mouvement Social*, no. 152 (July–Sept. 1990): 7–30.

4. Regina Lee Blaszczyk, *American Consumer Society, 1865–2005: From Hearth to HDTV* (Wheeling, IL: Harlan-Davidson, 2009).

5. Carolyn Goldstein, "Educating Consumers, Representing Consumers: Reforming the Marketplace through Scientific Expertise at the Bureau of Home Economics, US Department of Agriculture, 1923–1940," in *The Expert Consumer: Associations and Professionals in Consumer Society*, ed. Alain Chatriot, Marie-Emmanuelle Chessel, and Matthew Hilton (Aldershot, UK: Ashgate, 2006), 73–88.

6. Matthew Hilton, *Prosperity for All: Consumer Activism in an Era of Globalization* (Ithaca: Cornell University Press, 2008), 3, 10.

7. Raewyn Connell, *Masculinities*, 2nd ed. (Oxford: Polity Press, 2005). See also Carol Gould, ed., *Gender: Key Concepts in Critical Theory* (Amherst, NY: Prometheus Books, 1997), and Simon Malpas and Paul Wake, eds., *The Routledge Companion to Critical Theory* (New York: Routledge, 2006).

8. Howard Chudacoff, *The Age of the Bachelor: Creating an American Subculture* (Princeton: Princeton University Press, 1999).

9. Daniel Miller, *A Theory of Shopping* (Ithaca: Cornell University Press, 1998).

10. Geoffrey Jones, Akiko Kanno, and Masako Egawa, "Making China Beautiful: Shiseido and the China Market" (Harvard Business School Case 805-003, rev. ed., 2008).

11. Amy Lippert, "Visual Culture in San Francisco, 1848–1865" (PhD diss., University of California–Berkeley, 2009); Jonathan Coopersmith, "Does Your Mother Know What You *Really* Do? The Changing Nature and Image of Computer-Based Pornography," *History and Technology* 22.1 (2006): 1–25.

12. George Chauncey, *Gay New York: Gender, Urban Culture, and the Making of the Gay Male World, 1890–1940* (New York: Basic Books, 1994).

13. Jannette Rutterford and Josephine Maltby, "The Widow, the Clergyman, and the Reckless": Women Investors in England, 1830–1914," *Feminist Economics* 12 (2006): 111–38. See also Anne Laurence, Josephine Maltby, and Janette Rutherford, eds., *Women and Their Money, 1700–1950: Essays on Women and Finance* (London: Routledge, 2008).

14. Christina Lubinski, *Familienunternehmen in Westdeutschland: Corporate Governance und Gesellschafterkultur seit den 1960er Jahren* (Munich: C. H. Beck, 2010). See also Christian Eifert, *Deutsche Unternehmerinnen im 20. Jahrhundert* (Munich: C. H. Beck, 2011).

15. Diana Henriques, *The White Sharks of Wall Street: Thomas Mellon Evans and the Original Corporate Raiders* (New York: Scribner, 2000).

16. Marie-France Etchegoin, *Un Milliard de Secrets* (Paris: Robert Laffont, 2011). A 2011 settlement left Mme. Bettencourt in control of her estate, but with some restrictions on spending.

17. Wendy Gamber, *The Female Economy: The Millinery and Dressmaking Trades, 1860–1930* (Urbana: University of Illinois Press, 1997); Gamber, *The Boarding House in 19th-Century America* (Urbana: University of Illinois Press, 2007); Arwen Mohun, *Steam Laundries: Gender, Technology, and Work in the United States and Great Britain, 1880–1940* (Baltimore: Johns Hopkins University Press, 1999); and for France, Claude Ferry, *La Blanchisserie et Teinturerie de Thaon (1872–1914)* (Nancy: Presses Universitaires de Nancy, 1992).

18. Claude Fischer, *America Calling: A Social History of the Telephone to 1940* (Berkeley: University of California Press, 1994). See also Venus Green, *Race on the Line: Gender, Labor and Technology in the Bell System, 1880–1980* (Durham, NC: Duke University Press, 2001).

19. Jean Rabaut, *Marguerite Durand: "La Fronde" féministe, ou "Le Temps" en jupons* (Paris: L'Harmattan, 1996).

20. Karen Ho, *Liquidated: An Ethnography of Wall Street* (Durham, NC: Duke University Press, 2009).

21. Virginia Scharff, *Taking the Wheel: Women and the Coming of the Motor Age* (New York: Free Press, 1991).

22. See Chudacoff, *Age of the Bachelor*, for the results of extensive research in census records.

5. Professional Services

Mainstream business history studies have focused chiefly not just on big business but also on big *manufacturing* enterprises. Whereas many scholars have studied merchant houses, securities exchanges, insurance companies, and banking firms (though few focus on real estate,[1] the last segment of FIRE [Finance, Insurance, and Real Estate]), again giants draw their attention (Allianz, Deutsche Bank, Metropolitan Life)[2] and are not explicitly conceptualized as *service* sector competitors. Economists have expended considerable energy documenting and analyzing the advancing "service economy," noting that, for example, service firms' share of total value added in the United States rose from 60 to 80 percent circa 1950–80.[3] If accurate, this finding should be galvanizing for American business historians, given that we have largely overlooked enterprises whose productivity may have contributed as much or more to making the American Century than manufacturing, agriculture, mining, logging, and fisheries combined. As our social science colleagues strive to determine what the engines of innovation in services have been,[4] we could well undertake to remedy silences in organizational and sectoral histories through historical research.

Though historical studies of the business side of service enterprises in hotels, commercial laundering, or cooking are now available,[5] we propose research on professionals in business as another entry point into engaging services historically. The classical professions (law, medicine, the clergy) shunned any notion that their practitioners were "in business" in any pecuniary or competitive sense. Of course, professionals needed funds for food, housing, and other basic needs, which parishioners and clients provided in recognition of the special capabilities lawyers, healers, and clergymen brought to bear on their problems. Professionals served the law and the state, defended human bodies and health, and delivered God's goodwill toward humanity, at least in the best cases. This polite fiction did not entirely avert cupidity, avarice, ambition, and greed, however, as scandals emerged when restraints on professionalism faltered. More crucially, across the nineteenth and twentieth centuries major changes ensued along three dimensions of activity and organization. Newcomers claimed the mantle of professional standing (within the original trio and beyond, e.g., engineers, scientists, accountants, managers, advertising and public relations specialists);[6] then clustered professionals of all vintages sought to erect barriers to entry; and finally, institutions emerged that gathered scores, even hundreds of physicians and lawyers (though not clerics) into self-governing, profit-seeking alliances.[7]

In France, professional, state-chartered *notaires* long served as "transaction supervisors," working with real estate, family inheritances, marriage agreements, and administrative and company law. Traceable back at least to the era of St. Louis (Louis IX, 1214–70), these geographically anchored independent agents continue to be central to exchanges in more than twenty European countries and in Quebec.[8] In the transnational arena, we should take note of international business law firms as well, a specialization that appears to have originated in late-nineteenth-century New York City, before multiplying globally.[9] Architects as well have begun to operate through international partnerships. These were (and are) businesses, and their histories deserve close scrutiny from business historians.

We know relatively little, as yet, about these profession-centered, revenue-gathering, and funds-distributing institutions. This is the case for both the associations that certified professional credentials and for the partnerships and corporations that reaped the economic harvest professionalism offered, though it does seem that the sole proprietor doctor or lawyer has become something of an endangered species. What professionals professed, in order to distinguish themselves from cooks and laundry workers, was that they provided expertise, not just garden variety service.[10] This of course demeaned the knowledge bases of gardeners, cooks, and clothes washers, but no matter: control of certification, and hence entry, elevated professionals' expertise above competitive scrimmaging. Moreover, the assertion of expertise posited the need for laymen to purchase (or better, rent) experienced advisers, as well as, in Anthony Giddens's terms, providers' "expert systems," whether embodied, technological, or organizational.[11]

International differences in profession formation also deserve attention: for example, in France, advertising specialists have created an association that defines who is inside and who is outside the boundary, but American advertising features no comparable certification or control.[12] Likewise, France took a different route from the United States in attempting to deal with competition among physicians as the medical profession emerged. From the 1880s, rather than empowering a private association, the state oversaw creation of doctors' unions (*syndicats médicaux*), organizations reframed several generations later as orders of physicians recognized by law and authorized to exclude those lacking proper credentials.[13] Given that legitimizing expertise is bounded temporally and spatially, it is surely far from conflict free, whether the specialized services are offered through consultancies and general contractors,[14] lobbying firms, think tanks,[15] or enterprises devoted to mobilizing knowledge about computers, accounting, telecommunications, aerodynamics, design, or nonprofit administration. In this light, seeking a conceptual unpacking of "expertise" as claim and category would be helpful; we believe help can be found by exploring Harry Collins and Robert Evans's recent sociological study *Rethinking Expertise*.[16]

In general, then, historical research on professional businesses can develop at three basic levels: (1) case study accounts of enterprises and their practices in different places and periods—organization, management, client relations, hiring and firing, professional development, profits and their uses, competition, and failure; (2) broader projects that explore the rise and transformation of professional sectors as businesses, political forces, credentialing organizations (regionally, nationally, and transnationally)—focusing on their leadership, arguments for claims of competence, and relations with other professions, services, and industries; and (3) critical generalizing initiatives that analyze professional trades' processes of legitimation, exclusion, classification, training, codification, and their exercise of authority in social, political, and economic domains. Promising social science work on these matters has been developing over the last several decades; business historians' interventions will enrich ongoing debates.

NOTES

1. But see Jeffrey Hornstein, *A Nation of Realtors: A Cultural History of the 20th-Century American Middle Class* (Durham, NC: Duke University Press, 2005), and Alexia Yates, "Why Is There No MLS in France? Information and Intermediaries in the Parisian Housing Market in the 19th and 20th Centuries" (paper presented at the Hagley Museum and Library conference, "Understanding Markets," 31 Oct. 2009).

2. See, for example, Gerald Feldman, *Allianz and the German Insurance Business, 1933–1945* (Cambridge, UK: Cambridge University Press, 2006), Christopher Kobrak, *Banking on Global Markets: Deutsche Bank and the United States, 1870 to the Present* (Cambridge, UK: Cambridge University Press, 2007), and JoAnne Yates, *Structuring the Information Age: Life Insurance and Technology in the 20th Century* (Baltimore: Johns Hopkins University Press, 2005). For a study treating emergent, often small insurers, see Sharon Murphy, *Investing in Life: Insurance in Ante-Bellum America* (Baltimore: Johns Hopkins University Press, 2010).

3. Francisco Buera and Joseph Kaboski, "The Rise of the Service Economy" (NBER Working Paper 14822, Mar. 2009), 2. Accessed at www.nber.org/papers/w14822 14 Oct. 2010.

There is considerable debate about how to assess both such value-added and service-sector productivity, not least because methods based on industrial (primary and secondary) classifications do poorly in evaluating performance in tertiary arenas (notoriously, computing and computer-aided activities such as online retail).

4. See Faïz Gallouj and Olivier Weinstein, "Innovation in Services," *Research Policy* 26 (1997): 537–56; Faridah Djellal, Dominique Francoz, Camal Gallouj, Faïz Gallouj, and Yves Jacquin, "Revising the Definition of Research and Development in the Light of the Specificities of Services," *Science and Public Policy* 30 (2003): 415–29; and Faïz Gallouj and Maria Savona, "Innovation in Services: A Review of the Debate and a Research Agenda," *Journal of Evolutionary Economics* 19 (2009): 147–72.

5. Andrew K. Sandoval-Straus, *Hotel: An American History* (New Haven: Yale University Press, 2007); Molly Berger, *Hotel Dreams: A History of Luxury, Technology, and Urban Ambition, 1829–1929* (Baltimore: Johns Hopkins University Press, 2011); Arwen Mohun, *Steam Laundries: Gender, Technology, and Work in the United States and Great Britain, 1880–1940* (Baltimore: Johns Hopkins University Press, 2002); and Rebecca Spang, *The Invention of the Restaurant: Paris and Modern Gastronomic Culture* (Cambridge, MA: Harvard University Press, 2001).

6. For a company study on the last group, see Karen Miller, *The Voice of Business: Hill and Knowlton and Postwar Public Relations* (Chapel Hill, University of North Carolina Press, 1999).

7. Andrew Abbott, *The System of Professions: An Essay on the Division of Expert Labor* (Chicago: University of Chicago Press, 1988), Paul Starr, *The Social Transformation of American Medicine: The Rise of a Sovereign Profession and the Making of a Vast Industry* (New York: Basic Books, 1984), and Marc Galanter and Thomas Palay, *Tournament of Lawyers: The Transformation of the Big Law Firm* (Chicago: University of Chicago Press, 1994).

8. See http://fr.wikipedia.org/wiki/Notaire (accessed 23 Mar. 2011); Laurence de Charette et Denis Boulard, *Les Notaires: Enquête sur la profession la plus puissante de France* (Paris: Robert Laffont, 2010).

9. See Benjamin Coates, "Trans-Atlantic Advocates: American International Law and U.S. Foreign Relations, 1898–1919" (PhD diss., Columbia University, 2011), Virginia Keys Veenswijk, *The Life and Times of Coudert Brothers* (New York: Dutton, 1994) (a history of the United States' first international law firm, which closed in 2006 following a failed merger effort), and Yves Dezalay and Bryant Garth, eds., *Global Prescriptions: The Production, Exportation, and Importation of a New Legal Orthodoxy* (Ann Arbor: University of Michigan Press, 2002).

10. This remains a claim asserted by college and university educators, though it has been increasingly challenged in the current decade.

11. Anthony Giddens, *The Consequences of Modernity* (Stanford: Stanford University Press, 1994).

12. Marie-Emmanuelle Chessel, *La publicité: Naissance d'une profession (1900–1940)* (Paris: CNRS Editions, 1998). The profession includes both corporate in-house staff and independent agencies.

13. Confédération des Syndicats Médicaux Français, *Les Médecins devant la médecine sociale* (Paris: De Lagny, 1952).

14. Christopher McKenna, *The World's Newest Profession: Management Consulting in the Twentieth Century* (Cambridge, UK: Cambridge University Press, 2006); David N. Keller, *Stone*

and Webster, 1889–1989: A Century of Service (New York: Stone & Webster, 1989); and Layton McCartney, *Friends in High Places: The Bechtel Story* (New York: Ballantine, 1989).

15. For a tough-minded American journalist's account of Cassidy & Associates, see Robert Kaiser, *So Damn Much Money: The Triumph of Lobbying and the Erosion of American Government* (New York: Knopf, 2009). For think tanks, Alex Abella, *Soldiers of Reason: The RAND Corporation and the Rise of the American Empire* (New York: Houghton Mifflin Harcourt, 2008).

16. Harry Collins and Robert Evans, *Rethinking Expertise* (Chicago: University of Chicago Press, 2007).

6. Projects

We start with a quote from a recent discussion of projects in modern economies: "Currently, more than 20% of global economic activity takes place as projects, and in some emerging economies it exceeds 30%. World Bank (2009) data indicate that 22% of the world's $48 trillion gross domestic product (GDP) is gross capital formation, which is almost entirely project-based. In India it is 34%, and in China it is 45%. In many public and private organizations, some operating expenditures are also project-based."[1]

Yet projects are still rarely researched in business history because they usually represent temporary organizations, not durable structures; involve teamwork and uncertainties that do not fit well into managerial hierarchies; and frequently fail—they are over budget, late, conflict-ridden, and given to blame games (think of Boston's Big Dig, well profiled in its early phases by Thomas P. Hughes, the distinguished American historian of technology).[2] This condition accounts for why business history has largely ignored construction, the film industry, and subcontracting, for example, as well as most military technology acquisitions projects. Even so, a recent eBay search uncovered more than twenty-four hundred books and pamphlets on project management (not just projects) available for purchase,[3] while Amazon.com listed more than fifteen thousand books and downloadable reports or essays available on the topic.[4] Scholars in the *International Journal of Project Management* have argued for a vast increase in projects as a share of business initiatives since the 1960s (their estimate),[5] including firms sponsoring project-based units and other firms created as projects intended for sale or a rapid windup once the key goals of an effort have been reached (many go broke, of course).

Making sense of projects involves locating them within the range of activities businesses undertake. The table below represents a preliminary effort to do this.[6] Reflecting for a moment on this distribution suggests how distinctive projects can be from more standard operations and interactions; they demand different managerial orientations, work organizations, expectations, and authority relations, as so often they enter unfamiliar and uncertain terrains. As a result, attempts to manage projects through formal rules, preexisting standards, and bureaucracies may well fail.

From railway construction to television series, many projects have been and remain big business, perhaps diffused spatially or outsourced organizationally, but their temporary status has made them elusive or invisible to scholars in our field. They have a history worth investigating, not solely in the post–World War Two era; nor should our inquiries center on R&D activity, a far too narrow perspective. Perhaps we should consider that business projects demand (and generate) specific practices and varieties of knowledge that are relevant to larger concerns about organization and policy. Projects develop (at a minimum): time-sensitive, corrigible expectations and estimates; testing, planning, and program-change protocols; assessments of innovation needs, prospects, and accomplishments; contingent budgets, plus at times, rules for dealing with cost escalations; and program/project evaluations and histories. Some firms

Core Activity	Operations	Interactions	Projects
Location	Organizations: inside the boundary	Settings: across the boundary	Sites: beyond usual boundaries
Process	Routinized	Individualized	Exploratory
Flows	Hierarchical	Open-ended	Collaborative
Outcomes	Expected, predictable	Ritualized, dynamic	Unknowable
Rule Set	Protocols, standards	Reciprocities	Reflexivity and improvisation
Examples	Accounting, reports, production, line management, evaluation	Contracts, sales, patents, licensing	One-off problem solving, innovation trajectories, experimental development

(aerospace and computer specialist) have internalized the project model in order to sponsor or guide reorganizations, directional changes, and assessments of merger or acquisitions possibilities. Historians need to explore many of these aspects of projects, not just through case studies, which proliferate through the project management literature, but also through conceptually informed or thematically centered research that spans projects, sectors, and borders.

Projects have clearly been an element of business activity for centuries; virtually all shipbuilding, railway and bridge construction, power system development, and other infrastructure assets and capabilities have been created through projects. Earlier business historians have looked most commonly to the organizational "operations" that followed, but projects are not just about preparing for stabilized management. Indeed, in the current day, projects are generalizing and morphing into unexpected domains—our eBay list included books on projects in IT, pharmaceuticals, construction (of course), industrial engineering, R&D across varied sectors, aerospace, etc. None of these works asked historical questions, so it is surely time to begin putting context behind contemporary practice in a thoughtful if preliminary way. Has there actually been a rising tide of project-centered business practice, and if so, how has this arisen, where has it been promoted (and resisted?), and how much has this development altered the landscape of employment, management, and innovation? How are these patterns differentiated cross-sectorally and cross-nationally, and where do we find transnational projects (starting with the transatlantic cable and the Suez Canal?), with what shifting political, ideological, and technological foundations? How did the field of project management arise, and what led initial leaders to seek a social-scientific or management-science basis for professionalization (now being sharply challenged)? Where are there projects beyond business history that business historians can profit from encountering? Can there be an empirically based "theory of projects" within business history that might have value to businesses as well?

To be sure, getting a workable sense of what a project is represents a critical step. Practitioners in project management have made a series of efforts; one that seems simple and clear describes a project as "a unique, complex, one-time task [undertaken] within time, cost and quality constraints."[7] The difference between projects and everyday operations (see table above) can be noted as "the extent to which individual expertise, knowledge and judgment are brought into play."[8] At base, operations enact rules and routines; projects move into unfamiliar territory, where space exists for creativity, silliness, failure, breakthroughs, dead ends, and profound insights (this last not as often as is wished).

Repeated attempts to theorize projects have had no better results than efforts to draw a bright line around what constitutes a firm. The sensible alternative to hammering definitions into stone is to deploy efforts to instantiate and exemplify the operations and problem-solving functions of most firms and most projects, respectively, then look carefully for the overlaps between them and for the silences remaining.

As in the American film industry, a succession of formats may be observable, from the early twentieth century, with scores of filmmakers creating diverse projects (of uneven quality), through the mid-century studio system, in which B pictures were ground out like car wheels—each designed to do a job (fill seventy-five minutes on a double bill, for example) and if not standardized, at least formulaic. Antimonopoly interventions that stripped studios of their theater chains in the 1950s shifted the balance back to project work and led to the rise of independent filmmakers and varied distribution channels that dominated the later decades of the twentieth century.[9] Yet consolidations of venues— movie "screens"—into ownership by giant distribution corporations (chiefly after 1980) reempowered studios as judges of mass entertainment values, even if they no longer had vast territories for shooting, captive actors, and powerful brand names to draw in audiences.[10] At this point, film projects needed to pass critical, corporate distribution filters before being completed for sale to mass audiences, just as your credit card needs to be "authorized" by a bank before you can carry off the goods. More recently, many film projects must be designed to be smoothly translatable to subsidiary sales, to television and DVD outlets (internationally), and to the Internet. This is ever more important as secondary or derived markets frequently make the difference between profit and loss. Unsurprisingly, the parameters within which projects in the same "industry" are executed shift substantially across time.

Finally, projects take place at all levels of spatial organization, adding to their interest for business historians. Many of them are quite local, taking place inside individual plants or company R&D units, at building sites, or through interfirm teams working at a production center. Others have a wider spatial reach, regional or national, as with building road, power, or data transmission networks. Project-centered institutions like Bell Labs or CNRS have national reach, and aerospace projects at NASA and EADS stretch well above terra firma and are routinely international, as well. Likewise, trade agreements represent international projects, like the Eurostar train and its Channel Tunnel, in their creation phases, which gave way to operations. Transnational projects are a special case, not being arranged between nation states but rather across and above them, for example, in the framing of air traffic controls or the specification of communications spectra, chiefly developed by NGOs, then validated by governments.

Projects as temporary organizations thus intersect (and have intersected) with operating companies focused on control and reliability, triggering uncertain outcomes. In this complex and contingent process, there is no one directionality (from project to operations, for example) but instead a much more elaborate and uneven dynamic. We believe that focusing on projects, especially from the inside out moving forward,[11] will help business historians reassess the value of firms, the utility of procedures, and the durable challenges of innovation.

NOTES

1. Christophe Brédillet, "Blowing Hot and Cold on Project Management," *Project Management Journal* 41.3 (2010): 4010.

2. Thomas P. Hughes, *Rescuing Prometheus: Four Monumental Projects That Changed the Modern World* (New York: Vintage, 1998).

3. Under "Books" on eBay, search term "project management," executed 1 Sept. 2010.

4. Under "Books" on Amazon.com, search term "project management," executed 8 Sept. 2010. This search excluded "project" alone and "management" alone as terms. A search for "project management, history" yielded 272 exemplars, among which was Peter Morris's classic *The Management of Projects* (London: Thomas Telford, 1997), which has a well-crafted, if brief, historical overview of projects, especially in construction and defense areas. Most of the other "history" hits were tangential, such as "The Wild Turkey in Virginia: Its Status, Life, and Management," which suggests both the historical thinness of work on projects and a certain strangeness in Amazon's protocols for generating X+Y search returns.

5. See, for example, Johann Packendorff, "Inquiring into the Temporary Organization: New Directions for Project Management Research," *International Journal of Project Management* 11 (1995): 319–33; Sylvain Lenfle, "Exploration and Project Management," *IJPM* 26 (2008): 469–78; and Romain Beaume, Rémi Maniak, and Christophe Midler, "Crossing Innovation and Product Projects Management: A comparative analysis in the automotive industry," *IJPM* 27 (2009): 166–74.

6. Drawn from Philip Scranton, "Projects as Business History" (paper presented at the Business History Conference, St. Louis, MO, Apr. 2011).

7. Roger Atkinson, "Project Management: Cost, Time and Quality, Two Best Guesses and a Phenomenon," *IJPM* 17 (1999): 337–42.

8. Terence Cooke-Davies and Andrew Arzymanow, "The Maturity of Project Management in Different Industries: An Investigation into Variations between Management Models," *IJPM* 21 (2003): 471–78.

9. Michael Storper, "The Transition to Flexible Specialization in the US Film Industry: External Economies, the Division of Labor and the Crossing of Industrial Divides," in *Post-Fordism: A Reader*, ed. Ash Amin (Oxford: Blackwell, 1995), 195–226. See also Arthur DeVany, *Hollywood Economics: How Extreme Uncertainty Shapes the Film Industry* (New York: Routledge, 2003).

10. For a study of a film as a project, see Gilles Marion, "James Dean et *La fureur de vivre*: L'anticipation d'un nouvel horizon d'attente," *Le Mouvement Social*, no. 219-20 (2007): 131–48.

11. Svetlana Cicmil, Terry Williams, Janice Thomas, and Damian Hodgson, "Rethinking Project Management: Researching the Actuality of Projects," *IJPM* 24(2006): 657–86, and Jean-Paul Boutinet, *Anthropologie du projet* (Paris: PUF, 1996).

7. Reassessing Classic Themes

In addition to suggesting new directions, reimagining business history also involves returning to classical concepts, which animated research for generations, asking fresh questions and acknowledging novel perspectives, all in service of promoting scholarly initiatives. This entry will be a bit longer than the others, chiefly because we seek to explore four concepts here, though briefly in each case: growth, value, welfare, and markets.

Growth. First, historically, attempts to understand growth, the most inexplicable dimension of any economics focused on exchange and instantaneity, have been supplemented recently by discussions of "sustainable growth" in business policy, environmental studies, and corporate social responsibility forums. For business historians, one question would be: How were sustainability and social responsibility conceptualized and operationalized in earlier eras? This could involve reassessing paternalism as a business practice seeking long-term stability of workforces and communities, and the family firm as a device to ensure durability, responsibility, and the production of reliable futures. Historically, enterprises and communities were aware of the environmental impacts of growth (lawsuits against railways for agricultural damage and fires; rural movements to block automobiles' use of roads) as well as its human costs. Perhaps nineteenth-century safety campaigns represented early moves toward monitoring and improving a sustainable industrial environment.[1]

Second, a generation of research has demonstrated that multiple, nonlinear paths to growth have been traced by actors worldwide since the seventeenth and eighteenth centuries. This diversity persisted through the precapitalist era of manufactories and state *fabriques* and in complementary specialty and mass production enterprise formats centuries later. Inasmuch as many of these initiatives succeeded and endured, while being far from highly efficient in using land, labor, and capital and failing to maximize growth (for personal, cultural, or resource reasons), we should reconsider narratives focused resolutely on best-practice exemplars. This is roughly analogous to David Edgerton's argument that historians of technology should step away from obsessing about innovation and embark on close studies of everyday practice.[2] As became plain by the 1970s, Fordist mass production held an ever-smaller proportion of manufacturing overall, offering a useless model for growth in fashion and high-tech trades, even as executives abandoned analyzing production (assigning this to lower-status engineers) and sought universal rules for management (rather than protocols tailored to specific situations) before moving on to regarding financial indicators as fundamental.[3]

In this vein, how can we evaluate growth in different modalities of capitalism? Consider on one side states based on the exploitation of resources, few of which have built a diversified economy—oil- and gas-driven post-Soviet Russia, Venezuela with its quasi-socialist consumerism, "wealthy" Nigeria riven by corruption, religious schism, and "rebel" gangs grasping for a share of the oil flows, or the Emirates and Saudi Arabia, financing high-modernist circuses and political extremists. (Norway is a notable exception. Can business historians explain why?) Looking back half a century in each place, massive change has taken place, including per-capita GDP growth, but without "growth" in the broader sense of institutional deepening or technical and sectoral diversification. By contrast, one can review the postwar arc of what has become the European Community with greater satisfaction (or fear), given the creation of complex regulatory frameworks, with inclusion of governance practices ranging from *dirigisme* and clientelism to social democracy and constitutional monarchy. Here social and political imperatives mattered to economic policy and enterprise decision-making. Yet, though the euro has convened a huge borderless market, it has not created a "free market" in the American ideological sense. So how do we parse growth in such territories, much less efficiency? In the United States, the rhetoric of free marketeering resonates widely, but national policies are replete with hidden (and not-so-hidden) state subsidies to agriculture, aerospace, home building, military technologies, etc. If we rely on growth estimates framed in percentages, estimates that wipe out contexts, how can we expect other than spurious regional or international comparisons? Here business historians could profitably invade neighborhoods poorly served by quantifiers from economics and economic history, in order to create comparisons that embrace narratives located in space and time.[4]

Value. On the value front, business historians have begun appropriating Michael Porter's "value chain" concept from the 1980s, an approach that argued that each of a firm's multiple functions had the potential (and obligation) to create value for buyers and users. However, some activities (transportation, perhaps) often represented bottlenecks, which reduced rather than augmented value. Hence, creating smoothly operating linkages among activities, including those located outside firm boundaries, and promoting coordination "can be a decisive source of competitive advantage."[5] Significant ambiguities attend this formulation, however, which historians will note rapidly: (1) no time dimension for these advantages is provided; (2) creating value for buyers may create loss or problems for others involved (shareholders, managers, suppliers, workers, local communities, emergent nations), thus inviting us to inquire, "value for whom and why?"; and (3) asymmetries of power and resources within the firm, which always exist, may be exaggerated by top-down pressure to prioritize serving clients. In considering value chains (or "supply chains," for that matter), we may need to place more emphasis and focus on "chains" as identifiable sources of constraints and conflicts than on expectations of increased efficiency and of fluid compliance with coordination schemes.

Two other items beckon: valuation or assessing value and controversies over accounting standards. From the nineteenth century, agencies rating firms' prospects and creditworthiness crafted socially constructed value profiles, which could have favorable or disastrous effects on enterprise futures. Little wonder that ill-treated US firms and individuals sometimes sued Dun & Bradstreet, which guarded its informants' secrecy and claimed comprehensive objectivity.[6] (There was apparently no European practice of rating individuals, however—an intriguing silence worth investigation.) Now that recent ratings and valuations of complex securities have been shown as profoundly flawed, historical questions are worth asking about what *measures* actors have used for assessments, the grounds for their expected reliability, and their effectiveness or vulnerability in practice. Real estate transactions, loans, insurance policies, tax assessments—all involve valuation practices whose opacity matches their ubiquity. In a neighboring domain, recent battles between US and EU accounting standards and reports of negotiated settlements raise the longer-term issue of what accounting systems measure and how they justify their assumptions.[7] Current concerns about whether company valuations should be made in terms of the market price of their shares or in terms of assets, real and intangible, have historical roots, as does the tortured course of cost accounting, with its many variants. Peering into the engines of value assertion, tracing their national or sectoral origins, the dynamics of practice and innovation, and their wider circuits of influence and challenge, can bring substantial rewards.[8]

Welfare. Concerning welfare, we would encourage a resocialization of the concept, stepping away from economistic definitions (Pareto optimality) that yield narrow ahistorical and misleading analyses. Rather, business historians could inquire what actors thought (and think) welfare was (and is), what foundations for these beliefs they have specified, and what implications for practice different formulations have had (and may have). Historically, welfare has had a religious dimension as well. Some entrepreneurs were and are deeply religious; hence notions of, for example, "Christian duty" informed relations with workers, families, and communities, especially in family firms. Such religious dimensions of action are also evident outside the West, in Asia and in Islamic societies.

Scholars have long recognized "welfare provisions" by firms as a blend of paternalism and the replacement of state or charitable functions by actions that may promote loyalty and reduce turnover.[9] "Modern" corporations have narrowed the boundaries of these relationships to wage contracts and payment-setting, but labor markets are more than money matters, offering key contacts to immigrants and youth and, in the past, serving as way stations for women in transition to traditional marriages.

A classic example of the cultural dimensions of welfare provision comes from recent research on Toyota, arising when the firm urged a plastic components supplier, who had never expanded internationally, to locate a new plant in China. The owner balked, but Toyota officials told him that as a long-term friend and partner, he must do this, despite his uncertainty about fragmenting his operations and the risks of operating in an unfamiliar milieu. Facing continuing resistance, Toyota threatened its "friend" with cuts in parts orders, so the owner agreed; but he demanded that he be allowed to do the job in his own fashion. Initially, in the planned manufacturing locale, his firm funded scholarships for Chinese students to attend universities and then, two years later, erected its factory. The scholarships created a favorable local climate, assuaging strong anti-Japanese sentiments dating to World War Two, and the enterprise flourished.[10]

We should also consider welfare-providing institutions like pension funds as businesses, including mutual societies, union-based, and state-based operations, for they are simultaneously significant employers, investors, and planners in national and international economic relations. In recent decades, their operations have become sources of controversy and targets for ideological challenges;

consider CalPERS, a US giant founded after a constitutional amendment in 1932 to provide retirement payouts for the state of California's workers and now a major investor in global equities and bonds, often embroiled in controversy. Was it ever such, or have there been long-term patterns distinguishing private from public provision or blurring such boundaries?[11] (See Opportunities, 8: Public-Private Boundaries.)

Markets. After the great smash of 2008, markets are no longer regarded as reliably rational or efficient, except by those defending failed economic models.[12] To have a general theory that works most of the time but fails spectacularly at irregular intervals does not induce confidence, nor is it a helpful guide for business historians, who are more likely to be intrigued by pratfalls than stolid transactions. Comparable critiques of markets as efficient (for whom? by what measure?) or "free" (a utopian prospect) put them back into histories and polities, where mutable conventions, time-anchored regulations, and the interests of states, parties, factions, and institutions all mix with uncertainties to trigger contestable outcomes. So, if we regard markets as contingent historical phenomena, themselves subject to processes of change, what sorts of questions arise? Using the plural indicates that markets are multiple and differently constituted, so what follows from that insight? What relationships operated in what we may imagine as historically distinct financial, credit, goods, labor, and property markets? Which of these were "naturally" inclined to intersect (property, credit, and finance), and how were links fabricated, with what difficulties and slips? How did actors conceptualize and theorize markets, their boundaries, and their performance in nineteenth-century Vienna or eighteenth-century Paris? How would a comparative history of real estate markets be framed and implemented?[13] How are slave markets distinctive from contract-based "free" labor markets, as practice and as performance?[14] When and where have auction markets been preferable to negotiations between parties, and why?[15] How were market rules established and governed, within or beyond what institutions, and what patterns of private ordering developed to enable various degrees of self-governance?[16] After all, no markets can exist without regulations of some sort, whether they be political, conventional, or local.

On these and other classic themes for business history, openings for fresh thinking and creative research abound, particularly for scholars prepared to work their way through a literature in economics and social theory rich with assertions and critiques and not commonly alert to historical dynamics and their vagaries. Rehistoricizing concepts that have been "abstracted to death" is by itself a commendable goal.

NOTES

1. Mark Aldrich, *Safety First: Technology, Labor and Business in the Building of American Work Safety, 1870–1939* (Baltimore: Johns Hopkins University Press, 1997).

2. David Edgerton, *The Shock of the Old: Technology and Global History since 1900* (New York: Oxford University Press, 2006).

3. Wickham Skinner, "Manufacturing—Missing Link in Corporate Strategy," *Harvard Business Review* 47 (May–June 1969): 136–45; Skinner, "Operations Technology: Blind Spot in Strategic Management," *Interfaces* 14 (Jan.–Feb. 1984): 116–25; and Skinner, "Three Yards and a Cloud of Dust: Industrial Management at Century's End," *Production and Operations Management* 5 (1996): 15–24. According to Google Scholar, the seminal 1969 article (above) has been cited 1,147 times, overwhelmingly in management journals, not in business history. The Boston Consulting Group's George Stalk observed in 1988: "Today the leading edge of competition is the combination of fast response and increasing variety. Companies without these advantages are slipping into commodity-like competition, where customers buy mainly on price." George Stalk Jr., "Time—The Next Source of Competitive Advantage," *Harvard Business Review* 66 (July–Aug. 1988): 41–51.

4. This echoes the famed Hayes-Abernathy critique of portfolio analysis for offering "analytic detachment rather than the insight that comes from 'hands-on experience.'" See Robert Hayes and William Abernathy, "Managing Our Way to Economic Decline," *Harvard Business Review* 58 (July–Aug. 1980): 67–77.

5. Michael Porter, *The Competitive Advantage of Nations* (New York: Free Press, 1990), 40–44. For an overview of post-1940 approaches to strategy, see Pankaj Ghemawat, "Competition and Business Strategy in Historical Perspective," *Business History Review* 76 (2002): 37–74.

6. For a particularly drawn-out lawsuit, see Scott Sandage, *Born Losers: A History of Failure in America* (Cambridge, MA: Harvard University Press, 2005), 164–84. See also Louis Hyman, *Debtor Nation: The History of Red Ink in America* (Princeton: Princeton University Press, 2011).

7. Elliot Posner, "The New Transatlantic Regulatory Relations in Financial Services" (paper presented at the 1st Annual GARNET Conference, "Global Financial and Monetary Governance, the EU and Emerging Market Economies," 27–29 Sept. 2006), accessed online at www.garnet-eu.org, 17 Oct. 2010.

8. For guidance, see Richard K. Fleischman, Vaughan S. Radcliffe, and Paul A. Shoe-maker., eds., *Doing Accounting History,* vol. 6, *Contributions to the Development of Accounting Thought* (Oxford: JAI Press, 2003), esp. Paul Miranti, Daniel Jensen, and Edward Coffin, "Business History and Its Implications for Writing Accounting History," 121–46. For documentation of the overwhelmingly Anglo-Saxon character of research in this area, see Salvador Carmona, "Accounting History Research and Its Diffusion in an International Context," *Accounting History* 9 (Nov. 2004): 7–23.

9. Andrea Tone, *The Business of Benevolence: Industrial Paternalism in Progressive America* (Ithaca: Cornell University Press, 1997).

10. Oral history interview by Patrick Fridenson, 2006.

11. See on CalPERS, www.pionline.com/article/20070514/PRINTSUB/70511017, accessed 17 Oct. 2010. For a historical study, see Eric Nijhof, "Pensions and Providence: Dutch Employers and the Creation of Funded Pension Schemes," *Enterprise and Society* 10 (2009): 265–303.

12. Justin Fox, *The Myth of the Rational Market: A History of Risk, Reward, and Delusion on Wall Street* (New York: HarperBusiness, 2009).

13. Real estate, central to the crash of 2008–9, is seriously underresearched as business history, it seems. For examples of recent work, see Jeffrey Hornstein, *A Nation of Realtors* (Durham, NC: Duke University Press, 2005), and Alexia Yates, "Why Is There No MLS in France? Information and Intermediaries in the Parisian Housing Market in 19th and 20th Centuries" (paper presented at the Hagley Museum and Library conference, "Understanding Markets," 30 Oct. 2009).

14. Walter Johnson, *Soul by Soul: Life Inside the Antebellum Slave Market* (Cambridge, MA: Harvard University Press, 2001).

15. For a hugely popular game-theoretic answer, which bears no relation to, and has no interest in, actual auction practices, see Vijay Krishna, *Auction Theory*, 2nd ed. (New York: Academic Press, 2009). For recent history, realism, and grit, see Christopher Mason, *The Art of the Steal: Inside the Sotheby's-Christie's Auction House Scandal* (New York: Berkeley, 2004).

16. For insights here, see Alessandro Stanziani, *Rules of Exchange: French Capitalism in Comparative Perspective, Eighteenth to Early Twentieth Centuries* (New York: Cambridge University Press, 2012).

8. Standards

Standards surround us, so much so since the mid-nineteenth century that we often take them as natural elements of the environment. Yet standards are anything but natural; nature has no standards. Instead, it is useful to view standards as the outcome of contending interests at play, the rationales and contexts for which need historical explication. Standards have advocates and thus are evidence of the agency of historical actors. They often serve as weapons for or against particular practices and are replaceable, historically, especially when the scope of markets increases. Standardized inputs (cotton yarn) can facilitate innovations in final products (endless fabric design variations), but standardization of final products (incandescent light bulbs) may inhibit further innovation, until the market, technical, or regulatory environment changes. Given their importance to business for several centuries, we propose the investigation of standards along five dimensions: (1) form, (2) origins, (3) entrepreneurship, (4) internationalization and standards wars, and (5) failures in standard-setting.

Form. We must acknowledge that standards are immaterial and constructed, like laws (public) and rules (private), but they also differ from these in that they result from cooperation *after* competition. They are enforced, renewed, and revised through meetings and encounters in voluntary organizations.[1] In general, governments support this process, but states more often ratify rather than create standards. Markets have always had rules, but they don't necessarily have standards, which codify best practice in a particular time and place. To appreciate standards, one can use the economic theory of clubs, which focuses on voluntary or mobilized *adhesion*.[2] For business history, key questions include: Are standards generally irreversible, like the QWERTY keyboard, and are they flexible? In our view, standards are historical protocols but not transhistorical rules.

Origins. Standardization long existed without the name. In the eighteenth century, techniques for restoring oil paintings diffused across western Europe, and by adopting principles that reflected best practices, craftsmen installed a pattern of what might be termed proto-standardization.[3] Likewise, before 1800, interchangeability became a material form of standardization to increase functionality. Plans devised by Honoré Blanc for standard military muskets were visionary, showing that armorers could "achieve uniform standards," but they remained impossible technically until the creation, in the nineteenth century, of precise machine tools.[4] Similarly, engineering groups in the German lands agreed upon norms for railway operations during the 1840s and advocated adoption of their frameworks (including gauges) by enterprises in France, Britain, and Russia.[5] In all cases, standards originated through private collaboration and geographical extension; states were commonly indifferent or hostile, though at times they came late to the process to certify or legitimize its outcomes.

Entrepreneurship. Here we might ask, as a starting point: What are the varieties of standards, sectorally and temporally? How can we account for periodic campaigns to install, achieve, improve, or extend standards? When and where is standardization inappropriate and why? Standards arise at specific conjunctures historically, and these situations merit investigation. Some entrepreneurs of standards worked inside companies, and others operated as outside experts or professionals. Consider Britain's Charles LeMaistre, an employee of the Thames Iron Works and Shipbuilding Company (ca. 1900), who became assistant to the secretary of the newly founded Engineering Standards Committee. This group's appreciation for American standardization of steel rails and LeMaistre's intentions to devise British versions led to a dramatic expansion of discussions across multiple engineering societies and eventually to the creation of the International Organization for Standardization.[6] LeMaistre embodied Joseph Schumpeter's concept of the "political entrepreneur."[7]

Inside the firm, we have the example of Corning's Henry P. Gage. Applying technical expertise in optics and a decades-long commitment to improving quality, in the 1920s Gage developed performance standards, a crucial elaboration on material standards, which could freeze processes and product features even while markets and environments changed. The performance standard, which set a target that could be achieved in multiple ways and that could be upgraded, "allowed for more flexibility and adaptation in design and means of production. . . . Gage promoted an entrepreneurial approach to standards, representing performance standards as providing both the strategic opportunities to develop new products for new customers and the looseness to allow methods and processes to be changed."[8] Even as Ford's assembly line continued making Model Ts, Gage was designing a "post-Fordist" framework for versatile standardization.

More recently, outside the corporate sphere, Tim Berners-Lee followed his invention of the World Wide Web (at CERN,[9] 1989–91) by creating an institution aimed at collaboratively standardizing the web's fundamental technical features (1994). His W3C, a standards-setting consortium, positioned itself between two warring factions: dot-com enterprises seeking profit-making venues and open-source developers with ideological and practical commitments to the free circulation of ideas and free access to information. W3C proved to be "an organizational solution to a technological problem, the imminent balkanization of the web's core technical standards." This Internet-based, nonproprietary endeavor, oriented to nonmarket social cooperation, managed "to create an island of trust in a sea of competition and mistrust."[10]

Internationalization and Standards Wars. Local or national standards are likely to spread abroad as markets expand internationally. They may also confront competing standards, triggering contests over which system will prevail, or be recognized as inadequate when transnational technological change continues. British standards for wire gauges, achieved after long mid-nineteenth-century negotiations, gradually became Empire standards as Western technologies penetrated colonial domains.[11] In the United States, William Sellers, a machine tool builder, campaigned from the mid-nineteenth century to standardize screw threads and sizes, of course offering his practice as a model to the trades. A generation earlier, Joseph Whitworth had created his own range of standard screws, which many British railroads adopted, as did some North American firms. Sellers's design was a variant of Whitworth's, and in the 1870s the US government and major railroads adopted it, making it the "US standard thread." In Europe, metric standard threads also evolved, in part echoing Sellers's approach, expressed in English inches and fractions. Unsuccessful efforts to unify the standards spanned early-twentieth-century decades, but technical analyses identified the true complexity of this project. Major problems during World War Two with screw interchangeability among devices from Canada, the United States, and the United Kingdom led to an inch-based unification agreement in 1949.[12] Internationally, metrics were eclipsing English units, and the increasingly influential ISO (International Organization for Standardization) created a metric standard adopted worldwide, though irregularly in North America. By the early twenty-first century, almost no auto parts fail to meet the ISO metric standards, even those made in the United States.

Elsewhere, Danish national standards for welding practices, created by informal voluntary cooperation in the 1940s, spread first across Scandinavia through formal adoption in the 1960s and then to the rest of Europe, once the European Union had launched a "common technical standards" initiative in the late 1980s.[13] In another region, Japan created the VCR, both at Sony (Betamax) and JVC (VHS), and no internal agreement could be reached. So both firms sought international allies in a global race for market share, which JVC won, despite the technological inferiority of VHS. This created a situation that transformed a field in which engineers, firms, and governments were dominant to a situation in which consumers decided both business and technical outcomes. For its part, Sony abandoned the consumer market, but the technical qualities of its Betamax product so impressed professionals in the videotape world that Sony became a major supplier to users there.[14] In consequence, rather than a simple victory for JVC and establishment of a de facto standard through competition, this struggle yielded one standard for consumer viewers and another standard for professional videographers, splitting the domain.

Failures in Standard-Setting. At times, market expansion produced conflicts and failed efforts to build standards. For example, in black-and-white television, national standards were initially achieved, but attempts to create international agreements foundered twice. Black-and-white screens in Britain displayed 441 lines, in the United States 525, in Germany 625, and in France 819. France had the finest images, but given the absence of intergovernmental cooperation, no global television receiver could be created.[15] The same impasse arose for color TV. In the automobile industry, a 1949 UN Convention on Road Traffic urged drafting worldwide standards for auto safety, but instead different systems arose in North America, Europe, and Japan. Resistance from companies using their own or national standards was decisive. Similarly, during the 1950s, a cross-national continental European commission undertook a project to standardize and co-produce military hardware, especially small arms, but could not overcome national autonomy and the interests of arms makers who supplied individual military branches.[16] Two decades later, a plan emerged to standardize European truck wheel sizes, so as to reduce road wear while simplifying maintenance. This failed due to antagonism between German truck makers, who wanted their standard adopted, like Sellers a century earlier, and British and Italian truck builders, who refused to capitulate. Here competition, as so often, undercut collaboration.

Whereas governments and businesses can inhibit standardization for political, cultural, or economic reasons, their recalcitrance may trigger innovation and creativity. Should one standard become dominant, it can force stalemated firms out of business. Military interests may also be involved in standard setting, seeking reliability in maintenance and replacement of weapons, vehicles, or communications equipment, but they regularly oppose transnational standards that appear to threaten their autonomy. In sum, standards represent a complex and inviting arena for business historical research, which as the notes to this entry suggest, has begun.

NOTES

1. See Wolfram Kaiser, Johan Schot, and Dagmara Jajesniak-Quast, *Making Rules For Europe* (London: Palgrave Macmillan, forthcoming 2014).

2. James M. Buchanan, "An Economic Theory of Clubs," *Economica* 32 (Feb. 1965): 1–14.

3. Emmanuel Coblence, "Le 'Secret' de Robert Picault et sa standardisation malgré lui," *Entreprises et Histoire*, no. 51 (June 2008): 148.

4. Ken Alder, *Engineering the Revolution: Arms and Enlightenment in France, 1763–1815* (Chicago: University of Chicago Press, 1997), 223–25.

5. Allan Mitchell, *The Great Train Race: Railways and the Franco-German Rivalry, 1815–1914* (New York: Berghahn Books, 2000).

6. JoAnne Yates and Craig N. Murphy, "Charles LeMaistre: Entrepreneur in International Standardization," *Entreprises et Histoire*, no. 51 (June 2008): 10–27.

7. Adam Sheingate, "Political Entrepreneurship, Institutional Change, and American Political Development," *Studies in American Political Development* 17 (2003): 185–203.

8. Margaret B. W. Graham, "Henry P. Gage: Entrepreneurial Standards Setter for Corning Glass Works, 1911–1947," *Entreprises et Histoire*, no. 51 (June 2008): 27–43.

9. The European Organization for Nuclear Research, founded in 1954, now has twenty member states.

10. Andrew Russell, "Dot.org Entrepreneurship: Weaving a Web of Trust," *Entreprises et Histoire*, no. 51 (June 2008): 44–56.

11. Aashish Velkar, "How Did Markets Manage Measurement Issues? Lessons from 19th-Century Britain" (paper presented at the ISNIE annual meeting, Toronto, 2008), available at http://extranet.isnie.org/uploads/isnie2008/velkar.pdf (accessed 7 July 2011).

12. "Discussion in London, 22 June 1945," *Proceedings of the Institution of Mechanical Engineers* 155 (1946): 161–92.

13. Lars Heide, "The Danish Welding Institute and FORCE Technology: Technical Standardization and the Shaping of Business," *Entreprises et Histoire*, no. 51 (June 2008): 57–68.

14. Michael Cusumano, Yiorgos Mylonadis, and Richard Rosenbloom, "Strategic Maneuvering and Mass-Market Dynamics: The Triumph of VHS over Beta," *Business History Review* 66 (1992): 51–94.

15. See www.television.441lignes.free.fr (accessed 16 May 2011), and Jean-Jacques Peters, "A History of Television," European Broadcasting Union, 2000, available at http://arantxa.ii.uam.es/~jms/tvd/tv_history.pdf (accessed 7 July 2011).

16. Pascal Deloge and David Burigana, "Pourquoi la standardisation des armements a-t-elle échoué dans les années 1950?," *Entreprises et Histoire*, no. 51 (June 2008): 103–16.

9. The Subaltern

Subaltern is a term widely used to reference people who and practices that are socially marginalized, despised, confined, and silenced: slaves, tenant farmers, serfs, prostitutes, refugees, prisoners, mental patients, and for many generations, unconventional sexualities (gay, lesbian, and transgender) and behaviors (especially drug-taking). In a more complex reading, the subalterns were, historically, those whose degraded, despised presences were "crucial to the self-definition of the majority group." However, "subaltern social groups were also in a position to subvert the authority of those who had hegemonic power."[1] Those socially excluded from mainstream societies have been widely researched by colonial, postcolonial, cultural, and social historians, but this territory has only rarely and fairly recently drawn attention from business historians, a glimmer of a trend we hope will continue and broaden.[2] What sort of business history questions can be asked of such populations (and by whom)?[3]

For a start, what organizations and businesses were involved in transporting, feeding, policing, or healing Europe's displaced persons after both world wars, as well as following the Armenian massacres and the wholesale relocation of Greeks and Turks as the Ottoman Empire collapsed? Who made payments to meet these expenses, how and from where, and what networks for food and transport were mobilized? How did governments, enterprises (particularly in transportation), and nongovernment agencies (Red Cross / Red Crescent) interlink to define and address problems and crises? Were costs or profits calculated from such efforts—if so, on what bases, if not, why not? By extension, what about the business history of illegal immigration? One of our students, for example, in a project on unlawful early-twentieth-century Chinese immigration to the United States, discovered that American authorities regularly paid informants running boardinghouses and cheap hotels just inside the US-Canadian border for alerts about Asian arrivals.[4] What can we learn from exploring shipping businesses that legally transported millions of Europeans to the Western Hemisphere or hundreds of thousands of Chinese to South Asia, Indians to East Africa, and Japanese to Latin America? How did states oversee, regulate, tax (or extract bribes from) this commerce? How were fares determined, responsibilities and liabilities understood, and errors recoded into revised policies? Certainly there was a business of migration, global and shifting across time, which begs for attention.

Or, on a different track, what enterprises helped constitute and sustain gay and lesbian communities in cities worldwide, beyond the early twentieth century's Gay New York,[5] whose businesses included bars, bath-, and roominghouses? Surely specialized publishers responded to gay community needs for information and amusement, just as entertainment venues catered to decisively nonstandard tastes. As investments were made and money changed hands, this history was not solely about cultural matters. If there were enterprises that thrived through concealment (of a sort), there were others that prospered through confinement. Prisons, like hospitals, do not often come into the viewfinder of business historians, but both did and do a great deal of business. In America and Europe, prisoners were long "farmed out" to work in agriculture and mining, while others were put to work inside the walls, their menial labor generating goods on contract with merchants and users. Who supplied prisons (or hospitals) with food, clothing, furniture, sheets and towels, and technologies of humiliation and healing? When, where, and how did prison sales become a specialized business among food packers or metal furniture makers? How different a business is supplying the subaltern from supplying soldiers or students; and were the same firms involved in these markets?

Fortunately, recent scholarship has carved a business history portal in at least two segments of this challenging subfield—on one side, slavery, and on another, prostitution and pornography. Walter Johnson, currently professor of history at Harvard, completed *Soul by Soul: Life Inside the Antebellum Slave Market* in 1999,[6] thereby reorienting the research spotlight from the practice of slaveholding at plantations and in households to the transactional flows of slave trading: pricing, buying, transporting, marketing, selling. Johnson's work tracks slave merchants purchasing men and women in the upper South and conducting them, usually in chains, to New Orleans, the demand center for second-phase cotton expansion in Mississippi and Texas. The business of slavery was not simply a shameful matter of human trafficking. It was also one means through which white manhood and patriarchy were reinforced, and it provided narrow apertures through which slaves could affect exchanges and, at times, "choose" their new masters. Locating agency, however restricted, in commoditized subaltern people is one reason why this study is exemplary for business historians. Similarly, when surveying plantation operations, the UK's Bill Cooke argued that

> American slavery has been wrongfully excluded from histories of management. By 1860, when the historical orthodoxy has modern management emerging on the railroads, 38,000 managers were managing the 4 million slaves working in the US economy. Given slaves' worth, slaveholders could literally claim "our people are our greatest asset." Yet a review of histories of management shows ante-bellum slavery excluded from managerial modernity as pre-capitalist, unsophisticated in practice, and without non-owner managers identified as such.[7]

Cooke writes from an unusual quarter, framing a postcolonial vector in management studies and relying on secondary sources to develop his pathbreaking article. There is plainly room for business historians to pursue archive-based studies of the slave business, both within and far beyond the American South.

As for prostitution and pornography as enterprises, Klara Arnberg at the University of Umea is analyzing Sweden's sexually explicit publishing industry in the mid-twentieth century, and she presented a portion of her research at the European Business History Conference (2010): "Under the Counter: The Business of Pornography in Sweden, 1950–1971." Arnberg, along with European colleagues in sociology and communications, joined a 2008 meeting, "Globalization, Media, and Adult Sexual Content," but business historians have not as yet ventured into comparable research. Last, cultural historian Mara Keire has recently released *For Business and Pleasure*,[8] an extensively researched analysis of US red-light districts and their regulation from the late nineteenth century through the Great Depression. Historical studies of prostitution and of antivice crusaders are not unusual, but rarely have they explored the economic and operational angles Keire's work details. Certainly locating sources, developing conceptually rich research questions, and dealing with harsh realities and deep-seated prejudices will be constant challenges for business historians undertaking work with confinement, sex, slavery, migration, or concealment as enterprises. Yet the high-quality work already accomplished along these lines should serve as a stimulus to others seeking to research subaltern histories with business institutions and relations as central dimensions.

NOTES

1. Homi Bhabha, "Unsatisfied: Notes on Vernacular Cosmopolitanism," in *Postcolonial Discourses: An Anthology*, ed. Gregory Castle (New York: Wiley, 2001), 50.

2. Ricardo Soares de Oliveira, "Business Success, Angola-Style: Postcolonial Politics and the Rise and Rise of Sonangol," *Journal of Modern African Studies* 45 (2001): 595–619; Ruth Phillips and Christopher Steiner, eds., *Unpacking Culture: Art and Commodity in Colonial and Postcolonial Worlds* (Berkeley: University of California Press, 1999); and Robert I. Westwood and Gavin Jack, "Manifesto for Postcolonial Business and Management Studies: A Provocation," *Critical Perspectives on International Business* 3 (2007): 246–65.

3. There is a substantive debate among cultural historians and cultural studies scholars about the continuing problem of "speaking for" the silenced. Our position is that there are no "authentic" voices anywhere, but there are worthwhile questions to be asked from academic locations, questions and answers that may be critiqued but should not be discounted in advance.

4. Mary Haddock, "Expelling the Chinese: Immigration Cases in Philadelphia, 1900–1932" (master's thesis, Rutgers University, Camden, NJ, 2005).

5. George Chauncey, *Gay New York: Gender, Urban Culture, and the Making of the Gay Male World, 1890–1940* (New York: Basic Books, 1995).

6. Published by Harvard University Press. The study won six major prizes in US history, though not a business history prize.

7. Bill Cooke, "The Denial of Slavery in Management Studies," *Journal of Management Studies* 40 (Dec. 2003): 1895–1918.

8. Mara Keire, *For Business and Pleasure: Red-Light Districts and the Regulation of Vice in the United States, 1890–1933* (Baltimore: Johns Hopkins University Press, 2010). Dr. Keire is associated with the University of Oxford's Center for Research in United States History.

10. Transnational Exchanges

In economic life the local becomes permeated by the national and the global, but this process is not unidirectional. This is why it is more accurate to speak of transnational exchanges than of internationalization or globalization. Even Japan between the seventeenth and the nineteenth centuries and the Soviet Union under Stalin's rule were never wholly closed. Therefore it is necessary to encompass the variety of transnational exchanges, to periodize them, to assess the possibilities of tensions between the local and global, and to delineate their impact on politics and culture.

Technologies are a key element of transnational exchanges. This is not just technology transfer from more-developed firms, institutions, or areas to less-developed sites of reception. There may be unanticipated transfers from the periphery to the center that come from colonies (water-pumping systems for irrigation) or from independent places (movable type, woks, or chopsticks). In addition to high-profile technologies, like railways or machinery, less visible technologies of information have been exported from the West for several centuries, including newspapers, cable telegraphy and telephony, radio, television, satellite connectivity, and the Internet. With each of these, the "periphery" starts speaking back to the "center," finding local voices to challenge commercial domination, colonialism, and imperialism and to share ideas, programs, and resources among emerging nations. Such technologies can "bite back," as Edward Tenner has shown,[1] as when radio broadcasts served as a mobilizing technology for genocidal slaughters in Rwanda.

Moreover, we should not forget that many transfers involve quite humble artifacts: corrugated iron for construction, metal sewing needles, or blank books for accounts. David Edgerton explains that "corrugated iron is a truly global technology. Its cheapness, lightness, ease of use and long life made it a ubiquitous material in the poor world in a way it never had been in the rich world."[2] Transnational organizations also promote transfers, as when the World Health Organization circulates medical techniques, serums for vaccination, or pharmaceuticals.

UNESCO promoted television in the 1950s, as well. Often overlooked are technologies that move among less-developed regions, such as rice cultivation or
ceramics-firing practices.

Over time, as historian of technology Bruce Seely notes, scholars have "adjusted and extended their concepts of what it takes for nations, firms, and organizations to innovate, adopt and adapt technologies developed elsewhere."[3]
Still, the policy literature often "see[s] transfers as a relatively predictable process whereby recipient organizations acquire, assimilate and then improve foreign technology."[4] Historical studies have been integral to reconceptualizing
technology transfer as something far more intricate than this "linear adaptation model," which posits a finished good crossing into new users' space, where
the receivers adopt or reject it.

> Historical analysis emphasizes that successful transfers rest on the exchange of
> people, not just machines, drawings, blueprints, patents, or other technical liter-
> ature. Moreover historians found that transferring technology required creative
> efforts; avoiding dependency required [imaginative] adaptation, not blind adop-
> tion, of imported ideas and machines. Adaptation required not just basic levels of
> preparation, but also support networks. [We now appreciate] the important role
> of users in the successful introduction of technical systems, both consumer ori-
> ented and for industry.[5]

Thus, transfer is anchored in cultural practices, involves contingent feedback
loops, and is anything but linear or logical. Indeed, we have learned "how difficult technology transfer could be even when the social, economic, and technical gap was not large."[6]

Technological ideas are not the only ones moving across borders. Managerial
methods, accounting procedures,[7] economic theories, legal principles, and eco-
logical concepts have all been disseminated from Europe and North America
outward. In return, developing nations, particularly Japan, have exported ideas
about just-in-time production, collaborative workplace relationships, long-term
subcontracting, and sustainability. Congresses, conventions, and universities
have offered forums for fluid exchanges among managers, academics, politicians,
and pundits. So too, NATO and the Warsaw Pact facilitated military contacts and
exchanges, whereas the earlier Universal Postal Union (1874), the International
Civil Aviation Organization (1944), and the International Radio Organization
(1946) had acted comparably in nonmilitary domains.

International consultants carried ideas in all directions, starting at least in
the nineteenth century. Crédit Lyonnais hired engineers beginning in the 1860s

to investigate the international operations of firms in which the bank or its clients had invested.[8] In 1914, having studied scientific management in America, Italian engineer A. Morini established a consulting firm in Paris, an early sign of multinationalism *among* industrialized societies.[9] Although the postwar rise to prominence of the American "big six" consulting firms is well known, by the 1980s Japanese consultants began taking *their* particular areas of production management expertise overseas. Even so, consultants working within individual nations continued to thrive by offering services matched to local needs, as in Toulouse, where regional specialists advised small and midsized technology firms, rather than Airbus.[10] When considering direct investment or acquisitions, multinational enterprises often bring consultants from their home countries, especially to assess financial conditions. This produces an equivocal situation, in response to information asymmetries and uncertainties about trust in the credibility of local experts and their reports.

In the exchange of products and services, transnational feedback defines markets businesses are unaware of, as with French cosmetics multinational L'Oréal's American hair-coloring ad slogan, "Because I'm worth it." It had such unexpected impact on US sales that the firm brought the phrase home to France, then circulated it worldwide as an advertising mainstay for decades. For some products and services, national boundaries have to be traversed in the search for scale. European transnational electrical grids are a case in point. They linked Germany and France in the early 1930s, but Hitler's drive for autarky ended this. In the postwar period, building Soviet-governed grids in the East and mutually beneficial grids in the West was a key element in power infrastructures for both sides.[11] Transnational services also include logistics and shipping, which in colonial eras involved uneven exchanges but did open new venues entrepreneurs had not foreseen. For example, steamship firms in the Indian and Pacific Oceans learned quickly that transporting migrant workers seasonally was a profitable supplement to shipments of materials and products. (See Prospects, 3: From Empires to Emergent Nations.)

Megaprojects—huge construction schemes—regularly spawn situations in which local knowledge and outside expertise interact, as with Egypt's Suez Canal in the nineteenth century and its Aswan Dam in the twentieth.[12] Armaments contracts have been transnational back to the eighteenth century, and in the nineteenth, European militaries bought weaponry on open markets. The French automobile industry extended production operations before World War One to Italy but after World War Two no longer sent cutting-edge technologies abroad. Instead, car makers sold older, rebuilt machinery to foreign start-up firms and licensed production of models no longer made in France. Citroën, in the 1970s, tried to sell India on the notion of taking over manufacturing the Ugly Duckling, its inexpensive 2CV, but was rebuffed by officials arguing that India planned to produce luxury cars. (Forty years later, the Tata tiny car finally met this segment of demand). Volkswagen did successfully relocate its environmentally challenged "Beetle" to Mexico and Brazil, after production in more-industrialized countries had to cease. In both nations, making even outdated cars provided stepping-stones for workforces and consumers, squeezing value and production experience out of what would otherwise have been expired designs and dead capital.[13] These cases indicate the heterogeneity of exchanges, as neither US nor Japanese firms tried anything comparable. Their overseas car plants routinely featured state-of-the-art machinery and tools, a strategy that became standard practice in the global automobile industry. Business historians have also coined the term *pocket multinationals* to characterize either relatively small multinationals or larger companies with very limited international operations. In Italy they suggested that 350 SMEs fit the category.[14]

Businesses have pursued transnational strategies on other fronts—in recruitment of personnel, procurement, financing, R&D, services, and relations with consumers, social forces, intellectuals, public authorities, and education and research systems. Greek shipping companies established transnational networks staffed by Greek nationals, starting in the Azov Sea and the Mediterranean in the 1800s and expanding to the rest of the world in the next century.[15] Multinationals have proliferated during, at times been interrupted by, and at times been advantaged by, wars and crises. However, contrary to the 1960s and seventies literature depicting them as all-powerful agents of domination, we now know that these giant firms faced limitations in their global spread. On one side, the economies-of-scope rationale, which is at the heart of their strategies, did not mean that they could indefinitely stretch their capabilities spatially. From the nineteenth century to the present, multinationals have made spectacular withdrawals from host countries. Think of the French hypermarket Carrefour's failure in Japan and Walmart's shipwreck in Germany during the past decade.[16] On another side, many firms have gradually learned that they need to adapt to local conditions, including speaking the local language—not doing so was a major source of advertising giant J. Walter Thompson's difficult beginnings in postwar France. Companies also learned the hard way that it was necessary to promote executives from host countries nationally and globally,[17] create R&D or style centers in host countries, and become partners with local banks and suppliers.[18] Learning the ropes about providing bribes to state officials also often proved helpful.

However, the process of adapting to these multiple challenges is not straightforward, even for large and experienced enterprises, and often results in transnational tensions. How do firms, individually or collectively, with or without the state, attempt to overcome such stress points? Do they offer constraints or opportunities, or both, and in what combinations? How do these strains influence the ownership and management of firms? What are their consequences for society, for culture, for the environment, and for relations between public and private? What are the effects of cycles of regulation and deregulation? How do tariff barriers affect these tensions? Are religious institutions or scientific knowledge outside their orbit? What actors other than firms (including NGOs, trade unions, and foundations) play a role in unfolding transnational dynamics? How do regional organizations matter (the EU, NAFTA, and ASEAN) to outcomes? What actions do international organizations undertake (the ILO, the OECD, the WTO)? What models and doctrines for negotiation and resolution develop and diffuse? What is the role of geography, that is, of sites where advantages can be developed locally, but with a worldwide outlook? Are there lasting differences between sectors and regions? What are the characteristics and results of the successive waves of globalization? These questions must all be explored historically, with comparisons among regions and nations and branches of industry and firms being especially valuable.

Free-standing companies are especially interesting, as they have home offices in one country but all their operating facilities in other parts of the world. They practice foreign direct investment as a pure economic strategy, not as an addition to facilities in their home nation. Mira Wilkins has explored the behavior of these strange creatures, finding them to be transnational without conforming to our usual understanding of a multinational.[19] Originating in 1830s Britain, such firms have no home workforces to oppose outsourcing or downsizing, no aging facilities in industrial districts, and no regulatory disputes with home governments, which gives them competitive advantages that bear further investigation. General trading companies, import-export specialists, have a long pedigree (Hudson's Bay Company, Dutch East India Company) and an even more ethereal existence, as their life centers around transnational exchanges. Geoffrey Jones explains: "Trading companies are very amorphous and difficult to identify [because] they often engage in the provision of financial and transportation services, and it can be purely arbitrary if a firm is classified as a trading company or something else, like a merchant bank or shipping company. . . . Many pure trading companies became hybrid trading companies over time and sometimes evolved further into oil, chemical or other types of firm."[20]

Business historians, demographers, and social historians have all stressed the importance of population movements in transnational exchanges. Some major features: a majority of migrants, but by no means all migrants, moved from depressed areas to more prosperous or more developed national economies. They were either birds of passage or permanent settlers. Relocation gave a sizable minority of migrants the idea or opportunity to become entrepreneurs. This was true not only for skilled workers but also for displaced peasants (some of whom become microentrepreneurs, serving their enclaves) as well as for laborers, semiskilled workers, and even civil servants. A case in point is the German philosopher and sociologist Norbert Elias. Having fled Nazi persecution, he settled in Paris during the early 1930s as a small entrepreneur, producing and selling wooden toys. Many prominent engineers or entrepreneurs were migrants, bringing their specialties or capital to new locales, not least in Latin America. Finally, diasporas of either ethnic minorities or national groups mobilized family or proximity links, cultural strategies, and financial resources to create transnational networks or transnational firms. The Parsis, the Armenians, and the Jews belong to the first category.[21] Recent business history has focused on the second, underlining the skills and multifarious activities of Chinese entrepreneurs outside China, of Indians worldwide, of Greek merchants or ship-owners in Southern Russia, and of Syrian merchants and traders in Africa, South America, and Southeast Asia.[22]

Business historians' views on capital in transnational exchanges have changed a lot, in keeping with those of geographers, sociologists (notably Saskia Sassen), and political scientists, who now speak of a "new mobility of people and money."[23] First, scholars have underscored the existence—and fluctuations—of return flows from places of migration to motherlands since the very early history of migration. In the late 1970s they began to analyze the origins and destinations of the remittances sent by migrants to their emerging countries.[24] Second, they assess in new terms the workings of finance capital. On one side, they do not really believe any more in the key role of a few (Western) international banks as promoters of monopoly capital. In keeping with the previous sections of this entry, what we have to explain is diversity. Banks of host countries play a significant part in many transnational ventures. They are not the only ones. Industrial groups have created full-fledged multinational financial institutions, starting with German electrical technology companies at the end of the nineteenth century, continuing with other Western firms, and now expanding in other parts of the world. On another side, international banks themselves have proven to be more fragile in the long run than the ability of balancing risks and profits on several simultaneous fronts, the relative volatility of capital, and the promises of moving funds to less-regulated areas would have led us to believe. Finally, dividends move across borders, and most commonly they travel within developed countries or tax havens. We suggest, however, that now one might not think so much of transnational capital returns, including bonds and share prices, but should open up the question of investments abroad and their effectiveness. This would be a worthwhile element of business historians' contributions to much-needed publications on how both individuals and nation states can become parts of "global assemblages," show some amount of flexibility in that process, and probably have to pay a cultural and political price in exchange.[25]

NOTES

1. Edward Tenner, *Why Things Bite Back: Technology and the Revenge of Unintended Consequences* (New York: Vintage, 1997).

2. David Edgerton, *The Shock of the Old: Technology in Global History since 1900* (Oxford: Oxford University Press, 2006), 41.

3. Bruce Seely, "Historical Patterns in the Scholarship of Technology Transfer," *Comparative Technology Transfer and Society* 1 (2003): 7–48, quote from 9.

4. Michael Cusumano and Detelin Elenkov, "Linking International Technology Transfer with Strategy and Management: A Literature Commentary" (MIT Sloan School Working Paper #3371-92/BPS, Jan. 1992).

5. Seely, "Historical Patterns," 22.

6. Ibid.

7. China had an indigenous set of accounting systems from at least the first millennium BCE, but their development was very gradual and their dissemination beyond Chinese territories uncertain. "Western" accounting arrived first in the 1840s, having only minor effects on existing practice, and again in 1949, when the new Maoist government adopted Soviet-style double-entry bookkeeping. See the special issue "Accounting History: Chinese Contributions and Challenges," Wei Lu and Max Aiken, eds., *Accounting, Business and Financial History* 13 (2003), especially Xu-dong Ji, "Concepts of Cost and Profit in Chinese Agricultural Treatises," ibid., 69–81, and Z. Jun Lin, "Chinese Bookkeeping Systems," ibid., 83–98.

8. Marc Flandreau, "Caveat Emptor: Coping with Sovereign Risk under the International Gold Standard, 1871–1914," in *International Financial History in the 20th Century: System and Anarchy*, ed. Mark Flandreau, Carl-Ludwig Holtfrerich, and Harold James (Cambridge, UK: Cambridge University Press, 2003), 17–50. Re Crédit Lyonnais, Flandreau notes: "In the absence of

international agencies, private risk analysis played an essential role in bringing about financial integration before World War I" (20).

9. Matthias Kipping, "American Management Consulting Companies in Western Europe, 1920–1990: Products, Reputation, and Relationships," *Business History Review* 73 (1999): 190–220.

10. Christian Longhi, "A French Revolution: Technology Management in the Aerospace Industry, The Case of Toulouse," *International Journal of Technology Management* 29 (2005): 194–215.

11. Arne Kaiser, Eric van Vleuten, and Per Hogselius, *Europe's Infrastructure Transitions: Economy, War, Nature* (London: Palgrave Macmillan, forthcoming 2014).

12. Caroline Piquet, *Histoire du canal de Suez* (Paris: Perrin, 2009); Hussein M. Fahim, *Dams, People and Development: The Aswan High Dam Case* (New York: Pergamon, 1981); and Asit K. Biswas, "Aswan Dam Revisited: The Benefits of a Much-Maligned Dam," *Development and Cooperation* 6 (Nov.–Dec. 2002): 25–27.

13. Helen Shapiro, "Determinants of Firm Entry into the Brazilian Automobile Manufacturing Industry, 1958–1968," *Business History Review* 65 (1991): 876–947, and John Humphrey and Mario Salerno, "Globalization and Assembler-Supplier Relations: Brazil and India," *Actes du GERPISA*, no. 2 (1998): 41–63.

14. Andrea Colli, *Il quarto capitalismo: Un profilo italiano* (Venice: Marsilio editore, 2002).

15. Evridiki Sifneos, "'Cosmopolitanism' as a Feature of the Greek Commercial Diaspora," *History and Anthropology* 16 (2005): 97–111.

16. Yuko Aoyama, "Oligopoly and the Structural Paradox of Retail MNCs: An Assessment of Carrefour and Wal-Mart in Japan," *Journal of Economic Geography* 7 (2007): 471–90.

17. Neveen Abdelrehim, Josephine Maltby, and Steven Toms, "Corporate Social Responsibility and Corporate Control: The Anglo-Iranian Oil Company, 1933–1951," *Enterprise and Society* 12 (2011): 824–62.

18. This field is also attracting economists and management scholars. See, inter alia, Ravi Ramamurti, *Emerging Multinationals in Emerging Markets* (Cambridge, UK: Cambridge University Press, 2009), and Lourdes Casanova, *Global Latinas: Latin America's Emergent Multinationals* (Basingstoke, UK: Palgrave Macmillan, 2009).

19. Mira Wilkins and Harm Schröter, eds., *The Free-Standing Company in the World Economy, 1830–1996* (Oxford: Oxford University Press, 1998).

20. Geoffrey Jones, *Merchants to Multinationals: British Trading Companies in the Nineteenth and Twentieth Centuries* (Oxford: Oxford University Press, 2000), 1.

21. See Robert E. Kennedy Jr., "The Protestant Ethic and the Parsis," *American Journal of Sociology* 66 (1962): 11–20, and David L. White, "Parsis in the Commercial World of Western India, 1700–1750," *Indian Economic and Social History Review* 24 (1987): 183–203.

22. Abner Cohen, "Cultural Strategies in the Organization of Trading Diasporas," in *The Development of Indigenous Trade and Markets in West Africa*, ed. Claude Meillassoux (Oxford: Oxford University Press, 1971), 266–78; Claude Markovits, *The Global World of Indian Merchants: Traders of Sind from Bukhara to Panama* (Cambridge, UK: Cambridge University Press, 2000); and Ina Baghdiantz McCabe, Gelina Harlaftis, and Ioanna Pepelasis Minoglou, eds., *Diaspora Entrepreneurial Networks: Four Centuries of History* (Oxford: Berg, 2005).

23. Saskia Sassen, *Globalization and Its Discontents: Essays on the New Mobility of People and Money* (New York: New Press, 1998).

24. See Gildas Simon's pioneering work, *L'espace des travailleurs tunisiens en France: Structures et fonctionnement d'un champ migratoire international* (Poitiers: By the author, 1979), and his recent synthesis of his whole research career, *La planète migratoire dans la mondialisation* (Paris: Armand Colin, 2008).

25. Saskia Sassen, *Territory, Authority, and Rights in a Global Digital Age: From Medieval to Global Assemblages* (Princeton: Princeton University Press, 2006).

11. Trust, Cooperation, and Networks

Trust at a distance . . . was necessary for an international market in a new manufacture.

—*Adrian Johns,* Piracy

A world immune to Ponzi schemes is a world utterly devoid of trust, and no one wants to live in a world like that. Indeed, no healthy economic system can function in a world like that.

—*Diana Henriques,* The Wizard of Lies

For the eighteenth-century book trade as for twentieth-century investments, trust is essential to business operations and transactions alike, yet we notice it chiefly when it fails. So it is with cooperation and networks, too—seamless and invisible when effective, conflictual or even catastrophic when collapsing. As background and infrastructure conditions for social action, all three are difficult to study in the present, much less historically. Yet understanding shared issues and contexts can prepare the ground for investigating the development, performance, and transformation of trust, cooperation, and networks across time and space. They have become critical topics in management and organizational studies, to be sure, but historical research on them is widely scattered and thin.[1] It may be that distrust, competition, and hierarchies are simply more dramatic, as the Bernie Madoff fraud case suggests; but we should recognize, with Johns, that long-distance trust relations are fundamental to trade, innovation, investment, administration, and learning, despite their accompanying hazards.

Trust can be defined within five contexts, according to corporate strategist Larue Hosmer: individual expectations, interpersonal relations, economic exchanges, social structures, and ethical principles. Individuals make decisions to trust, expressing a "non-rational" optimism about an outcome that's uncertain; these are one-way relationships—trusting a father, an officer, an agency, sometimes dismissively called "blind trust," perhaps in error.[2] Interpersonal trust actively allows one person "and perhaps others to be vulnerable to harm in the interest of some perceived greater good." Here are the roots of cooperation and reciprocity, in which each trusted partner takes responsibility for the trusting partner's welfare. Drawing on an extensive literature, Hosmer identified five characteristics of reciprocal trust: integrity, competence, consistency, loyalty, and openness. Clearly, the interpersonal variant involves complex social commitments and benefits.[3] In economic exchanges, transaction-cost theory has claimed the low ground by presuming distrust as a default feature of interactions. This approach emphasizes the costs of contracts, controls, and information to defend against opportunism: "self-interest seeking with guile."[4] Others reject this cynicism, arguing that "price, authority and trust [are] independent methods that could be combined in a number of ways." Indeed, trust can strengthen both markets and hierarchies, not least by facilitating collaboration and networking.[5]

For business historians, a range of questions concerning trust can be advanced. Given that most trust within and between enterprises is short term and needs renewing and reinforcing, how did this take shape in markets, joint ventures, and projects?[6] What devices or activities came into play? What exactly is included in a trusting relationship? How are boundaries framed? More than transactions or investments are involved, for trust has noneconomic dimensions like reputation, quality, reciprocity, and specialized information. Historically, bankers and merchants established credit relations at a distance by generating means of assurance (letters of credit, bills of exchange). Such practices routinized and formalized trust, transforming both face-to-face and arms-length relationships. Hence, how does the formalization that branding represents reconfigure trust, and with what implications?[7] How do actors expand and negotiate trust to prevent defaults (and litigation)? When and how does the state play a role in this process, positively or not? For example, military actors regularly negotiate trust with other branches, with allies, with suppliers and politicians. In Asia and Europe, government agencies do this on nonmilitary issues as well, though commonly with mixed results.

As an example of negotiated trust, consider the two leading French electrical/electronics companies, Thomson-Houston and Compagnie Générale d'Electricité (CGE, now Alcatel-Lucent) in the late 1960s. Both were becoming international players, and the French government sought to confirm them as national champions, so as to compete globally, but not with each other. At the "Yalta of Electronics" in 1969, the firms agreed to a division of labor: CGE to focus on telephones and communications, Thomson on information technology for business and industry. They would jointly venture into new areas, saving the costs of competition by trusting one another's good intentions. The firms had dramatically different leaders: Thomson's had risen from within without much formal education, taking advantage of World War Two staff losses and displacements, whereas CGE's top executive was a highly-trained engineer with experience as a senior civil servant (*pantouflage*).[8] This cultural gap made sustaining trust difficult, but results also matter. After four years, Thomson judged that CGE's telephone strategy had not produced innovations but instead had created scarcities and increased prices to generate high unit profits. Thus Thomson executives tore up the Yalta agreement and resumed head-on competition.[9]

On another plane, is there such a thing as involuntary trust, given asymmetrical relationships in economies and societies, or do asymmetries distort the term so much as to make it inappropriate here? For example, as citizens we have little choice but to "trust" the currencies our governments issue (and their electronic representations in our accounts), that is, to trust their authenticity, validity, and continuing value. This one-way "trust" is established by statute, by fiat, not by relational negotiation. So what are the consequences of compelling "trust," and how have they materialized in different forms?

Whether trust is deep, shallow, or absent, businesses cannot operate without cooperation, which must be secured through consent or contract—informal (work groups, committees) or formal (associations, cartels). Cooperation may start out informally and develop a structure of agreements or, conversely, may begin with contractual terms and evolve into informal practices, as trust and confidence grow. The bases for cooperation, which extend beyond recognizing a mutuality of interests, include legitimacy, shared values, fairness, social standing, prior experiences (including with the proposed partners), and social and historical contexts. Cooperation is also practiced differently in diverse nations and regions, cultures, and legal environments.[10] As so often, when we focus on the firm, we can forget that firms and actors are embedded in situated social relations that are both complex and contingent.

Key historical questions would concern the dynamics through which cooperation emerges and is sustained, inside and among businesses, within sectors (hence, cartels), and through links among organizations distinctly constituted (commercial, nonprofit, and nonbusiness [churches, governments]). What external forces or opportunities, and what internal prospects or conflicts, bring people to seek cooperation, and how is opposition manifested? Is it true that "metaphors of competition as war and of success as winning no longer seem as valid in today's complex business environment as they did in earlier times"?[11] When, how, and why is cooperation improvised and how might leadership be proactive, supported, or even reconfigured in the process? What changes in enterprise, alliance, joint venture, cartel, or association practice does repeated or sustained cooperative work set in motion? Interviews with Nissan personnel indicate that cooperative initiatives increased participants' experience, know-how, and competencies, for example, yet when the effort was temporary, individuals often proved reluctant to return to their "old jobs." Successful cooperation between firms may lead to a desire to merge; unsuccessful, to mistrust and go-it-alone sentiments.

As the 1987 creation of SEMATECH indicated, the French state was not alone in actively fostering business cooperation, in this case among a sizable cohort of fiercely competitive companies. The US government legalized a multipartner research consortium in 1984 and funded it through 1996 to rescue the American semiconductor industry from ruinous competition with Japanese rivals. Aimed to develop new manufacturing techniques and processes, SEMATECH allied fourteen companies for a five-year project, which proved sufficiently productive that eleven of them renewed for a further phase.[12] The consortium went international in the mid-1990s, adding seven non-US firms to a project on tool standards. After twenty-five years, as management reported, "SEMATECH's R&D model has continuously evolved to incorporate broader industry participation—including equipment and materials suppliers, fabless companies, foundries, and packaging/assembly companies—as well as collaboration with universities, regional governments, and other consortia in order to foster technology innovation and accelerate the commercialization of new materials and nanostructures for future transistors."[13] Yet success stories like this are not as common as we might hope. As Anne Huff argued, scholars need to address "the puzzle of why alliances continue to flourish despite widely agreed statistics showing that at least half of previous efforts have failed, often miserably."[14] Inquiring about what conditions have favored durable cooperation would be a worthwhile historical task.[15]

Finally, networks. Here tons of material has been published,[16] much of it richly descriptive or intensely theoretical, so we have just a few questions to offer. How have people created knowledge about and through networks? For what purposes have individuals and organizations used networks? What resources and pitfalls have networks generated? Consider on the first point, networks of car dealerships. They gather knowledge about local or regional consumption patterns, regulations, tastes, politics, and about shifts in these and in area financial resources, or labor force earnings, sharing these with one another and with automakers. Now consider an imaginary online nationwide car dealers' chat room, which would address issues on a different scale: import trade rules, corporate policies, transportation, credit trends, pricing, or demand pattern for makes, years, and models. Perhaps implausible, but why? Well, the physical location and scope of a network conditions the forms and themes of its activity, as do the capabilities of its members and the reach of their interests. Culturally, car dealers may strike us as having a narrower knowledge-seeking compass than car makers, but as globalization intensifies, this may no longer be true.

Though networks usually transfer information, other purposes can readily be discerned. In the United States, major automakers' dealer networks reinforced hierarchies of power through asymmetrical contracts that required dealers to make sunk investments, even though the Big Three could add or cancel dealerships virtually at will. Only antitrust action in the early 1940s reined in such practices.[17] Two centuries earlier, during the calico craze in eighteenth-century India, networks of merchants developed strategies to adapt to and profit from the East India Company's economic overlordship, in the process gaining power over hand weavers and agriculturalists in cotton.[18] In nineteenth-century Japan, networks of employers refused to lose face by making layoffs in weak markets, so collectively they turned to the courts, securing judgments that transferred responsibility to the government for committing this unworthy act. Thus did Japanese networks express and instantiate culture. In twentieth-century France, Freemasonry represented a key network for managers at La Poste and France Telecom, providing them with useful resources at a modest cost. Such articulations are, we believe, preinstitutional and should not be confused with associations or enterprises, occupying as they do an ambiguous space between trust relations and organizations. Moreover, in our focus on networked societies, we have undervalued material networks that facilitate supply and distribution.

Networks complicate individualization, as well. Your chances of success rise if you participate in a workplace dining, reading, or sports club, where others pass on the results of experience and learning. One cannot be so easily singled out for demotion and can be more readily prepped for advancement if one is a member of an extensive professional or enterprise network. Such practices have a rich and at times unsettling history, to be sure.[19] However, such clusters can also provide misleading information, as when trade veterans share "knowledge" over card games and drinks, playing a game of deception and trickery with colleagues and apprentices. Network players may fiddle with trust, amusing insiders, mocking and deflecting outsiders, and sowing confusion among the uninitiated. From our perspective, these variations and ambiguities do not make networks a topic for origin seeking (e.g., thereby framing Internet-era teleologies). Instead, it may be promising to regard networks as a thick soup of intentions, arrangements, and connections that facilitated business activity, a dish whose historical recipes and forgotten chefs are worth rediscovering.

NOTES

Epigraphs. Adrian Johns, *Piracy: The Intellectual Property Wars from Gutenberg to Gates* (Chicago: University of Chicago Press, 2009), 95. Diana Henriques, *The Wizard of Lies: Bernie Madoff and the Death of Trust* (New York: Times Books, 2011), 347.

1. A classic, of course, is Louis Galambos, *Competition and Collaboration: The Emergence of a National Trade Association* (Baltimore: Johns Hopkins University Press, 1966), which focuses on organizing the Cotton Textile Institute in twentieth-century America. For contemporary business practices, see the essays in Roderick Kramer and Tom Tyler, eds., *Trust in Organizations: Frontiers of Theory and Research* (Thousand Oaks, CA: Sage, 1996), and Farok Contractor and Peter Lorange, eds., *Cooperative Strategies and Alliances* (Kidlington, UK: Elsevier Scientific, 2002).

2. On the faith-based anchor for all forms of trust, see Guido Mollering, "The Nature of Trust: From Georg Simmel to a Theory of Expectation, Interpretation, and Suspension," *Sociology* 35 (2001): 403–20.

3. Larue Hosmer, "Trust: The Connecting Link between Organizational Theory and Philosophical Ethics," *Academy of Management Review* 20 (1995): 379–403, quotes from 381, 383, 384. An acclaimed overview is Barbara Misztal, *Trust in Modern Societies: The Search for the Bases of Social Order* (Cambridge, UK: Polity, 1996). Extensive 1990s discussions of trust seem to have faded sharply after 2001 or so.

4. Oliver Williamson, "Economic Organization: The Case for Candor," *Academy of Management Review* 21 (1996): 48–57.

5. Hosmer, "Trust," 386–93.

6. Long- (or longer-) term trust holds together families, friends, ethnic and cultural groups, old boys clubs, religious collectives, and consumers' relationships with shops, brands, and service agencies. All can be broken, but an expectation of dishonesty, betrayal, or defection is not present.

7. See Teresa da Silva Lopes and Paul Duguid, eds., *Trademarks, Brands, and Competitiveness* (New York: Routledge, 2010).

8. The pattern wherein state administrators become private business leaders in France. See http://en.wikipedia.org/wiki/Pantouflage (accessed 7 June 2011).

9. Frank Dobbin, "Metaphors of Industrial Rationality: The Social Construction of Electronics Policy in the United States and France," in *Vocabularies of Public Life: Empirical Essays in Symbolic Structure*, ed. Robert Withnow (London: Routledge, 1992), 197–201, and Maurice Lévy-Leboyer, Patrick Fridenson, and Véronique Rostas, *Thomson's First Century* (Jouy-en-Josas: Campus Thomson, 1995).

10. Ken Smith, Stephen Carrol, and Susan Ashford, "Intra- and Interorganizational Cooperation: Toward a Research Agenda," *Academy of Management Journal* 38 (1995): 7–23.

11. Ibid., 9.

12. Larry Browning, Janice Beyer, and Judy Shetler, "Building Cooperation in a Competitive Industry: SEMATECH and the Semiconductor Industry," *Academy of Management Journal* 38 (1995): 113–51. See also Browning and Shetler, *SEMATECH: Saving the U.S. Semiconductor Industry* (College Station: Texas A&M Press, 2000).

13. See www.sematech.org/corporate/history.htm (accessed 7 June 2011). A "fab" is "a facility where the wafer fabrication process is performed. Fabs include a high-quality cleanroom as well as support systems such as ultrapure water, gas and chemical generation and delivery systems, waste water treatment, extensive HVAC equipment, as well as other support functions." Definition available at http://dictionary.babylon.com/fab/ (accessed 8 July 2011).

14. Anne Huff, "Preface," in Mark de Rond, *Strategic Alliances as Social Facts: Business, Biotechnology and Intellectual History* (Cambridge, UK: Cambridge University Press, 2005), ix. De Rond's ethnographic analysis of three pharmaceutical projects shows the profoundly nonrational messiness of collaboration at the edges of knowledge.

15. Some candidates for evaluation: sharing a long-term project; repeated briefer intersections; tasks that build tacit knowledge, external hostility, peer recognition and affirmation; and interactions that generate multiple plausible solutions.

16. For an overview, see W. Mark Fruin, "Business Groups and Interfirm Networks," in *The Oxford Handbook of Business History*, ed. Geoffrey Jones and Jonathan Zeitlin (New York: Oxford University Press, 2007), 244–67, and Asli M. Colpan, Takashi Hikino, and James R. Lincoln, eds., *The Oxford Handbook of Business Groups* (Oxford: Oxford University Press, 2010). For a bibliography on networks and network theory, see http://pegasus.cc.ucf.edu/~nkapucu/documents/Network%20Theory%20Bibliography%20Categorized.pdf (accessed 7 June 2011); for network economics, www.stern.nyu.edu/networks/biblio_hframe.html (accessed 8 June 2011). See also Dirk Messner, *The Network Society* (London: Cass, 1997); Manuel Castells, *The Rise of the Network Society* (Oxford, Blackwell, 1996); and Nitin Nohria and Robert Earles, *Networks and Organizations* (Boston: Harvard Business School Press, 1992). For a critique, see Peter Marcuse, "Depoliticizing Globalization: From Neo-Marxism to the Network Society of Manuel Castells," in *Understanding the City*, ed. John Eade and Christopher Mele (Oxford: Blackwell, 2002), 131–58.

17. Sally Clarke, *Trust and Power: Consumers, the Modern Corporation, and the Making of the United States Automobile Market* (Cambridge, UK: Cambridge University Press, 2007), chap. 7.

18. Prassanan Parthasarathi, *The Transition to a Colonial Economy: Weavers, Merchants and Kings in South India, 1720–1800* (Cambridge, UK: Cambridge University Press, 2001), chap. 1.

19. Pamela Laird, *Pull: Networking and Success since Benjamin Franklin* (Cambridge, MA: Harvard University Press, 2007).

PART FOUR

RESOURCES

Generative Concepts and Frameworks

1. Assumptions

One of the usually hidden and problematic dimensions of business history (or of any historical field) is the set of unexamined assumptions that animate and situate research and discourse. A discipline's shared assumptions facilitate exchanges, evaluations, and the integration of new findings with established understandings, while excluding nonconforming approaches, concepts, and questions. This is quite ordinary practice, what some commentators call the "boundary work" necessary to disciplinary integrity,[1] but there are situations when it is timely to expose local assumptions in order better to grasp broader shifts or unexplored terrains. Assumptions often stand forth as assertions—*statements* that establish foundational claims about "what we all know." A second level on which such claims are active features *concepts* that scholars regard as transparent, rarely needing either explication, contextualization, or defense.[2] The following paragraphs offer a number of items about statements for reflection and perhaps for critique. Examining concepts will be the theme of a separate section. (See Prospects, 7: Reassessing Classic Themes.)

What might be a reasonable cluster of the assumptions business historians carry into their work? Consider these candidates, a group more exemplary than exhaustive:

We know what business is (and what is not business); by extension, we know what *a* business is and what it is not.

Business activity yields both private and social benefits.

States/governments are not "in business."

Market competition promotes and is central to efficiency.

Regulation reduces optimal performance by businesses and industries.

Money is simply a conventional medium of exchange and measure of value, sustained by state guarantees and by users' confidence.

Inflation is bad for business (and for economies).

High interest rates discourage investment and entrepreneurship.

Pricing is fundamental to valuation and exchange.

Hierarchies promote order and efficiency.

Innovation is both necessary and productive for the business community and the public.

Firms are independent units that compete, and cooperation between firms is infrequent and minimal.

Management is a rational search for effective plans and operational protocols.

Accounts chronicle success and failure objectively.

Mergers and scale economies improve performance, at both enterprise and national and international economy levels.

Let us take up here just the first item in the above roster, namely, we know what business is and what *a* business is. What essential or core characteristics define doing business or being a business? Is it handling money or representations of money (credit cards, checks, promissory notes)? Is it exchange (which can be barter, involving no money)? Is it profit-seeking (but nonprofit enterprises handle money and do exchanges, including barter—museums trading artifacts, for example)? Are physicians "in business" (in many places they are salaried state employees, elsewhere partners or proprietors)? Is a project (making a film, exhibiting one's photos in a park) a business, a business but also other things, or perhaps a proto-business—a venture in a process of becoming? Does the state define who's in business and who's not through licenses, taxes, and such? If so, when did that practice start and why? Such questions lead away from simple clarity and into situational and historical complexities. That's what happens when assumptions are probed.

Of course, we could add additional assumptions, and of course, not all business historians would share each and all of those offered here. But this is surely the point. Exploring, revising, or objecting to these assumptions opens a dialogue about our collective sense concerning what is going on in business, what is historically salient for researchers and for practitioners, and how we can modify assumptions given substantial variability in empirical situations or their disconfirmation by real-world outcomes. For example, one of our colleagues, Michael Gibbert,[3] recently alerted us to research findings showing that a substantial majority of mergers and acquisitions reduce the performance of the resulting enterprise after initially boosting share prices and generate negative outcomes in the medium and long terms, depending on sector, acquisition cost, etc.[4] A related proposition might suggest that mergers often prove positive for those selling out, not for buyers, but we expect that this needs to be researched and tested. The central issue here is that is it not sufficient to be aware of our assumptions, but that researchers would do well to inquire about how we might verify, invalidate, or modify them. In that context, disciplinary boundary work shifts from a maintenance to a critical and imaginative mode.

How to go about exploring the limits and silences built into our assumptions? Three paths, at a minimum, are open. First, recognize that assumptions are simplifying devices and thus determine what diversity of conditions or actions is compressed within them and whether these variants can be construed historically as significant or not. If omissions seem substantive, consider what cluster of linked assumptions might be necessary for repair work. Second, explore the outliers and anomalies about which the assumptions are silent (e.g., state enterprises, profitable frauds, boundary cases about "being in business"), in order to acknowledge activity to which our approaches customarily turn a blind eye. Third, invert the assumptions and seek out examples of behaviors that fall within the newly-defined domain. Where might we find situations where market competition undercuts efficiency? Efficiency for whom? Moreover, isn't inflation good for debtors, whereas doesn't innovation hazard or crush trades that new products or capabilities surpass?

Such inquiries reinforce several aspects of the scholarly challenge. They remind us of the complexity of the phenomena we seek to understand and analyze, highlighting the potential costs of simplification. They underscore the intellectual value of critique, of taking neither "our" actors' statements nor our own frameworks of expectation at face value.[5] And they condition us to embrace the value of watchfulness, the suspension of confidence, and the value of identifying overlooked players, silences in the record, and contradictions between the elements that constitute our sets of assumptions.

NOTES

1. For a seminal contribution, see Thomas Gieryn, "Boundary Work and the Demarcation of Science from Non-Science: Strains and Interests in Professional Ideologies of Scientists," *American Sociological Review* 46 (1983): 781–95. See also Susan Owens, Judith Petts, and Harriet Bulkley, "Boundary Work: Knowledge, Policy, and the Urban Environment," *Environment and Planning C: Government and Policy* 24 (2006): 633–43.

2. For a formal analysis, see David Papineau, "Theory-Dependent Terms," *Philosophy of Science* 63 (1996): 1–20. For a broad effort to "unravel our confusions" about mind-brain relationships, incisive and witty, see Papineau, *Thinking about Consciousness* (Oxford: Oxford University Press, 2002).

3. Coauthor of *Strategic Management in the Knowledge Economy* (New York: Wiley, 2005) and professor of marketing at Universita della Svizzera Italiana, Lugano.

4. This is evidently a well-known phenomenon among business analysts, though it hardly seems to curb the appetite for mergers and acquisitions deals. See, for example, George W. Dent, "Unprofitable Mergers: Toward a Market-Based Legal Response," *Northwestern University Law Review* 80 (1986): 777–806, and Richard E. Caves, "Mergers, Takeovers, and Economic Efficiency: Foresight vs. Hindsight," *International Journal of Industrial Organization* 7 (1989): Special Issue, 151–74. Klaus Gugler, Dennis Muehler, B. Burton Yortuglu, and Christine Zulehener found that "those mergers that decrease profits and efficiency account for a large proportion" ("The Effects of Mergers: An International Comparison," *IJIO* 21 (2003): 625–53.

5. For useful perspectives on unpacking assumptions, see Helga Drummond, "Triumph or Disaster: What Is Reality?" *Management Decision* 30 (1993): 29–34; Ralph Killman, "A Dialectical Approach to Formulating and Testing Social Science Theories: Assumptional Analysis," *Human Relations* 36 (1986): 1–21; Tony Grundy, "Destroying Shareholder Value: Ten Easy Ways," *Long Range Planning* 28.3 (June 1995): 78–83; and David McClintock, Raymond Ison, and Rosalind Armson, "Metaphors for Reflecting on Research Practice: Researching with People," *Journal of Environmental Planning and Management* 46 (2003), 715–31.

2. Communities of Practice

The concept of practice connotes doing, but not just doing in and of itself. It is doing in a historical and social context that gives structure and meaning to what we do. In this sense, practice is always social practice. Such a concept of practice includes both the explicit and the implicit. It includes what is said and what is left unsaid, what is represented and what is assumed. . . . Communities of practice are the prime context in which we can work out common sense through mutual engagement.

—*Etienne Wenger*, Communities of Practice: Learning, Meaning and Identity

Communities of practice are formed by people who engage in a process of collective learning in a shared domain of human endeavor: a tribe learning to survive, a band of artists seeking new forms of expression, a group of engineers working on similar problems . . . a gathering of first-time managers helping each other cope.

—*Etienne Wenger, "Communities of Practice: A Brief Introduction"*

Thinking about communities of practice (CoPs) helps us understand that there are sites for business history other than formal organizations, other than hierarchies and networks, all of which tend to privilege structure over process.[1] CoPs are not simply occupational groups, nor are they affinity groups (like Arsenal fans) or subcultures;[2] instead, they are situated collectives of active learners who may be co-present (the managers above) or not (the engineers). As two IBM analysts observed, in contemporary settings they can be "institutionalized, informal networks of professionals managing domains of knowledge," but "they are neither organization units nor teams."[3] And they have a history.

Consider the long tradition of the *compagnonnage* in France—artisans touring the country to broaden their skills and knowledge and their understanding of a trade's conventions and mysteries, refining both the explicit and the implicit dimensions of craft.[4] Consider the Royal Society—gentlemen seeking to unravel nature's puzzles and to share and publish findings and procedures, thereby institutionalizing scientific practice.[5] Although the CoP is not an organization, it can lay the foundations for one. Consider chemical engineering, a profession invented after several generations of industrial practice, once a cluster of DuPont engineers had lobbied within the firm for recognition of their distinctive area of learning and knowledgeability, separating it from industrial chemistry as a research discipline.[6]

French chefs continued artisanal communities of practice into the twentieth century, moving among restaurants to refine their techniques and expand their capabilities. In recent decades this CoP has been decisively internationalized as journeymen chefs circle the globe, learning and preparing dishes in multiple cuisines, laying a foundation for creating "fusion" menus in new restaurants. Self-constituting and self-regulating, the community of chefs has exploded since roughly the 1970s, producing thousands of cookbooks and memoirs, television series, specialist magazines, institutes and schools, online advice and reference sites, gastro-tourism vacations, and dedicated food channels (in many languages, circulated worldwide). Some of the chefs with the highest visibility have started multiple restaurants in leading cities or have generated global "brands" and chains. Such business initiatives do not replace the chefs' CoP but rather monetize elements within it.[7]

Communities of practice are protean, unstable, and poorly bounded collectives. They can remain so, or formalization can be initiated in various ways: creating conferences or associations, devising training programs for novice members (leading to professional schools and disciplines), providing certificates (and thus identifying core practitioners as certifiers), or fabricating durable containers for accumulated knowledge (journals, textbooks, manuals). In emergent technical fields, knowledge transfer and sharing can mandate the frequent updating of textbooks: between the 1880s and 1920s, Carl Justus von Bach revised his *Elasticity and Resistance* through eleven editions and his *Elements of Machinery* twelve times after first publication.[8] Ongoing CoPs may also evolve continually with arrivals and departures, generating unexpected links between science and technology and new potentials (and power relations) for job markets and firms. New CoPs may exit from organizations as well as become transformed into them. Such was the case for chemical engineering's biomedical spinoff a half century ago:

> Biomedical engineering appeared in ChE because some enterprising physicians in Boston and New York had important medical problems that they were willing to discuss with chemical engineers. . . . Several early pioneers of the late 1950s and 1960s indicated . . . that their first association with biomedical problems was in response to medical needs by practicing physicians in local hospitals. Some of these problems were related to blood separation and purification, blood flow, measurement of viscosity or shear stresses or improvement with simple medical devices.[9]

First a community of practice formed between doctors and research-oriented engineers, followed by shared projects, research grant applications, and preliminary attempts to give a name to what practitioners were doing ("chemical bioengineering" was an early try). Once formalization arose, journals, graduate programs, and innovation-centered enterprises ensued.

Much the same pattern occurred in NATO's construction of military optronics (using electronic devices to control light), where state and private industry scientists in optics and electronics discovered they had practices in common and, rather than contending with one another, built allied interests through a shared quest. Again, finding a name for the effort took time, but crafting the name was itself a critical process in assembling the community, a discursive moment rising from practice. Thus did "materials science" come into being, due to converging Cold War research needs that both transcended and blended practices from metallurgy and polymer chemistry. This led to runaway creativity at times, as military-funded aerospace researchers "in the 1980s and 1990s . . . developed more than nine hundred new materials for the impossibly expensive B-2 Stealth bomber."[10] Such practice exhibits neither efficiency nor managerial control but rather a shared search for knowledge and solutions in a context of late Cold War political urgency.

These experiences raise a variety of questions. Once a community of practice has found a name or started a journal, does it remain open and protean? What conditions favor CoP emergence, and in what circumstances is this implausible? Creating movies after the decline of the studio system is one ideal process to study, as skilled "individuals come together to create a film, and once this is achieved they disperse, yet . . . remain members of the film-making community."[11] We might initially imagine that routine work (managerial, clerical, or industrial) would be a hostile environment, but Etienne Wenger disagrees: communities of practice do form in such situations, but members may focus on handling boredom, evading supervision, dealing with incoherent directives and opaque forms, or sharing assessments of what pace of work is acceptable.[12] Indeed, he has sketched key features that help define CoPs, though few will exhibit the full set:

Sustained mutual relationships—harmonious or conflictual

Shared ways of engaging in doing things together

A rapid flow of information and propagation of innovation

Absence of introductory preambles, as if conversations and interactions were merely the continuation of an ongoing process

Very quick setup of a problem to be discussed

Substantial overlap in descriptions by participants of who belongs

Knowledge of what others know, what they can do, and how they can contribute to an enterprise

Mutual definition of identities

The ability to assess the appropriateness of actions and products

Specific tools, representations, and other artifacts

Local lore, shared stories, inside jokes, knowing laughter

Jargon and shortcuts to communication as well as the ease of producing new technologies

Certain styles recognized as displaying membership

A shared discourse reflecting a certain perspective on the world[13]

Given these nonconformist characteristics, what do business hierarchies do with internal communities of practice (accept and engage, try to control or co-opt, try to eradicate?)? What to do about CoPs that connect actors across organizations in unknown ways, generating capabilities beyond management's reach? What does authority or leadership mean in a CoP, how does it develop, and how is this different from network or hierarchy authority? Are communities of practice peaceful or laden with conflicts? How are stresses within a

CoP resolved, that is, does the classic "exit, voice, loyalty" trio apply?[14] It is also useful at this point to recollect that practice is different from routine,[15] that it is not codified knowledge but a shared set of capabilities for action through recognized conventions, rituals, and gestures (but not rules), as Kevin Borg has shown historically for auto repair shops in the United States.[16] And of course, the payoff question: What issues in business history can be addressed by introducing the communities-of-practice concept?

Management scholars have embraced, studied, and recoded the concept over the last two decades. Consistent with the ongoing critique of top-down, putatively rational management for control and efficiency, communities of practice have joined networks and projects as vectors for rethinking operations from R&D to marketing and M&A (mergers and acquisitions). Yet in corporate settings, control can readily supplant learning as the main agenda. CoPs are not *directional*; they do not reliably support the corporate mission or the divisional plan, but when they are *directed*, they become teams or units, shedding many of Wenger's core characteristics. Joanne Roberts notes that "a business can establish a team for a particular project, which may in time emerge as a community of practice. But management cannot establish a community of practice."[17] Andrew Cox concludes, "the implication for management discovering CoPs . . . is that their energy can be channeled through rather familiar rationalizing processes." Corporate overseers perhaps understandably will aim to crush "free-thinking CoPs," which "are likely to diverge onto their own path and become an autonomous influence in organizational politics."[18] Hence management-created CoPs readily become policy instruments, setting boundaries to learning and creativity. Business historians' research into critical studies of such practices, their contradictions, and their evolution in relation to corporate strategies would provide longer-term perspectives than the policy literature currently fosters.

Finally, where are there opportunities to explore the communities-of-practice perspective within business history? When and where has social learning been supportive of CoP formation (or not), and how? We could profitably revisit salesmen's communities, from railway travelers to more settled auto dealerships, where members shared knowledge of clients, trade lore, specialist language, and an array of tricks and jokes. Telegraphers chatted with one another routinely in an earlier version of "online discussions" and entered transmission speed contests that were at once competitive and a means to solidarity. Racing-car mechanics from the 1920s onward traded information about speed and safety and built businesses that thrived on innovative postwar customization, specialized technologies, and word of mouth among users. From the nineteenth century, urban professionals (lawyers, journalists, social workers) shared news, rumors, and knowledge in coffee shops, bars, and the increasing number of specialized clubs started for dinners and meetings, much like AnnaLee Saxenian's Silicon Valley software engineers gathering for morning coffee and pastries to puzzle out cranky code and random crashes. Machinists, like printers, traveled through American industrial districts, sharing "shop kinks" and warnings about untrustworthy employers or half-baked apprentices trying to "steal a trade." Indeed, J. R. Williams's long-running *Iron Age* cartoon series provided a weekly look at jokes, conventions, and conflict in machinists' extraordinarily durable community of practice—supportive, combative, and expert discourse, which continues today online at *PracticalMachinist.com* and other much-visited websites.[19] The possibilities for framing an interpretive business historical perspective, positioning communities of practice as distinct from hierarchies, networks, and markets, are surely broad and appealing.

NOTES

Epigraphs. Etienne Wenger, *Communities of Practice: Learning, Meaning and Identity* (Cambridge, UK: Cambridge University Press, 1998), 47. Etienne Wenger, "Communities of Practice: A Brief Introduction," available at http://partnershipforchildhealth.org/mhip_intro_10_Communities_of_Practice-A_Brief_Introduction_by_Etienne_Wenger.pdf (accessed 13 June 2011).

1. Mark de Rond, *Strategic Alliances as Social Facts: Business, Biotechnology and Intellectual History* (Cambridge, UK: Cambridge University Press, 2003), 21.

2. Andrew Cox, "What Are Communities of Practice? A Comparative Review of Four Seminal Works," *Journal of Information Science* 31 (2005): 517–40.

3. Patricia Gongla and Christine Rizzuto, "Evolving Communities of Practice: IBM Global Services Experience," *IBM Systems Journal* 40 (2001): 842–62, quote from 843.

4. Etienne Martin Saint-Léon, *Le compagnonage: Son histoire, ses coutumes, ses règlements, ses rites* (Paris: Armand Colin, 1901).

5. Steven Shapin, *The Social History of Truth: Civility and Science in Seventeenth Century England* (Chicago: University of Chicago Press, 1994).

6. David Hounshell and John K. Smith, *Science and Corporate Strategy: DuPont R&D, 1902–1980* (Cambridge, UK: Cambridge University Press, 1988). The creation of the American Institute of Chemical Engineers in 1908 was an early step in the long process of professionalization. See also Terry Reynolds, *Seventy-Five Years of Progress: A History of the American Institute of Chemical Engineers* (New York: AIChE, 1983).

7. Noel Riley Fitch, *Appetite for Life* (New York: Doubleday, 1997); Gwen Hyman, "The Taste of Fame: Chefs, Diners, Celebrity, Class," *Gastronomica* 8.3 (2008): 43–52; Andrew Dornenberg and Karen Page, *Becoming a Chef* (New York: Wiley, 1995); Michael Ruhlman, *The Soul of a Chef* (New York: Penguin, 2000); Amy Trubeck, *Haute Cuisine: How the French*

Invented the Culinary Profession (Philadelphia: University of Pennsylvania Press, 2000); and Marc Stierand and Paul Lynch, "The Art of Creating Culinary Innovations," *Tourism and Hospitality Research* 8 (2008): 337–50 (a remarkable theoretical excursion by a veteran chef and a British business school professor). Interestingly, cooks in diners, bars, and fast food joints are workers and do not seem to fashion communities of practice, reinforcing the CoP's anchor in shared learning.

8. Pascal Le Masson and Benoît Weil, "Aux sources de la R&D: Genèse des théories de la conception réglée en Allemagne (1840–1960)," *Entreprises et Histoire*, no. 58 (2010): 11–50.

9. For the full story, see Nicholas Peppas and Robert Langer, "Origins and Development of Biomedical Engineering within Chemical Engineering," *AIChE Journal* 50 (2004): 536–46.

10. Patrick Fridenson, "Le rôle des petites entreprises, des grandes firmes et de l'Etat dans la percée de l'optronique militaire en France," in *Autour de l'industrie: Histoire et patrimoine. mélanges offerts à Denis Woronoff*, ed. Jean-François Belhoste, Serge Benoit, and Serge Chassagneal (Paris: CHEFF, 2004), 603–27, and Ivan Amato, *Stuff: The Materials the World Is Made Of* (New York: Avon, 1997), 88–103, quote from 103.

11. Joanne Roberts, "Limits to Communities of Practice," *Journal of Management Studies* 43 (2006): 623–39, quote from 634, and Peter Miskell, "Sustaining Creativity: What Can the Film Industry Teach Us about the Management of Creative Resources" (paper presented at the Association of Business Historians annual meeting, Reading, UK, July 2011).

12. Wenger, *Communities of Practice*, 16–41.

13. Ibid., 125–26.

14. Albert O. Hirschman, *Exit, Voice, and Loyalty: Responses to Decline in Firms, Organizations, and States* (Cambridge, MA: Harvard University Press, 1970).

15. For "routine," see Michael Cohen, Roger Burkhart, Giovanni Dosi, Massimo Egidi, Luigi Marengo, Massimo Warglein, and Sidney Winter, "Routines and Other Recurring Action Patterns of Organizations: Contemporary Research Issues," *Industrial and Corporate Change* 5 (1996): 654–98.

16. Kevin Borg, *Auto Mechanics: Technology and Expertise in Twentieth-Century America* (Baltimore: Johns Hopkins University Press, 2007); for a philosophical reflection on repairing things, see Matthew Crawford, *Shop Class as Soulcraft: An Inquiry into the Value of Work* (New York: Penguin, 2009).

17. Gongla and Rizzuto, "Evolving Communities of Practice"; Roberts, "Limits to Communities of Practice," 625, and Ash Amin and Joanne Roberts, "Knowing in Action: Beyond Communities of Practice," *Research Policy* 37 (2008): 353–69.

18. Cox, "What Are Communities of Practice?", 531, 535. Lars Lindkvist, taking account of the increasingly temporary character of employment, proposed a variation on CoPs— collectivities of practice, "groups consist[ing] of diversely skilled individuals, most of whom have not met before, who have to solve a problem or carry out a pre-specified task within tightly set limits as to time and costs." This brings the world of project management into focus, though again within a managerialist framework. See Lindkvist, "Knowledge Communities and Knowledge Collectivities," *Journal of Management Studies* 42 (2005): 1189–1210.

19. Timothy Spears, *One Hundred Years on the Road: The Traveling Salesman in American Culture* (New Haven: Yale University Press, 1995); Greg Downey, *Telegraph Messenger Boys: Labor, Technology, and Geography, 1850–1950* (New York: Routledge, 2002); David Lucskso, *The Business of Speed: The Hot Rod Industry in America, 1915–1990* (Baltimore: Johns Hopkins University Press, 2008); AnnaLee Saxenian, *Regional Advantage: Culture and Competition in Silicon Valley and Route 128* (Cambridge, MA: Harvard University Press, 1994); David Montgomery, *The Fall of the House of Labor* (New York: Cambridge University Press, 1989); and James R. Williams, *The Bull of the Woods*, 6 vols. (Almonte, ON: Algrove, 2002) (reprints of Scribner's published collections of *Iron Age* cartoons, now again out of print).

3. Flows

Strategy and Structure (1962), Alfred Chandler's classic historical analysis of four major US corporations, sparked a generation of business history research into the most prominent features of what Zygmunt Bauman has termed "solid modernity." In Europe, the Americas, and Japan, the century after 1870 brought the establishment of institutions, expectations, and behaviors that emphasized the deep investment of enterprises in people, production, and places; lifelong careers at increasingly massive companies; nation states as building blocks both for politics and culture and for brutal wars over territory and resources. Solid modernity "was the era of shaping reality after the manner of architecture or gardening; reality compliant with the verdicts of reason was to be 'built' under strict quality control . . . and first of all *designed* before the construction works begin."

That world is no longer with us, except insofar as we hold in our imaginations a range of solid modern "zombie concepts," dead ideas still walking about, long past their expiration dates.[1] Twenty-first-century actors inhabit a "liquid modern" world framed less by structures and more by flows—some moving at lightning speed globally, others at a slower or more erratic pace, and all disrupting, melting, and devaluing the solidity exhibited by increasingly eclipsed, earlier forms of modernity.[2]

Of course, there have always been flows in business history; indeed, making them quicker and more reliable was essential to the industries and technologies of the transportation and communications revolutions. Yet characteristically we have focused on institutions and devices, not on what was flowing and the ways shifts in the rates, volumes, values, and composition of flows conditioned business practice, both shaping and constraining opportunities. Think about what might be the range of "routine" flows, their scope ranging from the local and interpersonal to the transnational and impersonal, and their contents changing over time, each offering a venue for business historical research, each having institutional locations, orientations, and actors:

1. Funds—as capital investments, payments, loans, fees, fines, restitutions, remittances, handled by transnational financial enterprises, transfer agencies, regulatory advisers, smugglers, etc.

2. Information/knowledge—as documents, wired/wireless messages, transmissions, images, data, processed through book dealers, publishers (including governments), communications enterprises, or satellite image and data technologies, for example.

3. People—as migrants, job seekers, visitors, refugees, armies, spies, managers, agents, missionaries, merchants, sales reps, scientists, engineers, inventors, journalists, academics, physicians, students, consultants, and diplomats, whose movements are facilitated by transportation companies, labor recruiters, short-term housing providers, and mapmakers.

4. Culture and practices—as foodways, fashions, arts and music, protocols and standards, measurements, classifications, accounting, codification, procedures for making, using, repairing, and disposal, all circulated through commercial market relations, auctions, gift-giving, the work of nongovernmental agencies, standards authorities, and the like.

5. Artifacts and technologies—as tools, machinery, household, artistic, and personal goods, power systems, weapons, routinely translated to new terrains through technology transfer and adaptation, through conquest, colonial imposition, and collecting, that is, through both economic and political initiatives.

6. Services—including insurance, wholesaling, and distribution, haulage and shipping, investment and managerial consulting, legal and psychological counseling, all of which operate through well-known institutions.

7. "Natural" materials—like agricultural and extractive commodities (wheat, fish, timber, ores), animals (sheep, birds, insects), mold, bacteria, viruses, whose character, quality, and threat profiles are established by classification, inspection, and boundary-maintaining agencies and firms.

From this roster, it is not difficult to configure scores of research questions that reach far beyond the realm of studying diffusion (often focused on technologies) or immigration (which ignores most human movement) into analyzing diverse and intersecting flows, particularly insofar as they are elements in transitions into solid modernity, from solid to liquid modernity, and from predominantly local and national to transnational and globalized flows. Lest any linearity creep into exploring the history of flows and the "space of flows,"[3] we need only recollect the massive disconnects that twentieth-century wars, hot and cold, brought to existing flow patterns or imagine what a twenty-first-century tripling of transportation fuel costs would do to stall or reverse vectors within liquid modern trends.

One possible target for business history research into recent flows would be the implementation of barcodes as nodal sites for information flows at multiple levels: providing data on prices and quantities of goods sold, placed in inventories, shipped, etc., offering insights into consumers' preferences and practices (as individuals or in particular places), generating critically important accounting figures for enterprises, and when purchases are completed electronically, delivering consumption profiles over time to credit/debit card issuers.[4] Issues of design and costs, enterprise formation, marketing tactics, equipment development, the circulation of devices between different parts of the globe, then producer/packager/retailer resistance or acceptance of them, plus operational failures, implementation beyond retailing, and state policies about information gathering and use can all be built into a research design that probes the fabrication of high-speed, precision flows in the late twentieth century.[5]

Another multifaceted locale for flows would be ports, entrepôts where goods, people, information, technologies, funds, diseases, information, culture, and practices circulate and interact in transnational transactions. Looking seaward can provide a corrective to land- and structure-based teleologies centered on industrialization and deindustrialization dynamics, helping us to perceive the unpredictability (and unreliability) of ocean-based flows, a phenomenon as familiar to the adventurers of the seventeenth century as to the oil tanker owners of the twenty-first century (each facing hostile states and pirates). Regarding imports and exports as clusters of practices based on complex knowledge requirements, deep interpersonal relations, and often poorly understood markets may bring to life dull tariff debates, tired ideological postures, and mind-numbing tabulations of quantities and values.

Finally, working with flows invites consideration of themes and phenomena both common and unknown in business history: channeling and regulation; floods and droughts; blockages, contamination, and purification; pooling and turbulence; movement's rates and volumes—all of which have historical and spatial presences and dimensions across each of the seven classes sketched above. Pursuing intersections and interactions among them—for example, in relation to contamination brought by individuals, bacteria, degenerate practices, offensive goods, or fake money—could richly delineate cultural dimensions of situated business practices, their tensions, contradictions, and transformations.[6]

NOTES

1. Quote from Zygmunt Bauman, *Liquid Modernity* (Oxford: Polity, 2000), 47. Bauman credits "zombie concepts" to Ulrich Beck. See Bauman, ibid., 6, and Ulrich Beck and Johannes Wilms, *Conversations with Ulrich Beck* (Oxford: Polity, 2004), 19.

2. Late-modernizing regions may recapitulate elements of solid-style industrialization, as with reliance on coal for fuel and electricity generation in China and Central Europe, while earlier industrial powers now seek decentralized, even fluid, energy sources from sun, wind, and tides. Great unevenness in any broad-gauged transition like this is to be expected.

3. A term Arjun Appadurai coined. See his *Modernity at Large: Culture Dimensions of Globalization* (Minneapolis: University of Minnesota Press, 1996). Appadurai's work resonates with Bauman's approach, stressing the intersection between electronic communications and mass migrations, for example.

4. Stephen Brown, *Revolution at the Checkout Counter: The Explosion of the Bar Code* (Cambridge, MA: Wertheim/Harvard, 1997), was an early study. For an overview of the more flexible RFID system, which does not need line-of-sight scanning, see Chin-Boo Soon, "Radio Frequency Identification: History and Development," at http://64.225.152.8/down loads/excerpts/33350.pdf (accessed 11 Apr. 2011).

5. Katja Girschik, *Als die Kassen lesen lernten. eine Technikgeschichte des Schweizer Einzelhandels, 1950–1975* (Munich: Beck, 2010). Dissertation abstract available at http://e-collection .library.ethz.ch/eserv/eth:244/eth-244-01.pdf (Accessed 11 Apr. 2011).

6. Theoretical work relevant to this theme includes, Manuel Castells, *The Information Age: Economy, Society, and Culture*, 2nd ed., 3 vols. (2000; New York: Wiley, 2010); Arjun Appadurai, *Modernity at Large*; and Ulrich Beck, *Risk Society: Towards a New Modernity* (Thousand Oaks, CA: Sage, 1992).

4. Follow the Actors

Many scholars are in a way like business consultants: they like to design categories, to identify mechanisms, to apply laws or typologies. Viewed from such perspectives, human actors are puppets or automatons. They do not matter as such or very much. They just need to align their practices to "the one best way," as American engineer and consultant Frederick W. Taylor articulated it at the end of the nineteenth century. Otherwise they fail. The only capabilities that are decisive for managing such people are incentives and control. An interpretation from a different perspective leads nevertheless to the same conclusion. Here individuals are to a large extent represented as unconscious agents, who obey various hidden determinations that frame their actions. They do not, in general, understand what they are doing, much less why. These two characterizations are profoundly misleading.

First, the discourse of the actors in firms or associations is not a pure illusion. All sorts of actors want to express values and creeds, and it is by paying attention to them that some behaviors or moves can be explained. For instance, in the mid-nineteenth century, midwestern entrepreneur Leander McCormick refused to shift to mass production of reapers, as he had embraced an ideal of quality outputs, relying on skilled labor.[1] In Eastern France, the nineteenth-century glassmakers of Baccarat, fervent Catholics, were among the earliest enterprise owners to develop industrial hygiene for their wage earners.[2]

Second, actors who are not at the top of organizations are not merely subordinates of business leaders. They are sometimes able to conceive options that substantially add to the policy designed by top management. The young managers of General Motors' varnish and painting department proposed a decentralized structure in 1920 and experimented with it at a time when the CEO and main owner of the corporation, Pierre du Pont, could see salvation for the near-bankrupt GM only in increased centralization.[3] Actors who are not in command may have the imagination and the open space to innovate. In the early 1960s, a group of production engineers at Sochaux, the main plant of the French carmaker Peugeot, appeared to have created a new version of the assembly line, rather similar to the approach pioneered in Japan by Toyota. However, it was rejected by the corporate hierarchy. The designs were only recently discovered by a business historian, thanks to oral history interviewing.[4] Finally, various actors devise ways to challenge the orders they have received. Local agents of multinationals may resort to corruption to keep their operations active in an environment where bribes are expected, and under such circumstances they will do their best to conceal such practices from their principals. Alternatively, actors at all levels may ignore ill-designed directives because they judge that they know realities in the field (or "on the ground") better than their superiors, who may be distant, overburdened, underinformed, or striving for uniformity. In both cases, business historians can show that, contrary to conventional wisdom, strategies have failed or companies have survived due to the autonomy of some actors.

Furthermore, business history often demonstrates that minor actors can have the power to damage a firm's performance. They may ignore safety instructions, as nineteenth-century workers at Delaware's DuPont powder works did, in order to emphasize their masculinity, risking accidents.[5] They may retain for themselves information of major interest (and potential value) to the enterprise, imagining perhaps starting their own firm on the basis of a laboratory discovery or bringing down an overbearing boss by encouraging the defection of an important client to other providers. Historians therefore try to reconstitute both the public and the tacit knowledge actors have employed (along with identifying gaps in such knowledge). They strive to recreate and map the networks that actors create or in which they participate, as well as the ways in which hierarchies can be (and have been) bypassed.

Third, actors may be able to access resources outside the firm. These may be in other businesses: connections with suppliers, distributors, or bankers provide them means—or biases—that organizational charts cannot reflect. The resources may also be located in the larger society: being a graduate of an English public school like Eton (or an American one like Groton), an alumnus of a French engineering *école* or a Japanese imperial (later national) university may generate executive opportunities that sheer economic analysis could neither predict nor illuminate. Actors as well may have links based on region, ethnicity, religion, freemasonry, or fraternal organizations. This complexity stands at a great distance from either the managerial or psychological simplifications noted above. Thus, there is every reason for business historians to keep constantly in mind the precept coined by French sociologist Bruno Latour, "Follow the actors!"[6]

Yet, this central rule for understanding how business is created, works, and changes deserves a few comments. Following the actors is a valuable means through which to identify what today are often called the stakeholders in a business environment, some of whom are far from the operating center. These include, taking an enterprise as a base point, active and downsized workers, managers, board members, shareholders, retirees, company record keepers, legal counsel and financial advisors—all close to the core of the firm. However, other stakeholders are regulators and other agencies, bankers, mutual fund managers, community members, employees' families, environmentalists, preservationists, and politicians, nonprofits, or educational institutions in communities or nations where the business operates, and so on. Thinking broadly about what actors (and what intentions) can be articulated within and around a firm substantially alters our usual concepts of management, control, planning, and operations. Enterprise or project outcomes arise from complex, unpredictable interactions among multiple "players," which undercuts simplistic notions of strategy, compelling leadership, or management by the numbers.[7]

Moreover, different actors do not necessarily see or hear the same things, as their filters for gathering information reflect social background, life and work experience, position in the enterprise, fear, ambition, and much else. Thus it is often effective to write a business history of a process, an event, a program or project, a structure, or an object so that the multiple lenses and voices of actors can be represented. Moreover, by contrast, actors do not see or hear some things that take place in front of them, due to the same filters or to the fact that what is taking place is unanticipated, complex, or difficult to apprehend. In any situation there may be possibilities of which actors have no knowledge or awareness but which materialize over time. Here historians need to use collateral sources (external to the firm or project, for example), national or international comparisons, or the tools of other social sciences to contextualize actors' historical understandings, explanations, or errors. In short, they should mobilize both professional resources and their own imaginations.

NOTES

1. David Hounshell, *From the American System to Mass Production* (Baltimore: Johns Hopkins University Press, 1984).

2. Caroline Moriceau, *Les douleurs de l'industrie* (Paris: Editions de l'EHESS, 2009).

3. Alfred D. Chandler, *Strategy and Structure* (Cambridge, MA: MIT Press, 1962).

4. Nicolas Hatzfeld, *Les gens de l'usine* (Paris: Editions de l'Atelier, 2002).

5. Christopher McKenna, "Better Living through Chemistry: Industrial Accidents and Masculinity at DuPont, 1890–1930," *Entreprises et Histoire*, no. 17 (1997): 9–23.

6. Bruno Latour, *Science in Action: How to Follow Scientists and Engineers through Society* (Cambridge, MA: Harvard University Press, 1987).

7. For an effective analysis of such a complex dynamic, see Bruno Latour, *Aramis, or the Love of Technology* (Cambridge, MA: Harvard University Press, 1997). Aramis was a highly sophisticated, driverless transit system designed for Paris in the 1980s, and Latour here undertakes to show, through following the actors involved, why it was abandoned after considerable investment in planning and prototypes. Travelers at Paris's Charles de Gaulle airport ride between terminals and rail stations on an automated, driverless descendent of Aramis.

5. Futures Past

Recalling the past (remembering) occurs only with the intention of making it possible to foresee the future; we look about us from the standpoint of the present in order to determine something, or to be prepared for something.

—*Immanuel Kant,* Anthropology from a Pragmatic
Point of View

As the present no longer predictably emerged from the past, neither could the future be foretold from the present.

—*David Lowenthal, "The Forfeit of the Future"*

How are our ideas of the future constructed, and what role do they play in our present activity? How have "futures" changed over the centuries in the West, the East, and the South? Before the modern era, European futures were anticipated by extrapolating from the past, just as neoclassical economics still does, but that expectation collapsed with the wars, economic upheavals, and revolutions (political and intellectual) of the eighteenth century. The imaginary of progress replaced extrapolation and replication, but by what process?[1] What makes the future change, even as we learned through twentieth-century crises, dislocations, and disjunctures that progress is a chimera and tomorrow is no longer reliable? Why do historians conceptualize and write history differently in different eras? This is the domain of "futures past"—as historians recurrently mobilize different pasts to address present concerns and to highlight future possibilities.

Scholars engaging these questions see the Enlightenment as anchoring a crucial transition: "A future so radical in its openness and unpredictability annulled the present utility of past experience."[2] Henceforth, historians would mine the past in order to construct narratives relevant to the perceived dynamics of present change, rather than creating moral chronicles to reinforce transcendent values. (That older tradition survives in memoirs, not least those of business leaders.) Among American business historians, amid deep Cold War anxieties, a focus on major corporations and business-government relations served to restore confidence in leading businesses battered by the Great Depression, unionization struggles, and antitrust lawsuits. Similar perceptions of transitional economic and political dynamics animated Italian and German business history in the 1970s and French business history in the 1980s. Indeed, nothing so well indicates that business historians sought to emancipate their field from the dead hand of the past as the core German journal's name change from *Tradition* to *Zeitschrift für Unternehmensgeschichte* [Business History] in 1976). In the spirit of Reinhart Koselleck's "radical historicization of the historical interpreter,"[3] what we seek here is to open the door to a post–Cold War, globally alert business history, recognizing that historical fields that do not reinvent themselves periodically become unintentionally ahistorical.

Yet amid these shifting tides, one element of continuity is the "durability of the linguistic 'superstructure,' in contrast to a more fragile and changing 'base' of economic and social arrangements." In the flux of late-modern instabilities, narratives help sustain communities: "In times of turmoil and rapid change . . . meaningful interpretations of reality are precious resources to which people tenaciously cling."[4] In such circumstances language deeply matters to action and behavior, to the way we conceive of problems and contextualize them. What holds us together are frameworks of meaning that are simultaneously resources for action, with historians, among others, being culturally responsible for fashioning and updating such frameworks. In this process, Koselleck's reflections on how our concerns for the future invest our transformation of the past into histories are salient. Four dimensions of his perspectives concern us: temporal multi-layeredness, the space of experience and the horizon of expectation, events and surprise, and repetition as the basis for knowledge.

Temporal experiences are multilayered, involving at least three separate but mutually constituted "planes." First, we have the awareness of short-term successions, befores and afters, from a few minutes to several years in duration. These present severe difficulties for anyone attempting predictions. Second, we recognize "middle term trends deriving from the course of events [including] transpersonal conditions [which] exert an influence on what is happening." On this plane, we find wars and generational transitions, which often have repeated characteristics and permit historical "arguments by analogy." Third, we encounter "metahistorical duration," the domain where "anthropological constants . . . elude the historical pressure for change." These cultural residuals and processes provide "doctrines with direct instructions for action," like the proverb "Pride goeth before a fall." Moreover, in modernity the relations among the three have changed. Short-term prognoses have become even more problematic, "because the number of factors that must enter into them has multiplied." Middle-term "transpersonal constants" have "changed with increasing speed in the last 200 years" as technology and industry have penetrated societies, such that "presuppositions" about life courses "change more quickly." Last, "formerly long-lasting constraints," which stabilized mid- and short-term behavior, "have themselves come under increased pressure of change," with the compression of space, reshaping of gender roles, and radical expansion of access to information. We act inside all three temporal spheres, even when we are not aware of them. Moreover, as the preceding suggests, in light of present circumstances, we may identify a different long or middle term than our predecessors did, reorganizing our periodization of the past. Conversely, on occasion a moment arrives that actors agree is transformative, but this proves to be a misconception. Isn't it remarkable to see how 1989 has diminished as marking, globally, the end of an era?

For business historians, we might suggest that a useful set of long-, middle- and short-term planes could be: long term—capitalist development and commodification; middle term—incorporation and regulation (of course other middle-term planes are available); and short term—financialization and crisis. The short is nested within the middle (along with many other shorts), the middle within the long. For Japan, we could identify: long—learning from and then overtaking the West, 1870–2000; middle—imperial impulses and defeat, 1920s–1945; and short—creating precision watches for the military, 1938–1944.[5] Of what value is this exercise? At a minimum it shows that short-term phenomena are doubly situated within mid- and long-term planes, indeed perhaps in more than one of them. In addition, it reminds us that the "uniform and empty time" of modernity now gives way "to a composite and non-homogeneous temporality, full of 'holes, recesses, and gradients.'"[6] This understanding exemplifies "the typical late-modern awareness of the radical complexity of time, of its structural stratification which renders it constitutionally incapable of being reduced to the generalities of a common unit of measure."[7]

On the second theme, Koselleck observes that "every human being and every human community has a *space of experience* out of which one acts, in which past things are present or can be remembered, [yet] one always acts with reference to specific *horizons of expectation*."[8] This refers to anticipations and decisions that are activated by the intersection of a past that carries on and a future that crowds in—a present past and a future present. The space of experience configures "the available past for any given present," and the horizon of expectations represents "the cutting edge of future possibilities for any given present." Both are evident in historical acts or events, influence efforts to explain them, and change over time and in their relationship.[9] In sum, "it is the tension between experience and expectation which, in ever-changing patterns, brings about new resolutions and through this generates historical time."[10] So, how do business decisions reflect simultaneous appropriations from past practice and memory, along with expectations for possible futures? How might this help explain contests and crises in policymaking, as individual parties put in play incompatible perspectives? What might we learn from developing a cultural history of business visions for economy and society, in different eras and locales? Given that training encapsulates the past and prepares for the future, researching the history of vocational and corporate education schemes can identify key values, goals, and visions articulated by governments and enterprises alike, the choices made and the options discarded. After all, it appears that training has been expanding in recent decades, with a revival of apprenticeships in Europe, accompanied by the multiplication of corporate "universities" to instruct incoming employees and augment the skills of veteran workers.[11]

A related issue arises from the Ford Motor Company's 1949 decision to build a new engine plant in Cleveland, Ohio. Board members received an extensive briefing book, outlining a number of possible plans, but the plant that was built followed none of them; it was not a compromise among the options but was something substantially different. As there are no minutes available, there is a gap in our understanding of the decision process. Even were there a transcript, it wouldn't show heads nodding, fingers pointing, or eyebrows lifting during the discussion. As Naomi Lamoreaux explains, this "lays bare, in almost archetypal fashion, the existence of something that lies at the heart of all decisions—not just in business but in all human experience: what philosopher John

Searle calls 'the gap.'" This term references "the space between the reasons for a decision and the actual decision made. The gap exists because none of the reasons for taking an action is causally sufficient to produce the decision to act."[12] Individuals must consider alternatives and choose, but we rarely have access to this process. The reasons participants give may not be reliable, because people lie. Moreover, "under conditions of uncertainty, individuals cannot rank-order choices independently of the way the options are framed," in this case by those who defined and presented them. The result is post hoc justification (see Traps, 5: Retrospective Rationalization) for "the right course of action always seems clear after the fact."[13]

This surely poses a problem for narrative. There is an open space between the access historians have to the available past and the future possibilities entwined in decision-making. These elements "cannot be related to one another in a static way. They constitute a temporal difference within the here and now, by joining together the past and the future in an asymmetric way."[14] The past is known, at least partially, whereas the future is projected and unknowable. Known possibilities vanish once a decision is made, and that decision becomes a part of, while changing, a future available past. Thus historians have to work on a probability scale, trying to establish the most likely available past in a given situation by creating links among plausible actions; but this isn't the same as having access to the actors' available pasts, which will themselves be heterogeneous.

Experience is a crucial term in this domain, and like all other elements of this approach, it is neither uniform nor singular, not reducible to perception and movement. Three sorts of experiences constitute our historical sensibilities: "surprise at the unpredictably new, the realization of the repetition of what has already been well-known, [and] the reflexive awareness of directly unperceptible changes."[15] We notice the unexpected, which reminds us that it wasn't there some time ago—a time-consciousness sparked into life. This phenomenon helps account for why there is no business history of continuity; we always talk about change, but it's crucial to remember that continuities are sturdy carriers of meaning and agents for coherence. David Edgerton took this point fully in drafting histories of humble technologies that transformed or sustained lives.[16] Integrating studies of change and innovation with coexistent continuities in practice or meaning would be valuable.

This leads to the second variety of historically sensitizing experience, the realization of repetition. Here actors enter reflexive time by noting that they have encountered, used, fixed, or implemented this or that before, perhaps many times. Indeed, "we constantly sift events into patterns of recurrence and repetition to create a 'space of experience.'" Without repetition, information cannot graduate to knowledge; as Koselleck concluded, "knowledge is always *re*-cognition. But novelty signals disappointed anticipation, *anomaly*,"[17] as our expectation of stability is interrupted. Business historians might reasonably ask: What are the knowledge-generating repetitions in business, and whence do they come? How do enterprises respond to novelty or anomaly, brought to the nuclear power industry by Three Mile Island or Chernobyl or to jazz and swing bands by national radio broadcasts, challenging local live music venues?[18] Similarly, how are past and future combined in annual planning, as when, since the 1920s, radio broadcasters devised the next season's grid of shows, scheduling that was part repetition and part novelty?[19]

Finally, departments, businesses, and associations on all scales plan for the future and have done so for centuries. In one of the earliest business plans, from the hand of Pierre-Samuel du Pont (ca. 1800), he developed key themes for exploration, experimentation, and simulation at his growing gunpowder works.[20] A new stage in this development surfaced in the early twentieth century, with published handbooks of business plans (1916) alongside accounting manuals and compendia of business forms. This pattern remains true even in the present age of standardized management tools, from checklists and worksheets through sophisticated systems for strategic planning.

Nonetheless, a business plan is never a stabilization of conditions but rather an opening to possibilities, because it organizes the circulation of information and encourages both reflexive thinking and some level of inventiveness. These tools appear during a time of uncertainty and individuation, offering a lifeboat to anxious managers seeking to control the future, but they rarely are capable of achieving this. Planning schematics are not only implemented by large corporations; they have also been utilized by more modest firms, like grocery stores, flower shops, and gasoline stations. Plans may not travel well, however. As head of Nissan in Japan from 1999 to 2005, Carlos Ghosn executed two planning cycles with remarkable results, but when he moved to Renault and implemented the same planning process in France, it failed to be effective. In recent decades, according to Henry Mintzberg, strategic planning has experienced a gradual decline;[21] but, as with scientific management or value engineering in the mid-twentieth century, it will either be reconstructed or succeeded by novel formulations for "handling" present complexities and "assuring" profitable futures.

NOTES

Epigraphs. Immanuel Kant, *Anthropology from a Pragmatic Point of View* (Carbondale: Southern Illinois University Press, 1978), 77, quoted in Reinhart Koselleck, *The Practice of Conceptual History: Timing History, Spacing Concepts* (Stanford: Stanford University Press, 2002), 133. David Lowenthal, "The Forfeit of the Future," *Futures* 27 (1995): 358.

1. For studies of the history of the future, see Simon Schama, *The American Future: A History* (New York: Ecco, 2009), and Lawrence Samuel, *Future: A Recent History* (Austin: University of Texas Press, 2010).

2. John Zammito, "Koselleck's Philosophy of Historical Time(s) and the Practice of History," *History and Theory* 43 (2004): 124–35, quote from 127.

3. Ibid., 131.

4. Geoffrey Herf, "Multiple Restorations vs. the Solid South: Continuities and Discontinuities in Germany after 1945 and the American South after 1865," in *Different Restorations: Reconstruction and "Wieder aufbau" in Germany and the United States, 1865–1955,* ed. Norbert Finsch and Jürgen Martschukat (Oxford: Berghahn Books, 1996), 51–52.

5. Pierre-Yves Donzé, "The Hybrid Production System and the Birth of Japanese Specialized Industry: Watch Production at Hattori and Co. (1900–1960)," *Enterprise and Society* 12 (2011): 356–97.

6. Luca Scuccimarra, "Semantics of Time and Historical Experience: Remarks on Koselleck's *Historik,*" *Contributions to the History of Concepts* 4 (2008): 160–75, quote from 163–64.

7. Ibid., 172.

8. Koselleck, *Practice of Conceptual History,* 111, emphasis added.

9. Scuccimarra, "Semantics," 129.

10. Reinhart Koselleck, *Futures Past: On the Semantics of Historical Time* (New York: Columbia University Press, 1985; repr. Cambridge, MA: MIT Press, 1990), 275.

11. Scott Taylor and Rob Paton, "Corporate Universities: Historical Development, Conceptual Analysis, and Relations with Public Sector Higher Education," The Open University, 2002, available at http://oro.open.ac.uk/id/eprint/23734, and Peter Holland and Amanda Pymer, "Corporate Universities: A Catalyst for Strategic Human Relations Ddevelopment," *Journal of European Industrial Training* 30 (2006): 19–31.

12. Naomi Lamoreaux, "Reframing the Past: Thoughts about Business Leadership and Decision Making under Uncertainty," *Enterprise and Society* 2 (2001): 632–59, quote from 643–44.

13. Ibid, 644–45, 647.

14. Koselleck, *Practice of Conceptual History,* 127.

15. Scuccimarra, "Semantics," 172.

16. David Edgerton, *The Shock of the Old: Technology and Global History since 1900* (Oxford: Oxford University Press, 2007).

17. Zammito, "Koselleck's Philosophy," 129.

18. James Kraft, *Stage to Studio: Musicians and the Sound Revolution, 1890–1950* (Baltimore: Johns Hopkins University Press, 2003).

19. Susan Douglas, *Inventing American Broadcasting, 1899–1922* (Baltimore: Johns Hopkins University Press, 1997), and Gregory Lowe and Taisto Hujanen, "Broadcasting and

Convergence: Rearticulating the Future Past," in *Broadcasting and Convergence*, ed. Gregory Lowe and Taisto Hujanen (Goteborg: Nordicom, 2003), 9–25.

20. Martin Giraudeau, "The Making of the Future: An Historical Sociology of Business Plans," *economic sociology_the european electronic newsletter* 11.3 (July 2010): 78–79, available at http://econsoc.mpi-fg-koeln.mpg.de/archive/econ_soc_11-3.pdf#page=77 (accessed 11 July 2011).

21. Henry Mintzberg, *The Rise and Fall of Strategic Planning: Reconceiving Roles for Planning, Plans, Planners* (New York: Simon & Schuster, 1994).

6. Memory

History is memory cultivated in the interest of producing a "collective" past on the basis of which a collective identity can be forged.

—*Hayden White, "Guilty of History?"*

Attempting to remember has a truthful ambition and should not be criticized for that, as we have nothing better.

—*Scott Taylor, Bill Cooke, and Emma Bell,*
"Business History and the Historiographical Operation"

What one does not see and what one should not expect to see [in written archives] is what actors live and experience. What one sees remains social life in interaction: a thin interaction, but already microstructured.

—*Paul Ricoeur, La mémoire, l'histoire, l'oubli*

Memory is fundamental to history because remembering leads individuals and organizations to preserve documents and images as well as to fashion stories based in part on them. We begin here by outlining four dimensions of memory—private, professional, public, and organizational—before turning to their implications for the practice of business history. Private or individual memory should be regarded as partly voluntary (recall) and partly involuntary (unbidden flashbacks). It can never provide complete truth, but it does inform narratives, often drafted in memoir form. Individual memory is constantly revised; retelling events will induce changes because of each person's continuing experiences. Professional or historical memory also takes a narrative form and frequently relies on memories, written or oral; but it can also conflict with individual memory. Witnesses, for example, regularly claim greater understanding than historians. "I was there" or "I know better" for them is adequate justification. Like private memory, professional memory is revised in retelling, but it is governed by "sources," to which individuals can remain indifferent. Unlike individual memory, professional memory's links to education are deep, as education's formal structures are organized around historical conceptions that animate disciplines (e.g., improvement, progress, standing on the shoulders of giants, or genealogy). Moreover, "history is as much about forgetting as about remembering . . . a great deal of history has been written in order to cover over or hide or deflect attention from 'what really happened' in the past by creating an 'official version'" that repels critique.[1]

In turn, professional memory contributes to public or collective memory, as histories accumulate synthetic narratives of the past. When informing public memory, history has dual missions: to find and speak the truth and to sort truth from falsehood. To be sure, collective memories can be disrupted and dislocated by wars, forced migrations, and epidemics (at the societal level) and by downsizing, layoffs, and mergers (at the firm level). In addition, increased employee mobility, voluntary or not, and projects that pull people out of established groups and shift their experiences and commitments have a similar effect. Collective memory can be fragmented or largely erased, if a company or sectoral collapse is neither challenged nor memorialized. Indeed, when companies shrink or die or plants close, displaced workers experience individual grief and collective loss, though they may retain "continuing bonds," emotional and historical, with their former work sites.[2] In contrast to fragmentation and separation, communities of practice (see Resources, 2: Communities of Practice) foster all three dimensions of memory thus far introduced, which may well be one reason why some management scholars advocate that steps be taken to prevent their formation among employees (hiring many part-timers, moving staff frequently, or changing the composition of project teams).[3]

Nations, regions, and cities have what might be termed collective memories *of* businesses, which vary geographically, from dictatorships to republics or from stable or growing urban areas to distressed, decaying, or rebuilding cities. Think of Goodyear and Firestone as memory tokens for Akron, Citibank and J. P. Morgan for New York, or Toyota at Toyota City. Germans doubtless have conflicted, fragmented memories of leading corporations during the Nazi era.[4] Business historians might profit from inquiring about the purposes such memories serve and the mechanisms and incentives for their preservation and reinterpretation.

Organizational memory as a category was introduced as a spinoff from the "discovery" of corporate culture in the 1970s and 1980s. Its originators quoted Karl Weick as an opening gambit: "If an organization is to learn anything, then the distribution of its memory, the accuracy of that memory, and the conditions under which it is treated as a constraint become crucial characteristics of organizing."[5] James Walsh and Gerardo Ungson offered a definition in their keystone 1991 article: "Organizational memory refers to stored information that can be brought to bear on present decisions." Significantly, "an organization may preserve knowledge of the past even when key organizational members leave."[6] Useful questions include: Where is this memory located? By what processes is it "acquired, stored, and retrieved"? How does it matter and to what end (outcomes, planning, solidarity, efficacy)? Most commonly, organizational memory is kept or encoded in files, computers, archives, procedures, standards, expectations (behavior, hierarchy) and allocations (space, amenities, budgets). It is carried forward by individuals, organizational culture, work designs, formal and informal structures, and by outsiders (clients, consumers, former employees).[7] This form of memory also exists between firms. When Yuitiru Kojima, the Toyota supplier mentioned in another entry, resisted launching a parts plant in China, one of Kiichiro Toyoda's sons made this appeal to him: "You are one of the few remaining people who know and worked with our father. You cannot leave us on the basis of such a disagreement." Plucking, in Michael Kammen's terms, the "mystic chords of memory" worked quite well, and Toyota's China supply-chain program went ahead.[8]

When organizational memory is itself organized, the process is selective, purposive, and connected to power. Hence, memory in enduring organizations is regularly a matter of competition. Scholars have recently criticized the Walsh and Ungson version of organizational memory (OM) as presenting a "repository image," arguing that OM is actually politicized and unstable, "subject to the influence of powerful organizational actors." For example, Henry Ford II sponsored an early oral history project (some hundred and fifty interviews, all transcribed) to establish a definitive biography of the founder, but his hidden agenda was to document how the company had declined during the last decade of his grandfather's management.[9] Organizational memory is put to the test following mergers or acquisitions and spinoffs and needs then to be rebuilt or reconfigured, another political process. What happens to consumers' or stakeholders' memories when a company name, brand, or product line changes? When General Electric moved heavily into financial services, old hands in the engineering side of the firm were deeply disturbed. Likewise, when U.S. Steel invested capital, not to upgrade technology and facilities, but to purchase an oil company, morale among veteran managers sagged.[10]

Media enterprises are also contestants in struggles to control organizational and collective memory. These battles are political to the extent that memory shapes the environment for public or corporate policy, choice, financial allocations, and planning. Preservation and heritage initiatives are at times not just cultural conservation efforts; they may generate business opportunities and thus trigger broadly-political decisions about what to abandon and what to restore and exploit. Such activity creates material touchstones for business history. Venues abound for researching the politics of business memorialization in repurposed factories, museums, website histories, industrial films, war memorials, and commissioned histories.[11] Here it is important as well to appreciate that the accumulation of decisions and experiences alters the platform for later memorials. (See Resources, 5: Futures Past.)

Finally, is memory positive or negative for an organization? It can inhibit innovation or make a firm a hostage to routines reinscribing the past, yet according to Hirschman, memory can also be a foundation for loyalty. Consider the difference between executive suites with long rows of former leaders' portraits in their entryways or lining their corridors versus those decorated with company ads, plant views, or bland abstract art. Here the choice and placement of historical images along with changes in their use may tell a story about organizational memory different from that offered by the firm's public relations department or the packaged website history.

We may also look for organizational memory beyond the firm, seeking to identify key "professional memory builders" in the enterprise ecology. Credit raters, litigators and courts, banks, trade associations, newspapers, and journals all gather and archive organizational memories, even as other agents labor professionally to destroy them. Fashion industry firms have futures but no pasts (at least in business terms, except when attempting style revivals); consultants and law firms urge clients to discard or destroy records. In France, when Citroën moved factories and offices from southwest Paris to a suburb, all archival material was dumped, except for the Legal Department records, preserved to defend against future lawsuits. In the United States, by contrast, legal advisors differ about whether archived records open to discovery will facilitate litigation defeats or whether they are necessary for effective defenses.

These "memory building" exercises have a long history: by 1871, Crédit Lyonnais had established its own Department of Financial and Industrial Surveys, tracking opportunities presented by commercial and industrial firms, in and beyond France. Within a generation, the department had covered the activities and prospects of "51,000 companies and 243 local and national governments."[12] Another group of memory builders are the organizers and promoters of spectaculars, entertainments, and fairs (including expositions and world's fairs), from the time of the Crystal Palace to Disney's theme park mobilizations of history, as magnets for travel and consumption. However, the presence of Euro Disney and Cité des Sciences et de l'Industrie in and near Paris has drawn so many millions of visitors that neither Renault nor PSA (Peugeot Citroën) have opened their vast historic auto collections to the public—the threshold of profitability is too high and the competition too stiff. Thus does the commercialization of memory constrain the range of memories that can be commercialized.

Business historians considering approaching memory phenomena in research might wish to explore individual memory in and beyond organizations, social and cultural memories of products, brands, services, networks, or organizations (both of which are affected by market trends, crises, mergers and acquisitions, strikes, or bankruptcies), and objects, buildings, and landscapes that serve as sites for or carriers of memory. Further, when memory is voiced as testimony, ample source material for historical analysis emerges, as testimony is "the process of making memory documentary. . . . Memory is externalized in testimony, inscribed, preserved [in archives] and sometimes used by historians."[13] Hence a schematic might be drawn in which memory, testimony, archives, and history are linked to one another with multiple feedback loops, in which archives supplement testimony and can refresh memory, and in which histories both rely on testimony and archives and reshape memory as they are disseminated.

Business historians might well expand the four memory categories noted above to include visual and process memories, which, we would suggest, pertain chiefly to individuals and organizations. Visual memories are pointillist fragments of recall, not necessarily narratives, but that we store them in minds or files indicates their significance. We may recognize visual memories as something like still photographs or home movies, or indeed we may have recollections of actual photographs and family film presentations. Visual memories are thus a jumble of impressions, but they can be reorganized into narratives, as oral historians using visuals with respondents have shown. Visual impressions and discursive memories may inform operating decisions from the shop floor to the executive suite, perhaps more than we imagine. As Weick once slyly observed, "Any decision maker is only as good as his memory."[14] Process memories concern how to do things—a soldier's ability to take his rifle apart and reassemble it in the dark, a machinist's aural memory of a lathe being overtaxed by the job at hand, a manager's recollection of the steps needed to get a project proposal approved. For business history, this is how memory is linked to routines, which are, on the one hand, consolidated into manuals, forms, and flowcharts, but on the other, as here, performed by people at particular places and times for specific purposes.

Taylor, Cooke, and Bell offer an arresting insight, echoing White, with which we will close this entry: "We suggest that in business history there is a tendency toward 'over-remembering' of certain aspects of practice (for example, the actions of individual early industrialists, or more recently the decision making processes of senior executives in large organizations), and a forgetting of darker aspects of organizational and managerial pasts (for example, slavery or organizational engagement with totalitarian regimes)."[15] This imbalance will take long years to be corrected, even were we to build a "dark side recovery project," for while the shameful is repressed, the banal is reflexively forgotten, and usually rightfully so. Still, although our canons for what is "interesting"—deserving research attention—include both success and failure, crime and corruption rarely intrude, much less form the intellectual spine for an inquiry. (See Prospects, 2: Fraud and Fakery.) Nonetheless, seeking out questions that probe memories of injustice, deception, and corruption would be a worthwhile start.

NOTES

Epigraphs. Hayden White, "Guilty of History? The Longue Durée of Paul Ricoeur," *History and Theory* (May 2007): 233–51, quote from 235. Scott Taylor, Bill Cooke, and Emma Bell, "Business History and the Historiographical Operation," *Management and Organizational History* 4 (2009): 151–66, quote from 154. Paul Ricoeur, *La mémoire, l'histoire, l'oubli* (Paris: Le Seuil, 2000), 275. The English translation is from *Memory, History, Forgetting*, trans. Kathleen Blamey and David Pellauer (Chicago: University of Chicago Press, 2004).

1. White, "Guilty," 237.

2. Emma Bell and Scott Taylor, "Beyond Letting Go and Moving On: New Perspectives on Organizational Death, Loss, and Grief," *Scandinavian Journal of Management* 27 (2011): 1–10.

3. Joanne Roberts, "Limits to Communities of Practice," *Journal of Management Studies* 43 (2006): 623–39.

4. Richard Ned Lebow, Wulf Kansteiner, and Claudio Fogu, eds., *The Politics of Memory in Postwar Europe* (Durham, NC: Duke University Press, 2006).

5. Karl Weick, *The Social Psychology of Organizing* (Reading, MA: Addison-Wesley, 1979), 206.

6. James Walsh and Gerardo Ungson, "Organizational Memory," *Academy of Management Review* 16 (1991): 57–91, quotes from 61.

7. Walsh and Rivera, "Organizational Memory," 62–67.

8. Mr. Kojima's interview with Patrick Fridenson, 2006, and Michael Kammen, *Mystic Chords of Memory: The Transformation of Tradition in American Culture* (New York: Knopf, 1991).

9. Mary Ann Glynn, "Commentary: Collective Memory as Fact and Artifact: Cultural and Political Elements of Memory in Organizations," in *Advances in Strategic Management*, ed. James Walsh and Anne Huff (Greenwich, CT: JAI Press, 1997), 147–54, quoted in Charles Booth and Michael Rawlinson, "Management and Organizational History: Prospects," *Management and Organizational History* 1 (2006): 5–30. See also Elizabeth Atkins, "A History of the Ford Motor Company Archives, with Reflections on Archival Documentation of Ford of Europe's history," in *Ford, 1903–2003: The European History*, ed. Hubert Bonin, Yannick Lung, and Steven Tolliday (Paris: Editions PLAGE, 2003), 32–35.

10. One of the U.S. Steel veterans was Phil Scranton's father, who then headed specialty engineering at American Bridge. He retired soon after the Marathon Oil acquisition. For a careful reconstruction, see John Hoerr, *And the Wolf Finally Came: The Decline and Fall of the American Steel Industry* (Pittsburgh: University of Pittsburgh Press, 1988).

11. For one analysis, see Nick Nissey and Andrea Casey, "The Politics of the Exhibition: Viewing Corporate Museums through the Paradigmatic Lens of Organizational Memory," *British Journal of Management* 13 (2002): S35–45.

12. Patrick Fridenson, "Crédit Lyonnais and Stock Certification" (unpublished conference paper, 2006), available at www2.e.u-tokyo.ac.jp/~sousei/Fridenson.pdf (accessed 23 June 2011), quote from 3.

13. Taylor, Cooke, and Bell, "Business History," 156.

14. Karl Weick, *Sensemaking in Organizations* (Thousand Oaks: Sage, 1995), 184–85, quoted in Booth and Rawlinson, "Management," 11.

15. Taylor, Cooke, and Bell, "Business History," 162.

7. Modernity

For business historians the advent of modernity presented the discipline's foundation stones. In a long, irregular transition, freestanding capitalist enterprises emerged from a mélange of fleeting merchant adventures, royal or state monopolies, artisan guilds, aristocratic clientelisms, and church-governed estates and manufactories, marginalizing them all in a steadily industrializing economy. Modernity is our culture; we act within it and yet it is rarely visible to us without an effort to historicize and anatomize it, undertaken briefly here to help us gain perspective on the ocean we swim in.

In our view, three prominent features characterize modernity: the notion that humans can transform the world; the institutions that sustain industrialization and market economies; and the related political institutions that support and are nested within nation states. In consequence, "modernity is vastly more dynamic than any previous type of social order. It is a society . . . which unlike any preceding culture lives in the future rather than the past."[1] Its historical prerequisites included the disenchantment of the world, the advance of instrumental reason, and the elevation of the individual to social centrality. Disenchantment entails confining religion to spiritual matters, removing enforceable barriers to inquiry and requirements for orthodoxy, hence liberating sciences, states, marketeers, and consumers from constraints and rules based on transcendent mysteries or truths. Instrumental reason involves validating the search for optimal means to reach goals in any situation, without prescribing which goals are worth attaining—this is the core of market economics and of those sciences that harness nature to realize human intentions.[2] Spreading individualism subverts at least four forms of traditional authority: religious, princely, patriarchal, and familial, undermining persons, customs, and texts that sustained deference in exchange for unleashing dynamics of personal and participatory growth.[3] These facilitators generate striking historical consequences, as each concerns transforming our conditions of existence and action. Replacing these forms of authority is a new ascendancy of law, attuned directly to the needs of enterprises and bringing particular guarantees to wage earners as well. In the United States, corporations have even been transformed into persons by legal rulings,[4] whereas by contrast, neither czarist nor Soviet law was shaped to handle these tasks, representing instead the law of a royal, then a command economy. In both cases, investment and industrialization proved, at a minimum, awkward.[5]

Modernity in full flower features the institutionalization of a capitalist economy, including expansive commoditization, the development of new means to organize information and exercise administrative capability, the establishment of permanent military orders, and the articulation of a technology-based civilization. It is critical to realize that markets are not primal here but rather are components of multidimensional and simultaneously-emergent processes that are reshaping resources, information, power, and artifacts. For example, a capitalist economy features multilateral relationships up and down supply chains, rather than fixed, conventional sequences that restrict who can sell to or buy from whom, on what terms, where, and when.[6] These dynamics in turn reconfigure relationships in time and space such that distant events have increasingly immediate effects on many locales; such that organizations expect to survey and oversee workers, accounts, streets, flight paths, instantly and constantly; and such that trust becomes grounded technologically, in invisible expert systems.[7]

Constituted by motion, modernity entails continuous transformations. Business historians may find useful a recent effort to conceptualize two major phases of modernity's course, first the consolidation of a "solid" modernity, starting more than a century ago in the developed West, and then its devolution into "liquid" modernity, across the last third of the twentieth century. In both modes, businesses were organized in different ways, but the pathway to success has shifted in recent generations. Solid modernity was the lived counterpart to "heavy capitalism," which focused on "bulk and size" and had clear and tight boundaries. "In its heavy stage, capital was as much fixed to the ground as were the laborers it engaged." This was the age of big business, notably in manufacturing, requiring factories that "reduced human activities to simple routine," bureaucracies "in which identities and social bonds were deposited on entry," and oversight that "never dozes off, always keen and quick in rewarding the faithful and punishing" failures.[8] Solid modernity thus posited, in and beyond the firm, that "reality compliant with the verdicts of reason was to be 'built' under strict quality control and according to strict procedural rules and first of all *designed* before the construction begins." This world of production and control exhibits deep fault lines, however. "Wealth and might which depend on size and the quality of hardware tend to be sluggish, unwieldy and awkward to move. Both are 'embodied' and fixed, tied in steel and concrete." Moreover, driving toward utopias of planning and control meant that heavy capitalism "was endemically pregnant with the tendency toward totalitarianism."[9] Note how these features intersect with modernity as continuously expressed in business, administration, war, and technology to form a twentieth-century Juggernaut, manifested in World War Two, which before long came to pieces, as great armies, dominant giant enterprises, vast mass production facilities, unassailable seats of power, and lifetime careers all eroded unevenly during the Cold War decades.

A half century later we occupy a very different world, and one puzzle for business historians is to explore how we got here and what alternative tracks failed to thrive, supplementing popular lenses focused on politics and culture with others spotlighting enterprises and technologies. Mobile or flexible capitalism has replaced its rooted forebears, for "nowadays capital travels light . . . nowhere need[ing] to stay longer than the satisfaction lasts." Even contemporary mass production plants are seen as far more temporary that would have been the case in the mid-twentieth century (consider Volkswagen's Pennsylvania assembly site, which operated for just a decade and closed in 1986.)[10] Investors and their assets are "disembedded to an unprecedented extent . . . quite sufficient to blackmail territory-bound political agencies into submission." Nation states lose the ability to regulate now-globally maneuverable agents, whether corporations, speculators, refugees, hackers, or terrorists. However, it is possible that transnational institutions can secure some leverage over such actors, given the EU's strong challenges to Microsoft's practices in recent years.[11]

Moreover, in fluid or liquid modernity, "the settled majority is ruled by the nomadic and extraterritorial elite," political, economic, and cultural, among whose crucial skills is the ability to depart and thereby to shed responsibility for outcomes, places, and people. If solid-era management "focused on keeping the 'manpower' in and forcing or bribing it to stay put and work on schedule," contemporary managers strive to avoid long-term hires and keep workers ready to be replaced through downsizing or outsourcing. "Brief encounters replace lasting engagements." For workers, home ownership and family and community ties can shift from assets to liabilities, given a fluid, financialized economy. Now "we live in a world of universal flexibility, under conditions of acute instability, penetrating all aspects of individual life," and in consequence, "safe ports are few and far between and most of the time trust floats unencumbered."[12] (See Prospects, 11: Trust, Cooperation, and Networks.)

Ours is a modernity of globalized consumption, short-term mentalities, and surplus population, which seems to have produced a widespread eerie complacency. As production is social and consumption personal, even when conducted in public, liquid modernity defuses earlier societal divides (capital vs. labor, urban vs. rural) while encouraging group formation in ephemeral and low-commitment modes (Harley motorcycle owners, fans of Johnny Hallyday).[13] We realize that the "speed of circulation, of recycling, ageing, dumping and replacement" is crucial to profit and prosperity, whereas durability and reliability once featured large in a producerist mindset for purchasing goods. Both these portraits are stylized, to be sure, but to the extent that they resonate with broad patterns across the last hundred and fifty years, they trigger critical questions for business historians. We have spent a generation proposing explanations for the advent of solid modernity; we have a comparably demanding task to account for its devolution and the triumph of its light, liquid, unstable, and flexible successor.

NOTES

1. Anthony Giddens and Christopher Pierson, *Conversations with Anthony Giddens: Making Sense of Modernity* (Cambridge, UK: Polity, 1998), 94.

2. This has complex implications for moral philosophy and ethical choice, as, with the erosion of prescriptive rationality (where ends are authoritatively specified or proscribed in advance), we reach environments of heightened individualism and potential normlessness (*anomie*).

3. Patriarchial is different from clan or family authority as it refers to the commanding roles men take in society over women and children and those older men take over younger men, which extend beyond settings of communal or blood relation (in which women may, for example, exercise considerable authority).

4. Morton Horwitz, *The Transformation of American Law, 1870–1960* (New York: Oxford University Press, 1992), chap. 3. For a long-term review, see Sanford Shane, "The Corporation Is a Person: The Language of a Legal Fiction," *Tulane Law Review* 61 (1986–87): 563–609.

5. See Avner Greif and Eugene Kandel, "Contract Enforcement Institutions: Historical Perspective and Current Status in Russia," Center for Institutional Reform and the Informal Sector, University of Maryland, Nov. 1993, available at http://pdf.usaid.gov/pdf_docs/PNABR268.pdf (accessed 11 Apr. 2011).

6. See Sean Adams, "How Choice Fueled Panic: Philadelphians, Consumption, and the Panic of 1837," *Enterprise and Society* 12 (2011): 761–89.

7. This section draws on Giddens and Pierson, *Conversations*, interview 4. Zygmunt Bauman adds in this vein: "Modernity starts when space and time are separated from living practice and from each other and so become ready to be theorized as distinct and mutually independent categories of strategy and action" (*Liquid Modernity* [Cambridge, UK: Polity, 2000], 8).

8. Bauman, *Liquid Modernity*, 25, 58.

9. Ibid., 25, 47, 115. Bauman sees the concentration camp, gulag, and prison as expressing the capacity of powerful organizations to exclude "all those presumed not to be or found not to be malleable enough" (25). Of course, immense conscript armies have been replaced by high-tech professionals in the West.

10. Ulrich Jürgens, "The Development of Volkswagen's Industrial Model, 1967–1995," in *One Best Way? Trajectories and Industrial Models of the World's Automobile Producers*, ed. Michel Frevssenet, Andrew Mair, Kiochi Shimizu, and Giuseppe Volpato (New York: Oxford, 1998), 273–310. See also Jefferson Cowie, *Capital Moves: RCA's 70-Year Quest for Cheap Labor* (New York: New Press, 2001).

11. Eleanor Fox, "Monopolization, the Abuse of Dominance, and the Indeterminacy of Economics: The U.S./E.U. Divide," *Utah Law Review* n.v. (2006): 725–40, esp. 737–39.

12. Bauman, *Liquid Modernity*, 13, 122, 135, 149–50.

13. Atavistic surges of religious or ethnic activism remain, of course, aiming to undermine the global reach of liquid consumerism and to preserve purified enclaves, a task feasible if actors abandon nearly all of modernity's elements other than force-related technologies.

8. Risks

There can be no business without risks, not just because the future is unknowable but also, with Wittgenstein, because we have no access to other minds. This condition makes it important to appreciate the variety of risks enterprises may confront and the responses that, historically, companies, governments, and societies have found to address them. For example, in France exporting was considered a high-risk challenge, and thus twentieth-century companies and associations lobbied the state to provide a form of export trade insurance. This was judged to be a governmental task, as private insurance companies had no standing in disputes litigated in other nations.[1] Risks can be categorized along many overlapping spectra: long term versus shorter term, natural versus man-made, internal versus external, ordinary versus extraordinary. Just these four binaries suggest how truly elusive understanding risk and engaging risk can be. Risk may arise through accidents, defaulted payments, theft, espionage, cheating, unemployment, layoffs and strikes, interest- and exchange-rate movements, market crises and panics, shipwreck, fire, illness, epidemics, floods, eruptions, tsunamis, and in the broadest sense, politics, revolutions, erratic governments, war, technical change, and climate change. Given all these potential threats, why would anyone start a business? Precisely because enterprisers think they can make money on risks (or despite them) and because no one can stay focused on the many hazards that a specific situation can encompass.

Risks are different for the various stakeholders in an enterprise or project. Sorting this out means asking: Risks for whom? Second, the parties involved may well have different perceptions of the risks they face. This means asking:

How do actors calculate risks? Careers as well as money may be at issue; fear of litigation can drive strategy. Hence inequality is built into exposures to risks and to their analysis. For example, in Union Carbide's Bhopal disaster, the risk exposures of chemical plant workers and nearby residents, on one hand, and company shareholders and officers, on the other, proved dramatically different. A fully rounded inquiry would explore all forms of risk, their sources, and their consequences: here risks for health, employment, economic development, share valuation (leading to takeover attempts), and risks of litigation and financial loss.[2]

Individuals and organizations develop practices specific to working with risks. Joint ventures or cartels are mechanisms for voluntarily sharing risks, as are investment clubs, mutual funds, insurance firms, and up one level, reinsurance enterprises. The modern reinsurance industry developed in 1846, when German insurance companies had insufficient reserves to cover large industrial risks, yielding the formation of the Kölnische Rück, an institution to protect insurers against catastrophic losses.[3] In recent decades, reinsurance has internationalized dramatically, often in response to climate-related catastrophes or environmental disasters, the costs of which can run to many billions of dollars, pounds, or euros.[4] As at Bhopal, risks can be transferred from management to workers and citizens, rather than, as in other cases, reducing or eliminating them through safety devices, operational protocols, testing, and supervision. New institutions have been created in specific risk environments: in the 1880s, US manufacturers started a series of industrial fire insurance firms because existing insurance companies focused only on homes and shops with well-understood fire hazards. Late-nineteenth-century mutual insurance firms represented another alternative, in which the insured owned the enterprise, an attractive strategy at a time when many insurance firms were corrupt or insolvent. In various European countries, in addition to seeking insurance against export losses, trade associations founded other enterprises, to insure against the risk and costs of strikes. Even inside a group of practitioners (investors or workers), some actors prove willing to shoulder greater risks than others, enjoying the game or imagining greater returns. Other agents ignore risks, take precautions (limiting investments in unstable countries, declining dangerous assignments) or cover the risks through insurance, where possible.[5]

Conventionally, risk involves a known distribution of possible outcomes, many of which are not calculable. The unquantifiable is not the same thing as the uncertain, however; as with anticipating earthquakes along known fault lines, success or failure is all about timing. Thus all parties must take actions in consequence of such risks, reworking architectural regulations, for example. In this sense, there is a liminal space for perception and action between risk and uncertainty, which we believe is worth historical exploration. In this space we identify "requantification" as a widespread phenomenon since the eighteenth century, that is to say, that risks, once perceived, have promoted the growth of statistics and new professionals, such as actuaries. This meant replacing traditional, experience-based notions of risk (which were numerical—estimated percentages and proportions) by building a statistical foundation that facilitated identifying long-term patterns and situational variations, that is, revisionist quantification. Hence, it would be historically rewarding to investigate by what means we learned how to estimate the probability of probable outcomes. Over time, this wagering work has mobilized auguries, prayer, targeted religious or political donations, memory, records and documents, models, trend lines, consultants, sampling, and systematic polling, leading ideally to mathematical analysis that predicts the future on the basis of past events and patterns. None of this is reliable, but in "modern" cultures, the more quantitative the device, the more confidence we place in it. (Think of the algorithms that encapsulated the rational market thesis in finance and of the fat tails—a phenomenon in which what should be very rare occurences, at either edge of a bell curve distribution, empirically appear much more often than theories would predict—in securities markets. Too many large price jumps and falls than would be expected in a rational system exposed its investment guidance as a decontextualized oversimplification.)[6]

Ulrich Beck, in his widely respected *Risk Society*, has argued that in late modernity, risks have both accelerated and generalized spatially. On the first count, we find risk environments multiplying: from toxic chemical sites (newly discovered every year) and iatrogenic diseases in hospitals, to weather and crop failure hazards for agriculture (as pesticides force evolution of resistant bacteria, molds, and insects),[7] to catastrophic failures of nuclear energy plants, and more. This happens in a society that accepts more and more risks, even promoting risk-taking (unlike post–World War Two European welfare states), and that finds new ways to cover risks, for example, by extending the scope of reinsurance, insuring derivatives, and creating speculative contracts like AIG's famed credit default swaps (quite a nice paradox).[8] What has become risky that once wasn't? One new risk arises from demography, as the aging of most industrialized societies unsettles the foundation for many pension programs. Blood transfusions have joined the risk society, through a long chain of unintended consequences involving commercialization, hepatitis C, drug-using donors, and HIV.[9]

A key consideration is which risks can be insured and which are excluded. Acts of God and the results of warfare are uninsurable in almost all US property damage claims. When terrorists strike, are you covered? Here is the battleground over the incomplete contract. It is impossible to specify in advance all the things that can cause damage, loss of life, or liability; in this situation, legal interpretation becomes an art form.

Clearly, as noted above, risks that can be built into actuarial tables—classically, road and workplace accidents—are readily covered, not least because these datasets help insurers devise prices that can generate profits. In a different arena, Lloyds is famed for insuring "special situations," an actress's nose, for example, or an offshore oil rig. These are risks for which there is no possible data or just a scattered record of failure and consequence costs, and hence pricing becomes a portfolio play or an educated guess, as it was centuries ago. Of course, were ten thousand noses or platforms insured across some decades, the requantification sequence would likely occur. The relationship between new risks and insurability is time centered; hence health insurance for AIDS treatments lagged behind the incidence of the disease by many years, arguably again due to the ambiguities of pricing. Thus multinationals in sub-Saharan Africa created their own practices to deal with workers suffering from AIDS in the absence of an insurance market.[10]

Last, it is arguable that both welfare states and long-lived corporations become risk averse due to their large obligations to pensioners or to share- and bondholders. Embracing greater risk or a more diversified risk portfolio could energize both institutions. However, the underlying hazard is that those unfamiliar with risk-taking may make poor choices or become prisoners of advisers who are familiar with investing but cannot guarantee performance. Further, private attempts to underwrite welfare provisions have repeatedly proven unstable, as funding for programs in prosperous times fades toward zero when the economy craters.[11] A further institutional intervention has been more effective, however, as when philanthropies and foundations help individuals and institutions cope with enlarged risks both through direct funding of health care or food security and through research grants to reduce risks through innovation. Overall, the range of risk's meanings and the sites for its recognition and interpretation suggest multiple venues for creative research projects by business historians, stretching back to early modern times and reaching spatially across borders and oceans alike.

NOTES

1. Bernard Bobe, "Public Assistance to Industries and Trade Policy in France" (World Bank Staff Working Paper no. 570, Washington, DC, 1983); for the French agency COFACE, see http://fr.wikipedia.org/wiki/Compagnie_fran%C3%A7aise_d%27assurance_pour_le_commerce_ext%C3%A9rieur The UK and Japan have had similar programs.

2. Bridget Hanna, Ward Morehouse, and Satinath Sarangi, *The Bhopal Reader* (New York: Apex, 2005) (a documents collection), and Dominique Lapierre and Javier Moro, *Five Past Midnight in Bhopal* (New York: Warner, 2002) (a journalistic account). For a scholarly assessment, see Edward Broughton, "The Bhopal Disaster and Its Aftermath: A Review, Environmental Health 4 (2005): unpaginated html, available at: www.ehjournal.net/content/4/1/6/. Dow Chemical eventually purchased UCC and abandoned the Bhopal site. At least four novels and a play have been written about the tragedy, whereas local people have created an end-of-year carnival to commemorate the dead, in which giant puppets of corporate leaders are destroyed.

3. Edwin Kopf, "Notes on the Origin and Development of Reinsurance," *Proceedings of the Casualty Actuarial Society* 16 (1929): 22–91, details at 30–31.

4. Kenneth Froot, "The Intermediation of Financial Risks: Evolution in the Catastrophe Reinsurance Market," *Risk Management and Insurance Review* 11 (2008): 281–94, and Wallace Hsin-Chun Wang, *Reinsurance Regulation: A Contemporary and Comparative Study* (The Hague: Kluwer, 2003). Our colleague Christopher Kobrak is currently drafting a historical analysis of an industry leader, Swiss Re.

5. Andrew Yarmie, "Employers' Organizations in Mid-Victorian England," *International Journal of Social History* 25 (1980): 209–35.

6. Nassim Taleb, *Fooled by Randomness: The Hidden Role of Chance in Life and in the Markets* (New York: Norton, 2001).

7. Edmund Russell, *Evolutionary History: Uniting History and Biology to Understand Life on Earth* (New York: Cambridge University Press, 2011).

8. David Paul, "Credit Default Swaps, the Collapse of AIG, and Addressing the Crisis of Confidence," *Huffington Post*, 11 Oct. 2008, available at www.huffingtonpost.com/david-paul/credit-default-swaps-the_b_133891.html (accessed 11 July 2011). For a full review, see Roddy Boyd, *Fatal Risk: A Cautionary Tale of AIG's Corporate Suicide* (New York: Wiley, 2011).

9. Sophie Chauveau, "Between Gift and Commodity: Blood Products in France," *economic sociology_the european electronic newsletter* 11.1 (Nov. 2009): 24–28, available at www.people.hbs.edu/manteby/Economic%20Sociology_Euro%20E-Newsletter%20Nov%2009.pdf#page=24 (accessed 11 July 2011).

10. Philippe d'Iribarne, *Epreuves des différences: L'expérience d'une entreprise mondiale* (Paris: Le Seuil, 2009).

11. Andrea Tone, *The Business of Benevolence: Industrial Paternalism in Progressive America* (Ithaca: Cornell University Press, 1997).

9. Spatiality

> As both a material order and a cosmology, modernity has been
> constructed around the controlling center and the reasoning
> subject, around city, state, firm and the active participation of
> residents, citizens, and capitalists. The manipulation of
> apparently abstract, homogeneous space and time has been
> critical to both poles of the system. The proliferation of
> bureaucratic forms, together with ever-developing mecha-
> nisms of production, transmission, storage and transporta-
> tion of both signs and objects allows elites in those centers to
> project themselves over ever greater zones of space and time.
> —*Roger Friedland and Deirdre Boden,* Now Here

Business history by definition locates its analyses in time and space, but for both, our default setting often is an "apparently abstract" homogeneity—time as linear and irreversible; space as container, platform, enclosure. By contrast, in lived experience time is multiple: regimented clock time supplemented by cycles of days and seasons, punctuated by deaths or disasters, stretched by geology or culture, twisted and suspended in dreams, or inverted by historians who "predict the past."[1] As for space, while *distances* may be fixed, living and working spaces are fungible and dynamic, constituted by human action and reconfigured by technology, infrastructures, and institutions. Businesses, like states and armies, create and manage spaces, map and measure them, shrink and expand them, enshrine or abandon them. In this process, power and capital "project themselves" across terrains in highly differentiated ways that can be transformative—redefining wheat fields as commuter housing, linking cities by rail and air through passenger and freight routes, reshaping neighborhoods into slums through disinvestments.

Businesses, managers, and employees transmit authority and resistance through arranging and contesting spaces, by creating offices as separations within factories, then separating offices entirely from production sites, or by transforming open-plan office "pools" into asocial cubicles, both of which have been extensively satirized and critiqued.[2] Access to windows or bathrooms and the capacity for movement about the workplace symbolize the individual dimensions of spatial relations. All these rules and configurations have histories, which can hardly be explored unless space is taken as being fluid, not fixed—as a variable, as a force, as a moving target, or as an unstable component of actions or situations, rather than being abstracted away as an immobile framework.

One of the most likely ways in which contemporary business historians may encounter spatiality in research is when the topic of globalization heaves into view. Yet ironically, globalization erases space by totalizing it—in its simplest formulations, the global absorbs all "lower" levels of spatiality, and attention shifts to who gets what, how, and how fast. Space returns to being background scenery. In essence, globalization (and the accompanying instantaneity) completes the "annihilation of space by time," which Marx signaled in the *Grundrisse* and which Wolfgang Schivelbusch profiled in its initial, railway incarnation.[3] More critical inquiries have revealed, however, that globalization has limits as metaphor and as practice, that the national "remains the critical spatial scale for understanding contemporary political economies," and that "sub-national scales" remain "central nodes" within globalizing processes of information provision, capital mobility, operational extension, and product differentiation.[4] Geographer John Urry helpfully argues that these phenomena are far from determinate outcomes of liberal free-market policies but rather are perennially contingent, nonlinear, and complex, in the sense of not being reducible to propositions or formulas with predictive capabilities.[5]

A valuable way of grasping "space in history" has been proposed by the French sociologist Henri Lefebvre, who suggests that we mobilize space by exploring its *production* through the conceptual triad: perceived, conceived, and lived. Space *perceived* happens through "spatial practices," which delineate competence and performance. Building roads is a spatial practice, for example, both in process and in project and in the infrastructure created. Space *conceived* arises through "representations of space," which capture key elements of its meaning and our intentions. Thus maps, graphs, images, and codes (architectural, design, traffic, computer) all re-present spaces, usually translating three-dimensionality into two dimensions.[6] Space *lived* surfaces through "representational spaces," which carry the complex symbolisms humans invest in them—for example, the church, cemetery, market, and central square in a town. They are manifested in art, dreams, and advertising, each of which has a rich symbolic vocabulary.[7]

These three modes of apprehension might be summarized as spatial *operations*, spatial *images*, and spatial *signals*, which can be directly linked to business history concerns. Taking operations as a momentary focus, the production of space in, through, and by enterprises involves historical processes of drafting spatial rules and routines, designing and fabricating spaces for activities, exploring national spaces with marketing and patenting, or discarding wastes in toxic dumps.[8] Here is the domain in which historical business actors determined which potential clients were *near enough* to be worth soliciting for sales, a notion that is transformed once transportation and communications changes shift places once *far away* into places that become near enough. Activating operations necessitates spatial images—plans, blueprints, photographs—and again, their emergence and dissemination calls up historical questions. Hence we appreciate the economic significance of nineteenth-century railway maps and timetables (or transoceanic shipping routes and schedules), which allowed actors to conceptualize space visually. Businesses' spatial operations also conjured up experiences and symbolic representations that epitomized and stretched space—factory smoke meant prosperity in industrial districts (ca. 1900), whereas cheap Japanese metal and plastic toys signaled the postwar harmlessness of former enemies. Our vocabulary of commerce is thickly populated with cultural signals and symbols, which make "the shopping mall" or "the office" much more than descriptive terms. All three dimensions intersect in the production of space, Lefebvre affirms, and so too should they interact in inaugurating imaginative research projects. After all, "if space is produced, if there is a production process, then we are dealing with *history*."[9]

Circulation is a spatial phenomenon with temporal dimensions, and historians considering ways to integrate spatiality into their project designs might do well to consider it as a starting point. Circulation references the flows of capital, people, goods, services, information, standards, ideologies, techniques, and even nonhuman organisms across spaces and boundaries[10] (which are meaningless without a historical understanding of spatial processes). (See Resources, 3: Flows.) These patterned and situated movements are central to fashioning the expectations of businesses for delivery, payments, or meetings and their concerns about delay, misinformation, or fraud. Fundamental work in analyzing information flows as historical phenomena was undertaken more than forty years ago, when geographer Allan Pred documented how long it took antebellum newspaper stories about national events to reach coastal cities and interior spaces from New York and Washington. Mapping the spatiality of information and its changes across time once railroads and telegraphy had begun scattering links across the landscape generated unanticipated insights into markets and politics alike.[11] Just as Pred showed the spatial quietly at work in information circulation, analogous questions await business historians' attention along the variety of venues noted above.

NOTES

Epigraph. Roger Friedland and Deirdre Boden, *NowHere: Space, Time, and Modernity* (Berkeley: University of California Press, 1994), 9.

1. Barbara Adam, *Timewatch: The Social Analysis of Time* (Cambridge, UK: Polity, 1993); Adam, *Timescapes of Modernity* (London: Routledge, 1998); and Allen Bluedorn, *The Human Organization of Time: Temporal Realities and Experience* (Stanford: Stanford Business Books, 2002). See also Alfred Gell, *The Anthropology of Time: Cultural Constructions of Temporal Maps and Images* (New York: Berg, 1992), and Eviatar Zerubavel, *Time Maps: Collective Memory and the Social Shape of the Past* (Chicago: University of Chicago Press, 2003).

2. See, for example, www.flickr.com/photos/23968709@N03/4196757244/ or www.guter .org/typingpool.htm (accessed 19 Oct. 2010). Scott Adams's Dilbert cartoons (www.dilbert .com/) and *The Office* TV show, in both its British and American versions, satirize cubicle life and the power relations of workplace space. For a theoretical exploration of this theme, see Henry Wai-chung Yeung, "Organizational Space: A New Frontier in International Business Strategy?" *Critical Perspectives on International Business* 1 (2005): 219–40, and Wai-chung Yeung, "The Socio-spatial Constitution of Business Organizations," *Organization* 5 (1998): 101–28.

3. Karl Marx, *Grundrisse: Foundations of the Critique of Political Economy* (New York: Vintage, 1973), 539–40. The original text reads: "Thus, while capital must on one side strive to tear down every spatial barrier to intercourse, i.e. to exchange, and conquer the whole earth for its market, it strives on the other side to annihilate this space with time, i.e. to reduce to a minimum the time spent in motion from one place to another. . . . There appears here the universalizing tendency of capital, which distinguishes it from all previous stages of production." The original German text, written in 1857–58, was first published in 1939. See Wolfgang Schivelbusch, *The Railway Journey: The Industrialization and Perception of Time and Space* (Berkeley: University of California Press, 1987).

4. Ray Hudson, "On the Globalization of Business," *British Journal of Management* 13 (2002): 362–66.

5. John Urry, *Global Complexity* (Cambridge, UK: Polity, 2003), especially chaps. 4 and 5. See also David Harvey, *Spaces of Capital: Towards a Critical Geography* (New York: Routledge, 2001), and the excellent entry in the online Stanford Encyclopedia of Philosophy, http:// plato.stanford.edu/entries/globalization/ (revised June 2010, accessed 19 Oct. 2010). See also Henry Wai-chung Yeung, "The Limits to Globalization Theory: A Geographic Perspective on Global Economic Change," *Economic Geography* 78 (2002): 285–305.

6. The advent of CAD/CAM and video games opens the door to another dimension: representing three-dimensional spaces that do not exist except in their computer codes.

7. Henri Lefebvre, *The Production of Space* (Oxford: Blackwell, 1991), 33–45. For the advertising vocabulary of "space lived," see Roland Marchand, *Advertising the American Dream: Making Way for Modernity, 1920–1940* (Berkeley: University of California Press, 1985).

8. For a striking example of spatial practices regarding toxic outputs, see Zsuzsa Gille, "Socialist Waste vs. Capitalist Garbage: The Hidden East-West Relations in European Waste Practices" (paper presented at the panel, European Ways of Wasting, Final ESF Inventing Europe Conference, Sofia, Bulgaria, June 18, 2010).

9. Lefebvre, *Production*, 46. See also Henry Wai-chung Yeung's three part reflections on the firm and space: "Organizing 'the Firm' in Industrial Geography I: Networks, Institutions, and Regional Development," *Progress in Human Geography* 24 (2000): 301–15; "Regulating 'the Firm' and Sociocultural Practices in Industrial Geography II," *PHG* 25 (2001): 293–301; and "Producing 'the Firm' in Industrial Geography III: Industrial Restructuring and Labour Markets," *PHG* 26 (2002): 366–78.

10. For a classic study, see Alan Kraut, *Silent Travelers: Germs, Genes, and the Immigrant Menace* (Baltimore: Johns Hopkins University Press, 1995). A recent essay collection is Alison Bashford, ed., *Medicine at the Border: Disease, Globalization, and Security, 1850 to the Present* (New York: Palgrave Macmillan, 2007).

11. Allan Pred, *Urban Growth and the Circulation of Information: The United States System of Cities, 1790–1840* (Cambridge, MA: Harvard University Press, 1973). See also Pred, *The Spatial Dynamics of U.S. Urban Industrial Growth, 1800–1914* (Cambridge, MA: MIT Press, 1966), and Pred, *Urban Growth and City Systems in the United States, 1840–1860* (Cambridge, MA: Harvard University Press, 1980).

10. Time

Time in a business usually refers to tools: clocks and calendars are the oldest ones, eventually supplemented by agendas, deadlines, plans, programs, even by laptops and mobile phones. These tools by themselves suggest that time is uniform for everybody and that its use can be controlled entirely from the top as it flows continuously. Yet, while such tools are directly connected to work, agents are also confronted by other instruments, which cut time into slices, all related to money. Internally, they are the accounting systems and the meetings of owners, managers, or boards of directors for larger companies. Externally, they are the monthly or quarterly reports from twentieth-century financial analysts, advising their customers to buy and sell on stock markets, increasingly worldwide. On another side, they organize the tax payments set by local or national governments. All cast time in recurrent periods. Business historians should go further, to challenge naturalizing assumptions that these comprise all the relevant elements of time, for that approach reduces the depth of the temporal experiences made by men and women at work and in markets.

In work relations, rhythm and pace are always at stake. Speed is a requisite both for consumers outside firms and for managers, foremen, and supervisors inside. The latter group repeatedly tries to increase speed, in order to produce more and to deliver goods, services, or repairs faster. The Japanese auto manufacturer Toyota reached a celebrated new level in the 1950s by introducing "just in time production," that is, synchronizing production to a more regular provisioning of workshops by suppliers' networks. But scholars often neglect the opposite dimension of the time experience: the human tendency to slow down. This is not simply a matter of size, even though small and medium-size enterprises may "take their time" more easily. Even in large organizations, blue collars frequently react to speedups by discovering ways to re-create periods of slowness, while in another domain, since the 1850s, research and development people routinely ask top management, notably financial divisions, to distinguish the different scales of time under which they operate. However, when just-in-time-production was changing the blue-collar work experience, a major breakthrough was similarly observed in design activities. The introduction of project management, first by the US Air Force in the 1950s, then by Japanese industrialists, changed the tempo for the design of new products. (See Prospects, 6: Projects.) Some thirty years later, these time frames in turn were shortened by the implementation of concurrent engineering.[1] Therefore, business historians cannot restrict themselves to describing and explaining the emergence of general company guidelines and norms regarding time. They also need to direct their interest toward the variety of actual temporal practices different stakeholders within and outside firms developed and toward the success or failure of these adjustments or coordination efforts.

Second, time is an important part of the relations among firms. These practices include the sanctioning of delay or urgency in production and logistics— for example, penalties for late delivery, bonuses for early completion. The ways in which companies pay their bills are similarly diversified. They may prioritize some suppliers or follow a rule of payment after a certain time (like thirty or ninety days). Paying on time either creates a positive reputation effect or marks the firm as naive, in not taking advantage of an available system of delay. The latter option may be a way to shift the weight of time to other parties—a move even more frequent in crises (in 1920 Ford did this when it delivered Model Ts to its US dealers without orders having been placed).[2] Moreover, differences in visions of time may arise between a firm and its partners, clients, or workers. Bankers and industrialists often do not share the same horizons. At one mining company in southern France during the nineteenth century, peasant workers took more than sixty years to adjust to the management of time by urban-trained engineers.[3] Times of learning and resistance are also highly uneven.

Time's punctuation is an issue beyond factory walls. For trains, problems can surface regarding Sunday operations or the making and changing of schedules, as evidenced with the South Carolina Railroad during the 1840s. In the antebellum South, "time consciousness operated in a region not associated with industrial capitalism," and "multiple times could function simultaneously. While clocks were important to railroad operations, companies also had to address an array of non-clock times. Moreover, companies were never fully in control of their own time, but were in constant conflict and negotiation with various groups in the community."[4] In industrializing Meiji Japan, the railway authority's efforts to achieve on-time operations to control the movement of trains, as freight volume increased and traffic intensified, not only shaped employees' and passengers' time consciousness but also induced the spread of expectations about fixed-hour departures and arrivals and contributed to the establishment of standard time nationwide.[5] In markets, time is also differentiated, and possibly flexible, in several ways. Credit, an ancient practice, has evolved considerably since the nineteenth century. Debts can be analyzed as a means of pushing back the clock. Modern retail credit induces consumers to try and manage their use of possible resources. Finance entails a present discounting of future returns. Stock exchanges enable economic agents to buy and sell on different time scales as well.

Next, the connection between time and space is another recurrent and major issue for firms and their agents. Whether large or small, stores, offices, factories, and workshops all need to resonate with the pulse of their local communities. Yet simultaneously they follow the beat of the globe: information supplied by business correspondence or spread by the media, credit allocated by families, banks, firms, government institutions, directives set by multinationals, scansions of time brought about by the presence of migrants or immigrants, ruptures induced by the closing or opening of plants, and subsidiaries linked to developments elsewhere.

Firms or networks and actors related to them situate themselves along different scales of time. Some industries can make decisions that matter for a century at least: the selection of aluminum ore and smelter sites or the exploitation of coal mines (by the way, an industry whose output is still growing in the twenty-first century). Their consequences are wide ranging; they affect finance, employment, politics, and environmental issues. Others have a slightly shorter life expectancy. Such is the case for nuclear plants, which are doomed to be decommissioned, though debates about their safe life spans persist. So, despite common wisdom, not every industry is short-termist. Moreover, even short-term action intersects with other scales of time. As historian Joseph Corn has shown,[6] visions of the future are instilled into firms by exhibitions, travels, media, literature and art, and perhaps, since the 1950s, by think tanks.

Industrial or universal exhibitions specialize in designing tomorrow. In that game, technical magazines like *Popular Mechanics* in the United States are replete with futures that never arrived.[7] They still leave some kind of mark on at least some of the actors. They also change. Another historian, Lawrence Samuel, has outlined the successive images of the future that dominated America from the 1920s to the present. Positing that "the future is not a fixed idea but a highly variable one that reflects the values of those who are imagining it," he defines "six separate eras of future narratives" and argues that "the milestones reached during these years—especially related to air and space travel, atomic and nuclear weapons, the women's and civil rights movements, and the advent of biological and genetic engineering—sparked the possibilities of tomorrow in the public's imagination, and helped make the twentieth century the first century to be significantly more about the future than the past. The idea of the future grew both in volume and importance as it rode the technological wave into the new millennium."[8] For businesspeople, futures are more than a topic for speculative discourse. (See Traps, 5: Retrospective Rationalization.) They include a number of specific activities, most of which were not recently invented: prediction (regarding clients, accounts, and markets), prospecting (seeking resources, oil, or gold), education and training, sustainability (from the exploitation of forestry to planning with a green eye), maintenance, and the destruction or recycling of waste.

If in a number of sectors, the usual business horizon tends to cover a span of five years, in large enterprises and even in many small ones, there are also a series of bridges between the past and the future. Corporate culture (a concept prominent in the 1980s) may be considered one of them. Its references, language, and imagery can last for decades.[9] They may be transformed from the top down, after a change in ownership or in strategy, or partly from the bottom up after a conflict. But such modifications are not effective immediately, despite the impatience of consultants, businessmen, or managers. New owners or managers tend either to underestimate the depth of corporate culture or to not always see how its impact may be different in a new context. Furthermore, other elements of business life (agricultural activity, ethnic cultures, national identity) refer to much longer time horizons, which span centuries. Such insertions of business activities and actors into larger communities make using the works of cultural, social, and economic historians worthwhile in improving our understanding of attitudes toward and practices of time. Social theorists and sociologists can also contribute to our toolboxes.[10] In particular, cultural history indicates that historically and spatially, meanings of what is called "soon," "now," "in a while," are varied. It also documents that time can be falsified: changed date stamps on a document and back- or forward-dated checks are usual practices.

Historians of international relations have recently displayed interest in the process of standardizing the time of day worldwide. "Years, quarters, and months of calendars in use lacked the comparability accountants and business statisticians so craved. Chambers of Commerce and the National Association of Manufacturers in the US most actively supported the matter. Activities peaked in the years leading up to the [world] war but found continuation only in its aftermath in the 1920s. . . . But despite this interconnectedness, it was not just one world but many worlds that unifying time created." The process of strong cooperation and "unprecedented coordination" between more industrial countries that this transition entailed was indeed accompanied by tough competition and by the "intense protest from those whose schedules they regulated" in "the ageing continental land empires and their own colonies," as well as in the Middle East.[11] On the whole, standardizing time globally served as a resource for both business interests and organized religion.

Historian Fernand Braudel has insisted that a plurality of times coexist at every moment. Beyond the "brief, rapid, nervous oscillations" of finance, war, and politics, and beyond mid-term elements like economic cycles and phases, he has stressed the importance of much longer-term determinants shaping visions and "limiting the possible" in everyday life. In publications between 1949 and 1958 Braudel defined these determinants as constituting the *longue durée*: the evolution of landscapes, climate factors, geology, the relations between men and their milieux, and "old attitudes of thought and action, resistant frameworks dying hard, at times against all logic."[12]

Half a century later, building on the researches of German historian Reinhart Koselleck, François Hartog has shown how much the articulation between the categories of past, present, and future varies spatially and historically. Coining the notion of different regimes of historicity, he has emphasized that initially, the past "was authoritative for the present." From the late eighteenth century onward, the future "became the point of practical orientation." He dates the emergence of "presentism"[13]—only things judged significant to present prospects are valued—from the fall of the Berlin Wall in 1989. These displace-ments in the "temporalization of time" have far-reaching implications in the manner of living, speaking, and apprehending time. This raises the question of how large the relevant envelope of history can be for various business actors. (See Resources, 5: Futures Past.)

Therefore, both the collective action of agents, which is at the core of pro-duction and services, and their individual experience within organizations or in markets take into account, whether consciously or not, different levels of time. This is not to deny that, as the economic and business literature has shown, firms may be either responsive to events and changes in their environment or the opposite—path-dependent, at least for a while. Yet confining the analysis to such a bipolarization would be misleading. Not just individuals but also hierar-chies are steeped in multiple layers of time. It could even be argued that only a thorough assessment of the diversity of time horizons perceived within firms or networks or in markets at successive moments can illuminate various actors' margins of maneuver and potential for change.

NOTES

1. See Biren Prasad, *Concurrent Engineering Fundamentals: Integrating Product and Process Organization* (Upper Saddle River, NJ: Prentice-Hall, 1996), and M. Lawson and H. M. Karandikar, "A Survey of Concurrent Engineering," *Concurrent Engineering* 2 (1994): 1–6.

2. Thomas Dicke, *Franchising in America: The Development of a Business Method, 1840–1980* (Chapel Hill: University of North Carolina Press, 1994).

3. Rolande Trempé, *Les mineurs de Carmaux, 1848–1914* (Paris: Editions Ouvrières, 1971).

4. Aaron W. Marrs, "Railroads and Time Consciousness in the Antebellum South," *Enterprise and Society* 9 (2008): 433–56.

5. Naofumi Nakamura, "Railway Systems and Time Consciousness in Meiji Japan, 1868–2004" (working paper, Institute of Social Science, University of Tokyo, 2008).

6. Joseph J. Corn, *Imagining Tomorrow: History, Technology, and the American Future* (Cambridge, MA: MIT Press, 1986).

7. Gregory Benford and the editors of *Popular Mechanics*, *The Wonderful Future That Never Was: Flying Cars, Mail Delivery by Parachute, and Other Predictions from the Past* (New York: Hearst Communications, 2010).

8. Lawrence R. Samuel, *Future: A Recent History* (Austin: University of Texas Press, 2009).

9. For a Japanese example, see Toyohiro Kono, *Transformations of Corporate Culture: Experiences of Japanese Enterprises* (Berlin: Walter de Gruyter, 1998).

10. Barbara Adam, *Timewatch: The Social Analysis of Time* (Cambridge, UK: Polity, 1995), and Eviatar Zerubavel, *Time Maps: Collective Memory and the Social Shape of the Past* (Chicago: University of Chicago Press, 2003).

11. Vanessa Ogle, "The Many Worlds That Unifying Time Created: Temporal Standards in the Age of Global Comparison, 1881–1939" (PhD diss., Harvard University, 2011).

12. Fernand Braudel and Sarah Matthews, *On History* (Chicago: University of Chicago Press, 1982).

13. François Hartog, *Régimes d'historicité: Présentisme et expériences du temps* (Paris: Le Seuil, 2003), and Stefan Berger and Chris Lorenz, "National Narratives and Their 'Others': Ethnicity, Class, Religion, and the Gendering of National Histories," *Storia della Storiagrafia*, no. 50 (2006): 59–98.

Afterword

So here you are at the end of the book, having gotten to this point by reading straight through (we did tell you not to do this) or by hopping about (excellent!) or by turning to the final pages either first or early on, which is cheating when reading a mystery novel, but not here. We now offer you some final remarks on what we imagined we were doing when we began reimagining business history. First, one inspiration for this collection of extended aperçus (ostensibly clever insights) was Laurence Sterne's magisterial *Tristram Shandy*, an eighteenth-century quasi novel whose principal character announces that he will tell his Uncle Toby's story but spends hundreds of pages doing nothing of the sort. After four sections spent wandering about, Sterne's narrator presents the adjacent diagram, summarizing the flow of the book thus far, both linear and nonlinear, full of digressions, unexpected returns to earlier issues and places, and so on.

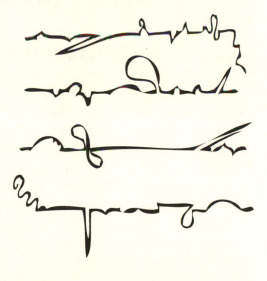

This image is an apt representation of our four parts as well, though it should have some cross-hatched lines connecting bits of each with bits of others, representing our references to other entries. Like Tristram Shandy, *Reimagining Business History* doesn't have transitions; it just jumps from one topic to another, and like Sterne's book, reading it straight through is a challenge, not least because his novel was parodying "the novel." Moreover, although neither that book nor this one "goes" anywhere, there is a great deal of traveling within them. In both cases, readers are invited to extract what they value, what they can use, and what provokes them on their own; there is no central message and no argument (other than "How about this?").

Surely some of you have considered tossing this book into a metaphorical fireplace because it fails to provide a core directive. You may still toss it after reading the afterword. After all, if we want business history reimagined, why don't we say just how? This we have refused to do. Instead, we offer dozens of suggestions, leading in all directions, echoing "the chaotic structure of the novel" Sterne has left us. Yet as the blogger ronosaurus explained:

> Although a straight line may represent an ideal plot line, no story can proceed so directly, without pauses for explanations, digressions that explore meaning, flashbacks that give context, or simultaneous scenes which are told consecutively. In fact, Sterne was not breaking the conventions of a novel by telling his story through digressions, he was only carrying a novelistic convention to an absurd extreme. . . . Even academic writing, as logical as it pretends to be, moving forward step by step, drifts and wanders, loops in upon itself.[1]

And so, in this spirit, we have carried an academic convention to an absurd extreme, offering a collage of loosely related scholarly observations that begins and ends, makes lots of points along the way, provides extensive references, but doesn't have a plot line.

Second, more fully echoing Tristram's style, your prospective historiographers close by providing a few lines of autocritique. We warned at the outset that business history is "too American" or "too Western," and this little book exemplifies that observation quite nicely. We're not capable of effectively presenting Asian or Latin American perspectives on the field, as we're too ignorant of languages, cultures, and scholarly literatures in both regions. It would be lovely were colleagues from beyond our domains to draft commentaries and responses to this volume, exploring *their* notions of reimagining.

Third, we have created a tottering straw creature, writing on occasion of "traditional" business history, when in reality the field has been moving out from under Alfred Chandler's shadow for years. Indeed, many scattered but vital new works, some cited above, many *about* business history but not written *by* self-conscious business historians, represent a wave of stimuli for this exercise.

Fourth, we opened the Introduction with two epigraphs that might rightly be regarded as expressing "business history imperialism," to wit: "As the field flexes its interdisciplinary muscle, almost everything becomes a part of business history."[2] We still like that idea, not least because it inverts economic history's "colonization" demeanor toward business history but also because, as one of our mothers often said: "If a thing's worth doing, it's worth overdoing." Making claims that place business and business history at the center of large events and dynamic processes, as well as at the heart of everyday performances in culture and society, is worth doing because it expands our imaginations, raises the stakes in our work, and calls us to speak widely in the world about issues fundamental to its future. We've finished here; now it's your turn.

NOTES

1. Ronosaurus, "Tristram Shandy ****s Up the Page," Metablog on Metafiction, 13 Mar. 2010, available at http://ronosaurusrex.com/metablog/2010/03/13/tristram-shandys-audacious-layout/ (accessed 12 July 2011). Sterne's diagram available at: www.cabinetmagazine.org/issues/13/timelines.php (accessed 12 July 2011); it is found on p. 152–53 of the novel's seventh edition, London: 1768. This version may be viewed at http://special.lib.gla.ac.uk/exhibns/month/oct2000.html.

2. Paul Gootenberg, "Between a Rock and a Softer Place: Reflections on Some Recent Economic History of Latin America," *Latin American Research Review* 29 (2004): 239–57, quote from 246–47.

Author Index

Subject Index